Praise for Recruiting & Retaining Employees For Dummies

"Contingency recruiters beware! Manning and Brugh have provided the recruiting advice that companies need to minimize outside agency fees while building the volume of high caliber candidates needed in an extremely competitive market."

— Susan Baerst, NEON Systems, Inc.

"This is the book every employee hopes management has read."

— Robert Mangin, Sun Microsystems

"Outstanding employees are a key characteristic of successful organizations. *Recruiting & Retaining Employees For Dummies* will show you how to develop the best strategies to attract talented people and keep them motivated."

— Stuart Page, NetworkOil, Inc.

"This book captures the essentials of effective recruiting combined with innovative techniques geared for the new millennium. It combines textbook knowledge with real world experience to create an outstanding reference for successful recruiting."

— Tiffany C. Nguyen, Context Integration

"A quick, reliable resource for the busy recruiting professional. Great recruiting ideas for any experience level, and a great refresher on what really works in the recruiting process!"

— Alysia Shahady, NetIQ Corporation

"*Recruiting & Retaining Employees For Dummies* is an excellent resource for finding and, more importantly, keeping the right employees for your organization. This book cuts to the heart of what's important in the recruiting process and does an excellent job of identifying tips and techniques in a clear, easy to follow format. We will use this book as a guideline for all of our recruiters and human resource staff to help them make our recruiting and retention programs as effective as they can possibly be."

— Colby Thames, EnFORM Technology

Recruiting &
Retaining Employees
FOR
DUMMIES®

Recruiting & Retaining Employees FOR DUMMIES®

by Paula Manning and Jennifer Brugh

Hungry Minds™

Best-Selling Books • Digital Downloads • e-Books • Answer Networks • e-Newsletters • Branded Web Sites • e-Learning

New York, NY ◆ Cleveland, OH ◆ Indianapolis, IN

Recruiting & Retaining Employees For Dummies®

Published by:
Hungry Minds, Inc.
909 Third Avenue
New York, NY 10022
www.hungryminds.com
www.dummies.com

Library of Congress Control Number: 2001089317

ISBN: 0-7645-5374-7

Printed in the United States of America

10 9 8 7 6 5 4 3 2 1

1B/SY/QW/QR/IN

Distributed in the United States by Hungry Minds, Inc.

Distributed by CDG Books Canada Inc. for Canada; by Transworld Publishers Limited in the United Kingdom; by IDG Norge Books for Norway; by IDG Sweden Books for Sweden; by IDG Books Australia Publishing Corporation Pty. Ltd. for Australia and New Zealand; by TransQuest Publishers Pte Ltd. for Singapore, Malaysia, Thailand, Indonesia, and Hong Kong; by Gotop Information Inc. for Taiwan; by ICG Muse, Inc. for Japan; by Intersoft for South Africa; by Eyrolles for France; by International Thomson Publishing for Germany, Austria and Switzerland; by Distribuidora Cuspide for Argentina; by LR International for Brazil; by Galileo Libros for Chile; by Ediciones ZETA S.C.R. Ltda. for Peru; by WS Computer Publishing Corporation, Inc., for the Philippines; by Contemporanea de Ediciones for Venezuela; by Express Computer Distributors for the Caribbean and West Indies; by Micronesia Media Distributor, Inc. for Micronesia; by Chips Computadoras S.A. de C.V. for Mexico; by Editorial Norma de Panama S.A. for Panama; by American Bookshops for Finland.

For general information on Hungry Minds' products and services, please contact our Customer Care department; within the U.S. at 800-762-2974, outside the U.S. at 317-572-3993, or fax 317-572-4002.

For sales inquiries and resellers information, including discounts, premium and bulk quantity sales and foreign language translations, please contact our Customer Care department at 800-434-3422, fax 317-572-4002 or write to Hungry Minds, Inc., Attn: Customer Care department, 10475 Crosspoint Boulevard, Indianapolis, IN 46256.

For information on licensing foreign or domestic rights, please contact our Sub-Rights Customer Care department at 212-884-5000.

For information on using Hungry Minds' products and services in the classroom or for ordering examination copies, please contact our Educational Sales department at 800-434-2086 or fax 317-572-4005.

Please contact our Public Relations department at 212-884-5163 for press review copies or 212-884-5000 for author interviews and other publicity information or fax 212-884-5400.

For authorization to photocopy items for corporate, personal, or educational use, please contact Copyright Clearance Center, 222 Rosewood Drive, Danvers, MA 01923, or fax 978-750-4470.

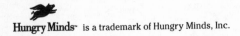

Hungry Minds™ is a trademark of Hungry Minds, Inc.

About the Authors

Jennifer Brugh and **Paula Manning** are co-owners of Triad Resources (soon to become IQ:IT), a $4-million-a-year Texas recruiting firm that specializes in placing information technology professionals. Between them, they have more than 13 years of experience in placing employees in both high-tech and non-technical fields.

Paula joined her first recruiting firm while still in college and, before starting Triad Resources, worked for firms handling recruiting for legal, accounting, administrative, clerical, light industrial, and information technology positions for Fortune 1000 firms. Her satisfied clients, past or current, include Continental Airlines, AIM Management, Enron, Exxon, Fulbright & Jaworski, McKinsey & Company, Merrill Lynch, Shell, the Methodist Hospital, Reliant Energy, Vinson & Elkins, and NetIQ Corporation.

Jennifer previously worked as a technical recruiter for Decision Consultants, one of the largest and most prestigious consulting firms in the country. Her past or current clients include Nortel Networks, Ameritech, United Airlines, Blockbuster, Enron, Williams Energy and Communications, and TIBCO Software.

Together, Paula and Jennifer now place hundreds of employees each year atfirms ranging from Fortune 1000 companies to start-ups and consulting firms. The key to their success: Working extensively with each company to design a personalized recruiting strategy that targets the right candidates for thatcompany. For more information about Triad Resources, check out their Web site at www.triadresources.com.

Authors' Acknowledgments

First, a big "thank you" to our wonderful agent Margot Maley Hutchison of Waterside Productions, Inc., for convincing us to tackle this project, and to her colleagues David Fugate and Wendy Lyons for their invaluable input and advice.

Our heartfelt thanks also go to Mike Kelly, our outstanding project editor, whose wise editing and creative suggestions vastly improved our book; to Jill Alexander and Holly McGuire, our acquisitions editors, for making the book happen; and to all of the other production and editorial staff at Hungry Minds who worked so hard to make this project a success. Special thanks to Alison Blake for making our dream a reality. To Nicole Dogruel, our research manager, who spent months helping us write, edit, and research this manuscript, our appreciation for all your hard work.

In addition, we'd like to express our gratitude to our colleagues Carrie and Wayne Consolvo, Jeff Driskill, Nick Tran, Dea Van Patten, Kwame Satchell, Annette Weaver Judice, David Williams, Stephanie Littel, and Colby Thames, for generously volunteering their time and expertise. Thanks also to our friends and families for their patience with us when we abandoned them to put in extra hours on the book!

Dedication

To Nicole Dogruel, whose talent, intelligence, dedication, and expertise have played an integral role in making Triad a success. Thank you for your help in writing this book — we couldn't have done it without you!

Publisher's Acknowledgments

We're proud of this book; please send us your comments through our Online Registration Form located at www.hungryminds.com.

Some of the people who helped bring this book to market include the following:

Acquisitions, Editorial, and Media Development

Project Editor: Michael Kelly

Acquisitions Editor: Holly McGuire

Editorial Manager: Pam Mourouzis

Editorial Administrator: Michelle Hacker

Editorial Assistant: Carol Strickland

Cover Photos: © Ed Taylor Studio/FPG International

Production

Project Coordinator: Maridee Ennis

Layout and Graphics: Jackie Nicholas, Julie Trippetti, Jeremey Unger

Proofreaders: Laura Albert, TECHBOOKS Production Services

Indexer: TECHBOOKS Production Services

General and Administrative

Hungry Minds, Inc.: John Kilcullen, CEO; Bill Barry, President and COO; John Ball, Executive VP, Operations & Administration; John Harris, CFO

Hungry Minds Consumer Reference Group

Business: Kathleen Nebenhaus, Vice President and Publisher; Kevin Thornton, Acquisitions Manager

Cooking/Gardening: Jennifer Feldman, Associate Vice President and Publisher; Anne Ficklen, Executive Editor

Education/Reference: Diane Graves Steele, Vice President and Publisher

Lifestyles: Kathleen Nebenhaus, Vice President and Publisher; Tracy Boggier, Managing Editor

Pets: Dominique De Vito, Associate Vice President and Publisher; Tracy Boggier, Managing Editor

Travel: Michael Spring, Vice President and Publisher; Brice Gosnell, Publishing Director; Suzanne Jannetta, Editorial Director

Hungry Minds Consumer Editorial Services: Kathleen Nebenhaus, Vice President and Publisher; Kristin A. Cocks, Editorial Director; Cindy Kitchel, Editorial Director

Hungry Minds Consumer Production: Debbie Stailey, Production Director

◆

The publisher would like to give special thanks to Patrick J. McGovern, without whom this book would not have been possible.

◆

Contents at a Glance

Cartoons at a Glance

By Rich Tennant

page 95

page 231

page 7

page 261

page 47

...

page 297

page 157

Cartoon Information:
Fax: 978-546-7747
E-Mail: richtennant@the5thwave.com
World Wide Web: www.the5thwave.com

Table of Contents

Chapter 30: Keep the Competition from Stealing Your Employees 291

Part VII: The Part of Tens 297

Chapter 31: Ten Keys to Being a Successful Recruiter 299

Chapter 32: Ten Biggest Interviewing Mistakes 303

Introduction

• •

Your company's new software could revolutionize the business world. Investors are lining up, wallets in hand, waiting to see proof that your product performs. You're only 20,000 lines of Java code away from success.

And you can't hire a Java programmer to save your life.

Or maybe you're the head of an understaffed sales department, the VP of a biotech firm that needs a dozen good lab technicians yesterday, or the human resources director for a large group of physicians — all of them screaming, simultaneously, for competent receptionists.

No matter what your company does, or which employees you're trying to recruit, you already know two facts. One is that the success of your current project, or possibly even the future of your company, hinges on finding the right employees for your jobs. The other is that those employees can be mighty tough to find.

Doesn't Anybody Out There Need a Job?

Actually, there *are* outstanding employees out there, but there aren't enough to go around — and the situation isn't going to change any time soon. The demand for information technology (IT) professionals, for example, is expected to outstrip availability by almost 425,000 jobs in 2001 in spite of a slowing economy, and the shortfall of IT candidates will last at least until the year 2006. Even with recent layoffs, dot-com failures, and bumpy economic times, top talent is still hard to locate.

Moreover, it's not just "techies" who are hard to find; in a time when many baby boomers are leaving the job market and unemployment remains low, it can be hard to fill any position, from janitors to junior VPs. So whether you need a carpenter, a clerk, or a computer programmer, your work is cut out for you.

But wait, it gets worse! As a recruiter, you're not only competing with other companies' human resources departments. You're also competing with the "big guys," professional recruiting firms (like ours) that know the best tricks for finding and placing job candidates. In fact, you're competing with an entire *nation* of recruiters. That Java programmer you're looking for, for example, will probably get calls from tech recruiters in San Diego, Boston, and Houston — in addition to every recruiter in your hometown.

To add to your challenge, you're also likely to compete against bigger, wealthier firms offering potential employees better benefits than your business can ante up. Everything from stock options and 401K matching to Foosball and free food is on the table these days, and employees aren't shy about asking, "Is that all you have to offer?"

Need still more stress? Even if you do beat the odds and find the perfect employees you're seeking, other firms will actively try to steal your stars away. In particular, if you're in the high-tech industry, where competition for personnel is cutthroat, your programmers or systems administrators may be lured away by better offers even before their business cards get back from the printer.

About This Book

Don't tell us . . . you're ready for some *good* news. And luckily, we have it. As experts in the field of recruiting, and owners of a (may we brag?) highly successful recruiting agency, we know the insider secrets of locating, wooing, and placing employees. In this book, we share our top time-tested techniques for finding qualified job candidates and getting them to say "yes." And since top talent is always hard to find, and the employee crunch may not be going away any time soon, we offer both tips for filling your current openings *and* strategies for long-term recruiting success.

But finding employees is only half the story. Once you get them to say yes to your job offer, it's equally important to keep them happy. That's why we also offer expert advice on creating a workplace environment that will keep your employees satisfied, productive, and loyal to your firm — even when other employers try to lure them away.

In addition, we offer powerful strategies to simultaneously enhance your recruiting *and* retention stats. For example, we tell you how to create an employee referral program — a technique that brings in new recruits relatively inexpensively and rewards your employees for finding them. We also give you a basic how-to course in branding, the art of making your company stand out from all the rest.

Foolish Assumptions

If you're a top recruiter for Volt or Manpower, you can pass on this book. (Of course, there's a good chance we know a few tips you haven't learned!) But we're assuming that your experience in recruiting isn't much more extensive than placing help-wanted ads in the local paper, or posting positions on Monster.com. If so, you need help. Fast. And we can offer it. The information in this book will be invaluable if you're one of the following:

- ✔ A human resources director
- ✔ A company recruiter
- ✔ A small business owner seeking qualified candidates
- ✔ A department director or company vice president who needs qualified employees for high-tech positions, sales or secretarial jobs, executive positions — you name it

If you have some training and experience in hiring, we offer advice on finding better employees — faster. And if you're completely new to the game (for example, if you're still asking, "What *is* Monster.com, anyway?"), we offer a step-by-step introduction to the world of recruiting.

How This Book Is Organized

Recruiting & Retaining Employees For Dummies is divided into seven sections that take you, step by step, through the recruiting process — from the day you realize that you're short a few good men or women, to the day you persuade your new employees to sign on the dotted line. In addition, we offer advice on retaining key employees, as well as tips for creating a streamlined process that will generate new leads for you well into the future. Here's what you can find in the following pages:

Part 1: The Recruiting Wars: Can You Compete?

To do battle in today's dog-eat-dog recruiting world, you need the "right stuff" — but do you have it? In this part, we list the basics your company needs, from competitive salaries to well-targeted perks and benefits, in order to win against stiff competition. In addition, we tell you how to maximize your offer, even if your salary is not up to par and your benefit package isn't all it could be. And we discuss how telecommuting options, flex hours, and other "lifestyle benefits" can make your offer sexier.

Part II: Sell Yourself! How and Where to Advertise Your Jobs

It's a favorite cliché: All of the good employees are already working. But every day, thousands of employees put themselves on the market — and in an age of shaky start-ups, underfunded dot-coms, and economic change, today's happily employed can easily become tomorrow's job seekers. However, these job-hunters won't come knocking on your door. You have to hunt them down, and fast — and we tell you how to do it. Also, you discover how *e-cruiting* works and why advertising on the major job boards isn't enough. In this part, we talk about the major online recruiting resources (and the little-known boards where the gems sometimes lurk), and we explain how to target your job-board dollars and write your ads for maximum benefit, as well as how to use the power of your own web site to pull in candidates. In addition, we explain why traditional recruiting methods, from newspaper classifieds to magazine ads, often out-perform the job boards.

Part III: Need More Power? Advanced Recruiting Tips

Advertising works, but it's not the only tool of your trade. In this part, we describe a host of other recruiting techniques, from college recruiting to corporate branding to cost-effective employee referral programs. Also, it's a dog-eat-dog world out there, but is it really okay to steal other companies' employees? Yes, and we explain a) when and why it's ethical, and b) how to do it. In addition, we tell you how to think "outside the box" and find the great employees other recruiters overlook, as well as how to select the best outside agencies when you need to call in reinforcements.

Part IV: The Nibble: How to Hook a Hot Prospect

She's bright. She's dependable. She's creative. She's just the person you need. But how do you convince her that you're just the company *she* needs? In this part, we explain how to make a good first (and second) impression, how to speed up the interview process, and equally important, how to make sure she's really as good as she looks on paper. Also, we show you the legal landmines to avoid in interviews, during reference checking, and on application forms.

Part V: Reeling in Your Catch: The Closing

The last few days of the recruiting game are the scariest. Will Jane get a better offer from another company? Will Tom discover that his doctor isn't on your medical plan, find out that his parking place isn't covered, or decide that he hates the color of your office? Maybe, but if you follow our advice on writing persuasive offer letters, countering counteroffers, and defusing discontent, your odds of keeping your candidate hooked will improve dramatically. We also talk about the *spouse factor,* and why recruiting an employee often means winning over a wife, a husband, or even an entire family.

Part VI: Once You Catch Them, How Do You Keep Them?

Recruiting is tough work, and you want lasting results, which is why hiring an employee is just the first step in your efforts. In this part, we explain how to create a company culture that makes your employees want to stay, and how to spot problems that might make them want to pack up and leave. We also tell you how to guard your back and keep your competitors from stealing your talent away.

Part VII: The Part of Tens

From the best recruiting tips to the worst interview mistakes, our lists of ten will give you a chuckle — and provide you with some good advice on recruiting do's and don'ts.

Icons Used in This Book

To make *Recruiting & Retaining Employees For Dummies* even handier, we've used special icons to direct you to ideas and information you may find particularly useful.

When you need to get back to the basics of the business, look for this icon.

This icon highlights real-life stories of what works, and doesn't work, in the world of recruiting.

Every *For Dummies* book offers plenty of tips. We also include some advanced tips — secrets even the pros don't always know.

This icon alerts you to talk the language, the lingo of the recruiting world.

Cautions about wrong moves that can instantly undo weeks of recruiting efforts.

Discover the stats you need to know about the job market, both present and future.

Where to Go from Here

Feel free to skip around as you read this book, because each chapter can be read on its own. If you're more interested in one section than another, simply dive in wherever you want.

Also, remember that attitude can make or break your recruiting efforts, and begin your hiring quest with these thoughts in mind:

- ✔ **Employees are out there — really!** Even in today's competitive hiring market, we find them every day, in every field.

- ✔ **Little guys *can* compete.** Surprisingly, big bucks and eye-popping benefit packages aren't the only incentives that draw top-notch employees. We've placed thousands of employees at small firms, start-up companies, and even mom-and-pop businesses.

- ✔ **Success snowballs.** Every recruiting success translates into a new employee who'll pass on the word about your company to friends and acquaintances — and that makes the job a little easier each time.

So arm yourself with the insider knowledge we offer in *Recruiting & Retaining Employees For Dummies* and expect great results. With the tips and techniques we outline, you can compete with the best and the biggest. Good luck!

Part I

The Recruiting Wars: Can You Compete?

The 5th Wave   By Rich Tennant

"Our indirect pay package includes your choice of company car or company skateboard."

In this part . . .

*H*ow do you make job seekers flock to your door? In this part, we discuss the importance of putting the basics in place, before you even start hunting for employees. Our first two chapters offer advice on creating a tempting salary and benefits package, and tell you how to play up your company's strong points and compensate for your weaknesses. Chapter 3 describes how to design a recruiting plan that brings in the most employees, in the shortest time, for the least expense. Finally, Chapter 4 tells you what you need to know about your company, your products or services, and the *lingo* of your field in order to find and attract the best candidates.

Chapter 1

The Right Stuff: How Your Package Stacks Up

*Y*our dream candidate shouts with joy when she opens your offer letter. "Stock options!" she says happily. "Twice the salary I'm making now! Fantastic perks and benefits!" Grabbing your hand and shaking it, she says, "Thank you! Thank you so much!"

And then you wake up, because unless you're recruiting for Microsoft, the scenario we just described only happens in your dreams. More likely, you're growing accustomed to job candidates saying, "Just got your offer letter. Is that salary negotiable? And does that on-site gym come with a personal trainer?"

As a recruiter, you're caught in a tough situation. There's a limit to how much your company can spend on employees if you expect to have money left over for the rest of your bills. Yet today's employees expect bigger-than-ever salaries, especially if they're in healthcare, IT, engineering, and other in-demand fields. And they expect a bounty of benefits — not just the standard health and life insurance, but everything from free bagels to on-site gyms.

How do you resolve these conflicting needs? Simple:

✔ Do your homework before setting salaries.

✔ Target the benefits that best match the employees you're recruiting.

✔ Pick powerful and cost-effective perks.

In the following sections, we explain how to accomplish all three of these goals.

How Much Should You Pay?

If you offer your employees double the going rate, you'll go broke in a month. Offer them less than the going rate, however, and you'll have an empty office. But how do you determine what the going rate is?

Start by analyzing your own company's track record. Think about your best employees. Are they staying? Leaving? Physically there, but thinking about looking for other jobs?

If your workforce is happy, then don't tinker with success. Offer your new employees salaries comparable to what current employees doing the same jobs are earning.

But make sure the jobs and candidates *are* similar — often they aren't, even if they sound the same. For example, a programmer with two years of experience with Java can command more money than one with two years of experience with COBOL, and a bilingual receptionist can expect extra compensation for her language skills if she'll be using them on the job.

If you're experiencing heavy turnover, however, find out if salaries are the problem. Conduct exit interviews with departing employees, and if money is their primary reason for leaving, talk with management. Compared to the high cost of turnover (see Chapter 27), increased salaries can be cost effective. Of course, you'll need to beef up the paychecks for current employees as well, because nothing lowers a long-time employee's morale faster than discovering that the newbie is making $1,000 a month more.

If you're not sure how competitive your current salaries are, or you're hiring employees in new job categories, there are several ways you can find out how much to pay. We recommend one or more of the following:

- ✔ Pay for salary surveys.

- ✔ Search online sites (for example, www.salary.com) for free salary surveys. Also, check out the Bureau of Labor Statistics (http://stats.bls.gov).

- ✔ Check the Internet job boards, where employers post job openings online (see Chapter 6), and find out what your competitors are offering. Be sure to factor in cost-of-living expenses if you're comparing competitors in different areas.

- ✔ Join online forums for recruiters and HR professionals, and ask recruiters in your geographical area what their companies are paying for different positions.

Remember that there's often more than one way to make a salary competitive. For example, if you're recruiting sales people and you're operating on a shoe-string budget, offer high commissions to compensate for low base salaries. Also, consider not placing a cap on commissions. You'll attract more job candidates, and sell more of your product as well.

Benefits: Start with the Three "Must Haves"

To have a fighting chance in the hiring game, you need to offer three basic benefits: a medical plan, paid time off, and some type of retirement plan. Trying to attract employees without offering these standard features is like trying to sell a car with no tires and no steering wheel: You won't get many takers! In the following sections, you can find, in a nutshell, what you should offer in each of these categories.

Basic benefit #1: Your medical plan

Whether your company is big or small, health insurance is a must. Moreover, a minimal plan won't do in most cases. A cut-rate health insurance policy is a little better than none at all, but employees are getting increasingly savvy about evaluating health plans before they accept jobs.

Because many employees want to choose their own doctors, your firm should offer a plan with an HMO (Health Maintenance Organization) option *and* a POS (point-of-service) or PPO (Preferred Provider Organization) option. The latter two allow employees to use doctors outside their plan, for a slightly higher deductible. The more of the policy's premium you can pay, the better. If it's at all possible, include coverage — preferably free — for dependents. Also consider these add-ons:

- Including vision and dental plans.
- Offering a more competitive salary if your employees must pay premiums out of pocket.
- Limiting the waiting period for coverage to 30 days, or offering a signing bonus to help cover COBRA costs until your policy's coverage starts. (For novice recruiters, COBRA stands for the Consolidated Omnibus Budget Reconciliation Act of 1985. Under COBRA, employees can continue to receive health insurance coverage through their prior employers at group rates, but the employees must pay the cost of this insurance themselves.)

Small companies often forego health insurance, believing they can't afford it. However, new laws make it harder for insurers to deny the "little guys" coverage, and require insurers to pool small firms, thus making health insurance far less costly. Also, contributions toward employee health coverage are tax deductible. Check with your legal counsel or tax consultant about the new laws and the tax code; you may be pleasantly surprised.

Basic benefit #2: Paid time off

Another essential, of course, is time off. Offer vacation, sick leave, and personal time, and consider lumping them all together as "paid time off" so that employees can use their days for any reason they want. Employees appreciate not having to tell those silly lies ("I'm so congested, and my fever's up to 102") whenever they want to play hooky and go to a ballgame. Also, offer paid holidays in addition to other time off.

How much time off is enough to tempt today's employees? Some rules of thumb:

- ✔ Two-week vacations, once the standard, are now considered skimpy. IT staff, for example, often receive three to five weeks of paid time off. Be sure your offer is on a par with what your competitors provide.

- ✔ Consider making vacation time and paid time off negotiable when you extend an offer of employment. If you can't budge on salary or other benefits, you may be able to offer more time off instead.

- ✔ If possible, pay employees for vacation time they don't use rather than sticking with the "use it or lose it" plan.

Get a good health plan — stat!

A bad medical plan will chase away good employees — and in the age of managed care, there are *lots* of bad medical plans out there. If human resources decisions are your responsibility, how can you choose a good medical plan, at a cost that you can afford? Check the Web site of the National Committee for Quality Assurance (NCQA) (www.ncqa.org), or review *U.S. News & World Report*'s HMO ratings (www.usnews.com). Also, ask for advice on HR forums; see Chapter 4 for tips on finding helpful online advice.

Even if you're strictly a recruiter, and not responsible for selecting your company's plans, it's smart to consult with your human resources staff to ensure that the plan they pick will attract potential employees.

Also, find a good insurance broker who will take your insurance needs to market and obtain quotes from insurance companies to find you the best rates.

Also, create a generous maternity leave policy that applies to both women and men. Consider offering "elder care leave" as well, if you're targeting baby boomer employees.

Basic benefit #3: A 401(k)

Today's employees know that Uncle Sam's Social Security program isn't going to cover their retirement costs. Thus, even young employees want 401(k) plans. If you can't match employees' contributions, a non-matching plan is better than none because it allows employees to contribute pre-tax dollars.

Hiring the Hard-to-Get

With a good health plan, generous vacation time, and a 401(k) plan, you can usually attract qualified administrative assistants or sales clerks. However, high-tech professionals, healthcare staff, engineers, researchers, and other people with highly specialized skills are harder to entice. To catch this elusive prey, you need an enticing benefit package. Can you provide it? Take our test in Table 1-1 to find out how you fare.

Make three copies of this list. On one, check off the benefits you provide. Then, on the other two, check off the benefits your top competitors provide. (You can usually find this information on their Web sites.) If you were a candidate, which package would win you over, yours or theirs?

Table 1-1	Score Yourself: How Many of These "Hot Bennies" Can You Put on the Table?	
Benefits	**You provide**	**Your competitor provides**
401(k) plans		
Matching 401(k) plans		
Health insurance (HMO only)		
Health insurance with HMO, PPO, POS, and/or traditional (fee for service) options		
Long- and short-term disability insurance		
Vision plan		
Dental plan		

(continued)

Table 1-1 (*continued*)

Benefits	You provide	Your competitor provides
Waivers for medical, dental, and disability packages, so that coverage begins immediately		
Life insurance plans		
Sign-on bonuses		
Stock options		
Early reviews		
Profit sharing		
Free training and education		
Long-term care insurance		
First-year raises		
Longevity bonuses		
Generous vacation time		
Paid maternity leave for new mothers		
Paid family leave for new fathers		
Domestic partner insurance coverage		

Done? Now, analyze your lists. What are your glaring weak points? What do you offer that your competitors don't? Do your strong points make up for your weak points? If not, schedule a meeting with the higher-ups and find out how you can beef up your benefit package to attract the talent you need.

Or, think about adding at least one or two benefits that your competitors *don't* offer. Different employees want different benefits, and sometimes you can often make up for weak areas by offering a benefit that's not available elsewhere. If you can't provide stock options or 401(k) matching, for example, look at your target market and think about cheaper benefits, such as extra vacation days or paid maternity leave, that might lure them. Or think about offering *cafeteria benefits,* that is, plans that let each employee select desired benefits and forego others.

The part-time question

Can you afford to offer benefits to part-time employees — and, if so, *should* you? More than 80 percent of employers now give part-timers vacation, holiday, and sick-leave benefits, and most offer healthcare benefits. If you follow their lead, you'll vastly expand your pool of potential employees. The downside? Your full-time employees may ask to cut back on their hours, if they know they won't lose benefits.

To help you decide, consider the number of part-time and full-time employees your firm uses, the cost of providing benefits to part-timers, and how crucial your part-time staff is to your success. One solution: Expand your part-time benefits but prorate them.

Perking Up Your Offer

Back in the good old days, you could hook an employee for life simply by offering good health insurance and a few holidays. Now, in addition to a loaded benefits package, employees want perks — and lots of them. The average small firm now offers at least three good perks, while larger outfits offer five or six at a minimum.

The good news is that perks are cheaper than benefits. (Some, such as casual days, are even free.) Thus, you may be able to use fun and creative perks to steal employees away from stuffier companies with bigger paychecks. Another plus of perks is that many, such as free food or errand-running services, allow your employees to stay at their desks longer. This translates into increased productivity, increased morale, and fewer missed deadlines.

How imaginative can you get with perks? Many employers go far beyond the old standards, such as cake for employee birthdays or reduced-price tickets to ball games. Table 1-2 offers a checklist of today's favorites:

Table 1-2	Score Yourself: Do You Provide Any of These Perks?	
Perks	**You provide**	**Your competitor provides**
Casual days		
Free food and sodas		
On-site gyms or health club memberships		

(continued)

Table 1-2 *(continued)*

Perks	You provide	Your competitor provides
Dry cleaning		
Attorney assistance		
On-site cash machines		
Internet access at work		
Paid time off for volunteering for charities		
Donations to employees' favorite charities		
Subsidies for childcare, or facilities for on-site childcare		
Tickets to sporting or cultural events		
Masseuses		
Spa days		
Discounts on the company's products		
Subsidies for elder care for aging parents of employees		
Adoption assistance		
Postal services (packaging and mailing)		
On-site health clinics or nurses		
Lactation rooms for nursing moms		
Concierge services		
Maid services		
Hair salons		
Car washes		
Permission to bring children or pets to work		
Assistance in paying off student loans		
Happy hours and parties		

Perks	You provide	Your competitor provides
Incentive plans — for example, generous gift certificates for Employees of the Month		
Contests		
Trips		

Needless to say, you can't offer every one of these perks. You'll need to provide at least a couple, however, and if you're recruiting in tight markets you'll need to be more generous. But while perks can be powerful, target them carefully:

- ✔ Perks that appeal mostly to women (free manicures, spa memberships, and so on) won't attract men, and vice versa.

- ✔ Childcare perks won't help employees whose kids are in school or grown, or employees who don't have children.

- ✔ Game rooms will attract fresh-out-of-college candidates, but not most working moms or seniors.

Be sure, therefore, that your perks accomplish two goals. First, they should attract your hardest-to-hire employee groups. (For example, offer childcare if you're recruiting nurses.) Second, as many perks as possible should appeal to all employees. Free food, casual days, and unlimited Internet access at work, for example, are almost always winners. Survey your existing employees to find out what perks they love and which they couldn't care less about, so you'll get the most bang for your buck.

Also, if you're tight on cash, think of inexpensive perks that create a warm, fuzzy, "I'm part of the family" feeling. For example, some firms pay night-shift employees an extra hour in the fall to compensate for daylight savings time, without docking an hour's worth of money in their paychecks in the spring — a cheap perk that generates good will. Others host monthly pizza lunches for employees, or give employees their birthdays off. None of these ideas cost much, but, as the old saying goes. sometimes it's the thought that counts.

If you're recruiting high-tech employees, however, forget about being cheap. You're competing against outfits such as the Houston software company that offers its IT employees hair salons, laundry and dry cleaning services, car washes, a gym with personal trainers, a stocked kitchen on every floor, private offices rather than cubicles, casual dress, on-site restaurants, an on-site bank and ATM machines, a basketball court, a volleyball court, and a putting green. You won't steal their employees away with a monthly pizza party!

What do employees want? Survey said....

According to a recent survey by Ceridian Employer Services, employers rate these work perks as the most popular:

- Casual dress: 82%
- Flexible hours: 60%
- Personal development training: 49%
- Employee entertainment/company product discounts: 40%
- Free food/beverages: 36%
- Telecommuting: 27%

- Fitness center: 16%
- Recreation facilities: 9%
- Bringing children to work: 7%
- Bringing pets to work: 5%
- Lactation room: 5%
- Concierge services: 2%
- Take-home meals: 2%
- On-site childcare: 1%

Telecommuting, Flex Hours, and Other "Time Perks"

Two of the most popular perks employers can offer involve time rather than money. For working moms, new dads, or "sandwich generation" employees caring for both kids and parents, flextime can be a powerful draw, and the option of telecommuting part- or full-time from home may be irresistible.

If your company can offer flex hours, then by all means, do so. It's virtually cost-free, and logistical problems usually are easy to solve. In fact, productivity often increases, because your employees have more brain cells available to think about work if they're not worried about juggling sitter schedules, getting Grandma to her seniors group, or finding time to rush to the bank or the doctor.

Another plus: Some employees are morning people, while others are naturally night owls. Let your employees work during the times they feel most productive, and you'll be far less likely to find them face down on their desks, catching some Zs.

Telecommuting, of course, is a more complex issue. On the upside, you tap into a large market that's missed by employers who don't offer this option. In particular, you get first dibs on talented moms and dads who want to be home for their kids, experienced boomers who care for aging parents, and skilled seniors with limited transportation. You also attract out-of-town, out-of-state, or even international candidates who aren't willing to relocate. Moreover, in an age of e-mail, on-line and video conferencing, and virtual private network (VPN) terminal servers with dial-in access, a remarkable amount of work can be done by employees who never set foot in the office except to pick up their paychecks.

Also, employees who work from home often spend extra time at nights, on weekends, and even during vacations and holidays, logging in to check e-mail and do some work. Employees are often more productive when they can work both from the office and from home.

On the downside, telecommuting arrangements don't always work out. In fact, according to a report by the Gartner Group, half of all initial attempts at setting up telecommuting programs fail. Among the reasons are declines in productivity and a lack of infrastructure.

 Our recommendation: Talk with the IT/networking department in your company to find out what's involved in setting employees up to work from home. How hard would it be? How much would it cost? If it sounds feasible, consider telecommuting as an option. Test it on a limited basis at first by allowing current employees to telecommute one or two days a week. And establish guidelines, so you can tell if your employees are productive. (For example, set deadlines, performance milestones, and weekly or monthly meetings in the office.) If your telecommuting program works, expand it and offer it as a perk for new employees.

Telecommuting is a particularly attractive option for IT employees — especially software programmers, who often are more productive at home than in the office. Luckily, many of these employees already have home offices loaded with high-tech tools, so the cost of setting them up to telecommute may be next to nothing.

What Matters Most to Employees?

Clearly, you have important choices to make when it comes to selecting perks and benefits. How to choose?

First, obviously, calculate how much you can spend. If the answer is "not much," offer a basic benefit package (medical insurance, 401(k), paid time off), and pick relatively cheap perks, such as free bagels, or one-time benefits, such as car-loan subsidies. Also, offer free or nearly free perks including casual days, monthly pizza lunches, and gift certificates for employees celebrating birthdays. If you're working with a bigger budget, offer as many of the major benefits as you can afford, and some top-of-the-line perks as well — health club memberships and childcare, for example.

Second, identify your most desirable employees, *and* the ones who are hardest to attract and retain, and target your benefits and perks accordingly. Here's how some companies do it:

✔ **Hoping to hire Generation X-ers?** One Houston consulting firm offers a "Raise the Roof" program, which offers employees $10,000 toward the closing cost of a new home, and a "Hot Wheels" program that gives employees $400 each month toward a new car lease. Many firms targeting 20- to 30-year-olds provide on-site health clubs and masseuses. Also on Generation X-ers' list of favorites, lots and lots of free training.

✔ **Targeting baby boomers?** Some firms now chip in on the cost of day programs or nursing home care for employees' elderly parents, or even offer on-site multigenerational care. Others provide full benefits for part-time work, to attract boomers interested in partial retirement. You'll also want excellent life, disability, and health insurance.

✔ **Seeking new grads?** They're hard to tempt with practical benefits such as disability or life insurance, but they like signing bonuses to help them buy cars, assistance in paying off student loans, and lots of free training. Many companies also offer recent graduates something else they really want: free breakfast, lunch, candy, and sodas. Other companies supplement their basic benefits package with fun stuff that attracts recent grads, such as gym memberships, game rooms, movie passes, trips, and contests.

✔ **Targeting busy parents?** One biotech firm offers its employees family-sized meals to go, develops their film on-site, and even provides the services of a florist. Other companies provide lactation rooms for nursing moms, or extra time off to care for sick kids. Many firms offer dads flexible schedules, too. It's a smart move: According to a new Harris poll, nearly four-fifths of men between 20 and 39 say that more family time is the most important goal in their lives, and 71 percent of those surveyed say they'd give up some pay to get that time.

✔ **Looking for experienced seniors?** Some employers contract with local clinics to offer free on-site flu shots, blood pressure checks, cholesterol tests, and routine healthcare. Others offer to train older employees, recognizing that many outstanding seniors have trouble breaking into the job market simply because they're behind the curve in learning computer skills.

Remember, however, to target your perks toward both the employees you hope to attract and the current employees you're trying to retain. Stay abreast of what's important to your employees and what perks they consider worthwhile.

While you're evaluating your perks and benefits, evaluate something else: your environment. Is your office a drab, Dilbert-like cubicle farm? If so, talk to management about making the environment more welcoming. Inexpensive little touches — a kitchen area with a comfortable table and chairs, floor-length mirrors in the women's restrooms, even a new paint job — can enhance the impression you make on potential employees. Also, if you're after IT employees, maintain a library stocked with reference manuals and computer magazines, as well as a lounge area where employees can unwind and de-stress.

Get Your Story Straight

A final note about benefits: Be *100 percent sure* you know what you can offer. If you have any doubts, meet with your boss and get the information in writing. There's nothing more embarrassing (or damaging to your cause) than to promise a benefit and then be forced to recant. So ask these questions ahead of time:

- ✔ Exactly what benefits and perks do we offer?
- ✔ Do these benefits and perks apply to all new employees?
- ✔ Do they apply to part-time employees?

Be sure to get the answers from management in writing, so you'll be on solid ground when you offer that new employee free maid service or laundry services. Otherwise, you may wind up scrubbing her kitchen and folding her sheets yourself!

Relocation Packages: Can You Make Moving Worth the Effort?

Thanks to the Internet, your job postings are likely to attract candidates from all over the country, or perhaps even other countries. Sometimes it's pricey to relocate employees, but in many cases you'll more than make your money back. Why?

- ✔ You'll double or triple your candidate pool.
- ✔ You're more likely to find top-notch candidates.
- ✔ Turnover rates are lower for relocated employees, especially if they sign contracts requiring them to pay back relocation costs if they quit soon after they're hired.

Relocation costs depend on the type of employee you're moving, but they average about $50,000 for homeowners and $15,000 for renters. To decide if it's worth the cost, factor in the following:

- ✔ How difficult it is to find people with the skillset for the job.
- ✔ How long the position has gone unfilled.
- ✔ How critical the employee is to your company's success.

Before you offer to relocate employees, find out what's involved, both for you and for the potential employee. To find good information on relocation costs and cost-of-living comparisons, check out www.Homefair.com, www.jobrelocation.com, www.hruniverse.com, and similar sites.

Obviously, you don't want to offer relocation for all positions. But keep an open mind about hiring out-of-towners for your hardest-to-fill jobs, and especially for executive positions.

Chapter 2

So — Why Would I Want to Work for You?

In This Chapter

▶ Showing off your strong points

▶ Compensating for your flaws

▶ Identifying your hidden perks

*F*ollowing our advice in Chapter 1, you can arm yourself with the sexiest salary and benefits package your company can afford. It won't be perfect, of course — no package ever is — but if you're lucky, it'll be effective.

This chapter helps you figure out how you plan to promote this package, and your company itself, to potential employees. This is trickier than it sounds. Too often, recruiters fail to capitalize on their company's biggest selling points, or conversely, find themselves defenseless when a candidate points out shortcomings. That's why it's important to plan ahead and develop strategies for discussing your company's strong points and weaknesses with job candidates.

Defining Who You Are as a Company

The first step in this process is to educate yourself about your company. Do you fully understand your products or services? If not, spend time in each department, ask questions, and learn the lingo. Gain some insight into the technology each department uses, and get up to speed on current and future projects. (For more on becoming an instant expert, see Chapter 4.)

Next, familiarize yourself with your benefits. And by familiarize, we mean (ugh) that you need to read every single word of your insurance policies, as well as understand each detail of your other perks and benefits. Is your life insurance plan portable? Does your dental plan cover braces? What's the waiting period before your vision plan pays benefits? How many weeks does your short-term disability plan cover? What's the out-of-pocket cost for insurance for different categories of employees? How much will it cost them to cover their dependents?

Trust us: If there's a fact you don't know, someone will grill you on it. Candidates will compare your benefits carefully to other firms' when they weigh their options, so don't risk losing good prospects by failing to have the right facts at your fingertips.

Once you know everything there is to know about your company, it's time to answer two questions honestly:

- ✔ What will attract employees to our company?
- ✔ What will turn them off?

Accentuate the positive: play up your strong points

If you're like the rest of us, odds are you're a little less than perfect. Maybe your nose is a tad too long, or you're getting one of those little bald spots in the back. You can't change these minor flaws, but you can divert attention from them by wearing a well-cut suit, getting a fantastic haircut, or accentuating your big brown eyes.

Wooing job seekers is similar: If you can make them focus on your strong points, they're likely to forgive your weaknesses. Odds are that your company's package has a few shortcomings — possibly even some glaring ones. Maybe you offer a big salary, but not stock options. Maybe you have great perks, but no dental plan. Worse yet, maybe you're between rounds of financing, and your benefits package will be bare-bones until your cash flow improves. That's where creative selling skills will come into play.

Start by taking a tip from professional advertisers, who use focus groups to gain information about their clients' products. You can use the same technique, because you have a captive focus group: your current employees. You know which benefits and perks you value — but do you know which ones *they* value, and why? Ask around, and be sure to ask different employees — men and women, younger and older employees, singles and married employees, people with and without kids. Invite key employees to lunch and pick their brains. You're likely to uncover surprising reasons why employees like your company. For example:

- A working mom may tell you, "I like the medical plan, because the pediatricians are better than on the plan where I worked before."

- A baby boomer might say, "The life insurance has a portable option. That means I don't have to go 'bare' for a long time if I ever get laid off."

- The techie who maintains your computer network may volunteer, "I'm getting exposure to some cutting edge technology here — and the pool table is great!"

The more of these little gems you glean, the more you can drop casually into the conversation in interviews — and the more insight you gain into what sells different employees on your company.

As you talk with employees, think ahead and target those who clearly enjoy working for your company and like their work. Later, you can arrange to have these employees meet with job candidates. Keep an eye out for malcontents too, and steer clear of them when your candidate is touring your office.

Know the hidden perks

When you're answering the question "What makes us special?" be sure to look beyond the obvious. Salaries and benefits are important, but also make a list of the advantages that aren't written into your contracts. These can include the following:

- **Your project:** Is your company developing a new medical device that could save lives? A cutting-edge technology that will change the face of business? A fun gaming system that will entertain a generation of kids? Potential employees like the idea that their work will challenge them professionally, make a difference to the world, or even make them look "cool."

- **Your location:** Are you close to great restaurants and shopping? Or, conversely, are you out in the boonies where stressed-out employees can enjoy the peace and quiet? Are there jogging trails for lunch-time athletes? Day-care facilities close by? If you're asking job seekers to relocate, are you near great schools, ski resorts, or Disneyland? Is your office near public transportation, or in an area that's a short and convenient commute from the suburbs?

- **Your company's personality:** Can employees come to work in jeans and sneakers every day? Do employees keep track of their own hours, rather than punching a time clock? Are you generous about letting employees take time off for dental appointments or their kids' soccer games? Do you provide lots of social or charitable activities for your staff, and work hard to get everyone involved? A friendly, casual, sociable environment wins over many potential candidates.

Again, as you list these selling points, think about which ones will appeal to your target groups. Make a note, for example, to emphasize exciting technical projects to IT candidates, and convenient day-care centers to candidates likely to have young children. But try to mention all of your major assets at least briefly in every interview. Even if your candidate isn't interested in skiing or golfing or fine dining, a spouse or child may be.

Minimize the negative: compensate for your weak points

You can't be everything to everybody, so almost every employee will be disappointed with some aspect of your offer. The key is to downplay your flaws, which takes some creativity and planning. Think out your strategies ahead of time, and you won't be tongue-tied when candidates spot your weaknesses.

Perhaps, for example, you can't afford to offer generous life insurance. What will you say if a candidate mentions this? It depends, in large part, on who your candidate is. If he's a 50-year-old with health concerns, and you know that *you'd* want life insurance if you were in his shoes, simply be forthright. ("We hope we can offer it in the future, but right now we can't. I think, however, that our other benefits can make up for it.") Then move on to what you can offer. If life insurance is a make-or-break benefit, you'll lose the candidate no matter what you say. If not, the rest of your package may sell him. Talk, in particular, about other benefits that a candidate his age is likely to desire — do you offer a good health plan? An elder care plan for his aging parents? Retirement planning?

Now, picture this same scenario — but with a candidate who's under 30. In this case, a different approach makes sense. For example, you can tell your candidate that for a healthy person in his age range, life insurance costs next to nothing. (It might help to have some figures handy.) Also, you can point out how much your other benefits can save or earn him by comparison. For example, the amount of money he'd accumulate through 401(k) matching will dwarf anything he'd shell out for a life insurance policy.

Review each of your benefits, and imagine scenarios like the preceding ones we've outlined. Plan what you'll say when questions arise, and how to best compensate for weak points while being honest with your candidates.

In addition, try to think of solutions for your weaknesses. If there's a 6-month waiting period for health insurance coverage, can you offer a signing bonus that will cover your employee's insurance costs until she's covered? If a candidate complains that the drive to your office is too long, can you compensate with a slight salary increase to cover his gas costs? If a potential candidate says your project isn't challenging enough, can you offer free training in skills she wants to learn?

The important point, no matter what your company's Achilles' heel is when it comes to salary, benefits, or perks, is to achieve the following:

- ✔ Recognize and define your weak points in advance.
- ✔ Identify the employees most likely to slip off the hook because of those weak points.
- ✔ Plan ways to make your company look attractive in spite of your shortcomings.

To Thine Own Self Be True

It's important to believe strongly in your company, but it's also important to be honest. Ethics aside, if you fudge when describing your company climate, benefits, or projects, your candidate will find out. Candidates who find out before they're hired will drop you like a rock. Candidates who find out after they're hired will be e-mailing resumes to other firms within a month. They'll also bad-mouth you to other candidates, making your job that much harder.

So tell the truth, but make the truth sound great. Just remember: If marketers can convince a million people to buy Pet Rocks, you can make your company sound attractive, too.

Put yourself in your prospect's shoes

One middle-aged software programmer still chuckles about his last job-hunting experience. After two weeks of interviewing, he'd narrowed the field to two potential employers. Company One offered portable life insurance and a good disability policy, big pluses for a baby boomer. Company Two didn't. When he brought this up with Company Two, the recruiter — a young guy — kept repeating, "But we have Foosball! It's really great! Have you ever played?"

"I kept thinking," the programmer says, "what the heck good is Foosball if I have a heart attack or a stroke?" He took the other job. The ultimate irony is that the company he turned down had better health benefits, a selling point the HR recruiter could have promoted successfully. But he wasn't thinking like a 45-year-old programmer; he was thinking like a 28-year-old Foosball fan. The moral: You're selling the job to your candidate, not to yourself!

Chapter 3

Planning Your Recruiting Strategy

• •

In This Chapter

▶ Reviewing your stats: Is there room for improvement?

▶ Calculating your staffing needs

▶ Designing a winning recruiting strategy

• •

Are you part of a recruiting team? Or are you the Lone Ranger, single-handedly solving all of your company's hiring needs? Do you keep all your hiring efforts in-house, or outsource some positions to placement agencies? No matter what recruiting model you use, it's important to analyze your current efforts and ask yourself if your efforts are working, if they can be improved, and if it's time to call for reinforcements.

It's also important to map out a step-by-step recruiting strategy. If everyone in your firm knows their roles and sticks to a well-thought-out game plan, you'll improve your odds of hiring top-notch recruits. If not, you run the risk of losing the best candidates to more efficient firms. This chapter helps you get off to a good start.

Check Your Stats: Is Your Current System Working?

Start your self-analysis by taking a hard look at your recruiting statistics. Recruiters frequently refer to these statistics as *metrics*.

To measure your effectiveness, ask yourself the following questions, and answer them candidly. Your answers will tell you if you're meeting the three goals of recruiting: to hire the best people, in the least amount of time, for the least amount of money.

✔ What is your *retention rate* (that is, the number of hires still with your company after six months, one year, or two years) — or, alternately, what is your turnover rate?

- You can calculate your turnover rate using this formula:

  Turnover rate = Number of employees terminated in a given year divided by average number of full-time employees in this category in the same year

- To find statistics on what your turnover/retention rates should be, check the Web site of the Bureau of National Affairs (www.bna.com/bnaplus), which publishes data broken down by profession, company size, and geographical region.

✔ What is your retention rate for critical, hard-to-fill positions?

✔ Are you meeting your hiring goals?

✔ How long do your positions go unfilled?

✔ Which positions remain open the longest? Which fill quickly?

✔ What's your cost-per-hire? (For info on calculating this, see Chapter 27.)

✔ Are you hiring qualified candidates?

✔ Are you hiring a good mix of candidates, and meeting your goals of attaining a diverse workplace?

✔ Are recruiting problems impacting your production, and thus your bottom line?

✔ Is your company expanding rapidly? If so, are you having increasing difficulty keeping up with recruiting needs?

✔ How long does it take to respond to a good candidate who submits a resume?

✔ How long after a position opens does it take to field resumes to hiring managers?

✔ How long does it take to extend an offer after an interview?

✔ How much of your recruiting process is automated and/or electronic?

✔ How long is your entire recruiting process taking, from start to finish? How many steps does it involve? Can it be streamlined?

✔ Are you planning for the future by building a pool of candidates, establishing a network for referrals, and recruiting even when you don't have open positions?

If your answers reveal a healthy recruiting effort and you're meeting your hiring goals, keep on doing what you're doing (while keeping an eye out for ways to improve your efficiency). But if you see glaring weaknesses — positions going unfilled for six months, unqualified candidates, high turnover rates — then try to pinpoint the cause.

How not to manage your recruiting

We once worked with two different large Fortune 500 companies that had more than 100 open jobs each and employed many internal recruiters. Both had centralized recruiting processes and used outside agencies to fill many positions.

Time after time, we submitted qualified and pre-screened candidates to these companies, only to receive no responses. They failed to answer our e-mails and phone calls, or returned them weeks after we submitted candidates. We never knew if resumes reached the hiring managers, or simply got buried in a pile of paperwork in the recruiting department.

Therefore, feedback could not be provided to a candidate, which created a bad impression of the company in the candidate's mind.

Conduct focus groups every few months to ask your employees for ideas on improving your company climate. Consult with hiring managers to identify flaws in your recruiting plan. And analyze your process from start to finish to determine if you need to outsource some of your positions to recruiting agencies, hire additional in-house recruiting staff, try a different approach, or all of the above.

Is your recruiting model working for you?

Recruiting models come in two flavors, *centralized* and *decentralized,* and each has pros and cons. Here's a quick look at each system, and how to make it work faster and better. (Bear in mind that many companies use bits and pieces of both systems.)

In a centralized recruiting model, a single person (for example, the recruiting director) is the point of contact for recruiting. This person participates in all recruiting steps, from screening resumes to interviewing candidates, and all recruiters report to her.

- ✔ **Pro:** Centralization prevents duplication of efforts and keeps your recruiting process consistent.

- ✔ **Con:** If the primary contact isn't organized and informed, the recruiting process bogs down, leading to lost time and lost candidates.

- ✔ **Keys:** In a centralized system, it's crucial to *keep things moving.* Be sure your candidates, the agency recruiters working with you, and employees who make referrals get timely feedback — within hours, or at most within a day or two. Information also needs to flow quickly and efficiently from recruiters to hiring managers, and vice versa. The person who's your single point of contact must know everything there is to know about your company, and all of your open positions, and keep everyone else informed.

In a decentralized recruiting model, hiring managers handle their own recruiting needs, or recruiters report to individual hiring managers.

✔ **Pro:** Hiring managers have a sense of urgency and will work hard to fill their open positions.

✔ **Con:** Communication breakdowns may result in a duplication of efforts. For example, some positions may overlap, and candidates qualified for other managers' positions may go unhired.

✔ **Keys:** Making decentralization work requires hiring managers to stay in touch with each other and share information weekly about open positions and good candidates. Also, while resumes can go directly to hiring managers, copies should go to one central person who keeps track of which resumes went to which managers. And again, feedback is critical: Managers must work closely with recruiters and make their needs clear.

If you're a recruiter, take your hiring managers to lunch; if you're a hiring manager, take your recruiter to lunch. The better you understand each other's needs, the faster you'll fill your job vacancies.

Are you suffering from Superman (or Superwoman) syndrome?

A common cause of recruiting woes is over-extension. Too often, recruiters are overwhelmed by non-recruiting functions. (In one small company we know, the senior recruiter is also the human resources director — and the office manager!) Other companies grow so quickly that the recruiting staff can't keep up with new hiring needs.

To determine if you're understaffed, calculate the number of hours per week that you and your current staff spend on recruiting. Include every step, from writing job ads to interviewing candidates. Next, calculate the number of hours per week that you and your staff need to devote to other activities.

If you're averaging more than 40 hours a week per recruiter, and you're not meeting your hiring goals, it's time to bring in reinforcements. Consider hiring one or more of the following:

- ✔ A recruiting assistant who can post ads, run reference and background checks, maintain your resume database, and generate offer letters.

- ✔ An Internet researcher, to locate candidates online.

- ✔ A human resources specialist, to handle non-recruiting functions such as benefits administration and payroll.

- ✔ Additional part-time or full-time recruiters.

As you select new personnel, choose a team that's strong in areas where you may be weak. For example, if computer searches aren't your specialty, hire someone with strong online research skills. Have trouble inventing creative ads? Look for someone who's a talented writer. And if you're new to the world of high tech, hire someone who knows how to "talk the talk" of hardware, software, and engineering.

Can you keep your recruiting in-house?

It's tempting to handle all of your recruiting needs on your own, instead of outsourcing your positions. And even though we're recruiters in an agency, we'll be the first to admit that this strategy often makes sense. You'll probably do just as well on your own as you would with an agency, if you meet the following:

- ✔ Your firm is small, your workforce is stable, and you aren't planning any major expansions.

- ✔ You don't need many highly skilled or specialized (particularly high-tech) employees.

- ✔ You have plenty of time to devote to recruiting, without short-changing other critical responsibilities.

The Internet recruiter: A new specialty

More and more HR departments are hiring people solely to do cyber-recruiting. These specialists spend their time posting to the Internet job boards, qualifying and pre-screening active candidates who post resumes on the boards, and hunting down "passive" candidates (those who post their resumes on personal Web sites, but don't actively hunt for jobs).

According to a poll by the Recruiter's Network, more than a third of large companies (over 10,000 employees) have at least one full-time recruiter assigned solely to Internet recruiting.

However, if your firm relies heavily on hard-to-find employees or you have a lot of positions to fill quickly, it's smart to consider hiring a recruiting agency to tackle the job. (See Chapter 13 for tips on hiring a good agency and avoiding a bad one.) For many organizations, outsourcing the task of recruiting saves substantial money in the long run. Are you one of them? Consider how much it's costing your company to have key positions going unfilled for months, and you may conclude that an agency fee is worth the money.

In deciding whether to go with an outside firm, calculate the number of people you need to hire. Can you justify hiring a full-time recruiter who'll just sit and twiddle his thumbs (and probably wind up being laid off) when your busy hiring period becomes a lull? Does your business revolve around key employees with esoteric skills or advanced technical knowledge? Then an agency makes sense, because of the following:

✔ Outside recruiters work when you need them — not when you don't.

✔ Outside recruiters understand specialized and niche markets. Whether you need an operating room nurse experienced in open-heart surgery or an executive who can turn around a million-dollar-a-month cash drain, an outside recruiter knows where to start hunting. She can save you months of time and thousands of dollars in wasted efforts.

✔ Recruiting agencies know advanced techniques for locating currently employed candidates who are "shopping around" for new jobs. These are usually the most highly skilled and desirable candidates for your jobs.

✔ An outside agency qualifies and pre-screens candidates and checks their references. They also perform background checks if you ask them to. In addition, they educate candidates about your company's products, services, goals, and climate. Thus, candidates submitted by an agency are generally highly qualified and ready to interview, saving you time and effort.

✔ Recruiting agencies that charge contingency-based fees only get paid when they fill positions. They have a sense of urgency and a real motivation (money) to find the best candidates quickly.

✔ Agency recruiters spend huge amounts of time building a pool of candidates they can tap for jobs or referrals. To do this, they network and recruit 'round the clock. (Of course, we know you're doing this, too! But agency recruiters work with many different companies and often have the added incentive of working on a commission basis.)

Planning Your Recruiting Strategy

After you've assembled your recruiting team, and you've picked which jobs to outsource and which you can fill on your own, it's time to lay out a winning strategy.

Begin by listing the steps of your recruiting plan from start to finish. They include the following:

- ✔ Recognizing the need for new employees, and deciding what types of employees and how many you should hire.
- ✔ Finding qualified candidates.
- ✔ Receiving and evaluating resumes.
- ✔ Interviewing and screening candidates.
- ✔ Extending offers.
- ✔ Hiring new employees and introducing them to the workplace.
- ✔ Reviewing your results.

Analyze each element of your plan. Construct a flow chart, detailing your recruiting process. What's involved — and who will be responsible? Walk through your plan step-by-step:

- ✔ **Recognizing the need for new employees:** What is the procedure for requesting new hires? What request/authorization forms are necessary, and who will design them? Who will define the skills and qualifications of the employees to be hired?

- ✔ **Finding candidates:** Map out the approaches you'll use to attract candidates: your Web site, print ads, online job boards, job fairs, employee referrals, and so on. Who will handle each step? Will you post job openings in-house? If so, who will handle that phase of your recruiting plan?

- ✔ **Receiving and evaluating applications:** Who will receive applications? How will they receive them — e-mail, fax, regular mail? How will they review them? Enter them into a tracking database? Respond to applicants?

- ✔ **Interviewing and screening candidates:** Who will be the initial point of contact for candidates applying for jobs? How many stages of interviewing will you require (for example, initial phone screen, second interview, final interview)? Who will participate in each phase? Who will head the interviews and develop the questions to be asked? Who will be in charge of checking references and handling drug screening or background checks? Who will keep in touch with the candidate throughout this process?

- ✔ **Making offers:** Who has the authority to make an offer? Who will extend the offer? Who will generate the paperwork?

- ✔ **Hiring new employees:** Who will do new-employee orientations?

- ✔ **Analyzing your efforts:** Who will keep track of your retention and turnover rate, track which hiring approaches work and don't work, calculate your cost-per-hire and time-to-hire rates, and measure the quality of the employees you hire?

By developing a recruiting strategy, and putting it down on paper, you'll save yourself headaches and prevent miscommunication and mistakes down the road. In addition, you'll help protect your company against charges of discriminatory hiring practices by following the same steps each time you review, interview, and hire candidates.

Get everyone in the recruiting game

Once you've laid out your recruiting strategy, it's time to get everyone in management on the same page. Start by having your boss buy into your plan. Next, give each manager or supervisor a written flow chart describing exactly who's in charge of each step of recruiting. Also, draft a timetable. For example, let managers know how many days they can take to review resumes, and how many hours they have to respond to candidates following an interview. Last but not least, make sure you clarify who has the final authority to extend employment offers.

Assemble your recruiting tools

Your programmers have computers. Your lab techs have beakers. And just like them, you need the right tools to run a successful recruiting program. They include the following:

- ✔ A Web site, with current job postings and an online application form. (If you don't have a good one already, see Chapter 7.)

- ✔ A resume/candidate tracking system (see Chapter 16).

- ✔ Professional-quality promotional materials for job fairs and other recruiting venues, and a complete company information package for the prospects you interview. (Include benefits info, annual reports, and your company's marketing/promotional literature.)

And, of course, be sure you have that other important tool: money. Your budget should be big enough to fund online advertising, print advertising, job fairs, and even lunches with candidates. If it isn't, have a chat with your boss and see if you can free up some additional dollars.

Keep Evolving — Every Plan Can Get Better!

When you have your recruiting plan in place, you can go to work — but as you implement the plan you've designed, watch carefully for flaws. Is your advertising failing to attract enough candidates, or the right types of candidates? Are there bottlenecks in the interview process? Do managers take too long to make decisions — or, conversely, are unqualified candidates sneaking in because your screening process is too brief? Chart your successes and failures and see if the patterns suggest that changes are needed.

Also, as you're designing and refining your recruiting strategy, think ahead. Is your firm likely to stay the same size, or grow exponentially? Are you planning to launch new products, open new offices, expand to new cities? Think long-term, and let management know if you predict that your recruiting needs will outgrow your recruiting capabilities any time soon. While you may not have a crystal ball, you can make some educated predictions — and those predictions can help your firm avoid being caught unprepared in a competitive marketplace.

Chapter 4

Recruiting 101: Mastering the Basics

In This Chapter

▶ Getting up to speed about your company, your competition, and your industry

▶ Learning the lingo

▶ Resources for recruiters: seminars, e-newsletters, Web training, and more

*R*ecruiting is a walk in the park. After all, all you need are a few basic skills. They include the following:

- An ability to master a foreign language every time you're asked to recruit a specialized or high-tech employee. ("I'm looking at your resume, and it certainly looks like you're an expert in theodolite fabrication . . . .")

- An ability to locate three Java programmers, a network administrator, and two Oracle database administrators in two weeks — in a city with only four out-of-work IT professionals.

- An ability to tell a superstar candidate from a slacker or a potential axe murderer, without consulting a psychic.

- A grasp of employment law that would boggle the mind of a Harvard law student.

- An ability to read 50 resumes an hour, write ad copy better than a New York advertising agency, do Boolean computer searches, and field questions such as, "Can I bring my pet snake to work?"

We can't help you with all of these skills. (You're on your own with the snake question, for example.) Some basic recruiting skills, however, are easy to master, if you know where to look for help. Here's a quick look at what you need to know, and where to get answers.

Oops!

What happens when a recruiter isn't up to speed? One startup company we know lost several excellent candidates because the company's recruiter was misinformed about what the company does and what technologies it uses. For example, she insisted that all development would be done in C++, when the company was seeking Java developers. Because she was the first point of contact for candidates, her lack of expertise gave candidates a negative impression of the company.

A second horror story: Recruiters in another company failed to work with an outstanding

candidate to determine what the candidate's out-of-pocket insurance costs would be for himself and his family. (The company did not cover 100 percent of the insurance cost and wasn't able to provide even a ballpark estimate of what the employee's share would be.) Unable to get a clear answer, the candidate chose to work for another company that provided this information quickly.

As the saying goes, you get only one chance to make a good first impression. Don't blow it!

What Do You Need to Know?

What should you know about your company? In a nutshell, everything. You should have a good understanding of what your company does, and about its past, present, and future. Among the facts you need to find out are

- ✔ If you're privately held, whom are you funded by, and how much funding do you have?

- ✔ If you're a public company, what's your stock price? Your stock symbol? When did you go public? What exchanges are you traded on?

- ✔ Who are your top executives, and what are their backgrounds?

- ✔ What are your company's major products and/or services?

- ✔ What are your projected growth and revenues?

- ✔ How many locations do you have? Where are they? Where are your corporate headquarters?

- ✔ How is your company organized? What are the different divisions or departments? How and where do different positions fit into your organization?

- ✔ Does your company have partnerships or alliances with other firms? If so, who?

- ✔ How many employees do you have?

✔ What are the specifics of your benefits and perks? (See Chapter 2.)

✔ What are your current job openings? Future hiring needs? What skills are you looking for?

Good grief! How can I find out all that stuff?

It's not easy — but it's not impossible, either. Set aside an hour or so a day to research your firm, and find answers to the questions we've listed. Read your annual reports, as well as the descriptions of your products or services in your company's manuals and sales brochures. Search for newspaper or magazine articles about your company on the Internet, and read back issues of your in-house newsletters.

Also, invite key employees out to lunch on your nickel and pick their brains. Don't be afraid to ask elementary questions; it's better to give your co-workers an occasional chuckle than to look bad in front of potential job candidates. Consult with management and HR personnel, who can explain how your company is structured and how your divisions fit together. In addition, meet with employees in different departments. For example, if you work for a hospital, talk to key employees in the emergency room, surgery, and other areas.

One good trick: Hang out occasionally in the break rooms in different departments and soak up inside information over coffee and bagels. Conversation tends to flow in a casual environment, and you learn a lot just by listening.

While you're at it, research your competitors, too. (It's usually easy, thanks to the Internet.) Find out how your products or services differ from theirs, and how they're similar. Keep up with trends: Are your competitors flourishing? Going through rough times? Know who's planning an IPO, who's expanding, and who's in trouble. You'll sound knowledgeable when you talk to job seekers, and you'll be better prepared to answer the question: "How does your product/service compare to the competition?"

To get the inside story on your competition, check industry-specific Web sites. For example, `Dirtpile.com` provides Web surfers with facts about more than 15,000 companies in the heavy construction industry.

You can also find good information on general Web sites. Hoover's Online (`www.hoovers.com`) offers profiles on major firms, as well as up-to-the-minute industry news. Check `Vault.com`, where you'll find everything from "Company Snapshots" to a thorough analysis of each business to "Uppers" (good news about the company) and "Downers" (bad news). Also, go to

WetFeet.com, and click on "companies;" you'll find financial data and industry profiles, and for a fee you can obtain "Insider Reports." Company Sleuth (www.companysleuth.com) will track down a wealth of information for you, ranging from SEC filings and analysts' reports to patent information. Northern Light (www.northernlight.com) is also an excellent source of information.

Be sure, too, to visit your competitor's Web sites on a regular basis. Read their press releases and latest news. Take a look at their employment site to see how it compares to yours.

In addition, visit Google's discussion group search engine (groups.google.com) to see what the informal scoop is on your company, your competitors, and your industry. Often it's an eye-opener.

Brush up on your business

Half the time, you may have no idea what your co-workers are talking about. Designing a container managed entity bean? Calibrating mass spectrometers? It's Greek to you. How can you talk like a pro about your firm's products and services when you're not a plastics engineer, a biochemist, a nurse, a lawyer, a programmer, or an archaeologist?

Begin by studying up on your industry. Suppose, for example, that your firm specializes in plastics. The plastics engineers you're interviewing won't expect you to be a guru — they're smart enough to understand that you deal with people, not with plastics — but they'll expect you to have an educated layperson's understanding of industry techniques. If you bone up on plastics development, manufacturing, and production, and where plastics engineers fit into this process in your company, you'll be more comfortable talking with them — and they'll be more impressed when they talk with you.

 To gain this information, read your industry's top trade journals. If you work for a large firm, these may be available from your company's library; if not, subscribe to at least one or two. To find out which journals are most useful, check with experts in your company, or check with local librarians. (University libraries can be especially helpful in helping you choose.)

Learn the lingo

In addition to knowing what your employees do, you need to "talk the talk" — and that means understanding the basic lingo of each department's employees. If you're recruiting programmers, for example, you should know what GUI is and what client/server means, and you should be able to talk intelligently about the programming languages, platforms, databases, and methodology your company uses. Recruiting candidates for a medical lab? Then you'll need to know the difference between a phlebotomist and a cytotechnologist, and understand what a CBC or lipid panel measures.

The more "insider talk" you master, the better you'll be at screening references, targeting job skills, and talking to candidates. Moreover, it's critical when you're writing job descriptions to include all of the right keywords so that candidates who are job hunting online can find you.

Where do you turn for help in mastering the jargon of your job seekers? Again, we recommend the Internet. Search on the major search engines using some basic terms of your industry, combined with the search terms "glossary" or "dictionary" or "FAQ" ("frequently asked questions"). If you're recruiting IT professionals, check out these helpful sites:

- ✔ Webopedia (`www.pcwebopedia.com`)
- ✔ ComputerUser.com (`www.ComputerUser.com`)
- ✔ Acronym Finder (`www.acronymfinder.com`)
- ✔ The FOLDOC Computing Dictionary (`http://foldoc.doc.ic.ac.uk/foldoc/index.html`)
- ✔ whatis.com (`http://whatis.techtarget.com`)
- ✔ Ask Jeeves (`www.ask.com`)
- ✔ TechWeb (`www.techweb.com/encyclopedia`)
- ✔ Bob Jensen's Technology Glossary (`www.trinity.edu/~rjensen/245glosf.htm`)
- ✔ NetLingo (`www.netlingo.com`)
- ✔ Geek.com (`www.geek.com`)

TIP

How do you compare?

Using the questions we outlined earlier in this chapter, create a spreadsheet and fill in your company's info. Then make a column for each of your major competitors, and fill in the same information.

Keep your chart updated; it'll give you a clear picture of how you compare to your competitors. It'll also be a handy tool, when candidates ask for specifics about how you stack up against other firms.

If you're recruiting in other fields, you'll find a similar wealth of information online. Excellent medical and scientific resources, for example, include the following:

- ✔ Virtual Hospital (www.vh.org)
- ✔ PDR.net (http://physician.pdr.net/physician/index.htm)
- ✔ Life Sciences Dictionary (http://biotech.icmb.utexas.edu)
- ✔ Encyberpedia (www.encyberpedia.com/glossary.htm)

If your field is small or unusual, simply enter some keywords on one of the major search engines — such as "horse training," "Roman art," or "flower arranging" — and you're bound to uncover useful sites (and better yet, sites that link to multiple resources). Also, if you're a novice in your company's field, explore sites geared to high school or college students. These sites, aimed at beginners, can help bring you up to speed on the basics of anything from geology to genetics. Last but not least, try the low-tech way to master high-tech talk: Visit your library or bookstore and pick up a few basic books and dictionaries. (If you're recruiting for IT positions, three basics are *Computers: Systems, Terms and Acronyms, The Computer Desktop Encyclopedia,* and *Client/Server Computing For Dummies.*)

Resources for Recruiters

Is there such thing as a free lunch? Yes, when it comes to helpful hints, in-depth advice, and networking with other recruiters. Surprisingly, even though we're all battling to find employees in a tight labor market, recruiters are a friendly bunch. Forums and Web sites abound, sharing everything from specialized tips ("Where can I find a DCOM expert who speaks Mandarin?") to hard-learned experience ("So-and-so's job fair was a bust last year — be careful!")

One of the best free sites we've found is the Electronic Recruiting Exchange, which offers everything from expert articles to a forum where recruiters can share their knowledge. (Be sure to skim through their vast collection of archived articles, which offer a mini-education in the most important recruiting topics.) You can sign up to receive daily e-mails, and you can use the forum to query members about everything from salary rates to orientation tips. Among recent topics: "Where can I find executive assistants in San Rafael?" "How can we increase diversity in our company?" "Are there interviewing tools for assessing job candidates' integrity?"

Other excellent forums, which we use frequently, include TechnicalRecruiter. com (www.technicalrecruiter.com) and the Recruiters Network Forum at Yahoo! Groups (http://groups.yahoo.com).

Search the Web under "recruiting" and "human resources," and you'll find dozens of other valuable and free sources of information. Some of the best sites that post free articles, news, e-newsletters, or other information include the following:

- hr-esource.com (www.hr-esource.com)
- HRhub.com (www.hrhub.com)
- Society for Human Resource Management (www.shrm.org)
- Electronic Recruiting Exchange (www.erexchange.com)
- HR Today (www.hr-today.com)
- HRfree.com (www.Hrfree.com)
- HR e-Group (www.hrsolutionsinc.com/egroup.htm)
- HRWorld (www.hrworld.com)
- Vault.com (www.jobvault.com)
- HR.com (www.hr.com)

Still more help

Once you've mastered the basics, where do you go from there? Consider training programs that can give you an inside edge on modern recruiting techniques. The Breckenridge Group, Dallas Training and Consulting Services, Interbiznet, Semco Enterprises, AIRS, and PowerHiring are some well-known groups offering seminars and workshops. Different seminars focus on different skills and industries, so ask around on recruiting forums to get feedback on which training programs best suit your needs. And consider purchasing one or two in-depth textbooks on recruiting — but be sure they provide current information, because the Internet and other high-tech developments make recruiting a constantly evolving game.

If you're not Web-savvy, make basic Internet training a top priority. *Researching Online For Dummies* is an excellent how-to for beginners who need to master online skills quickly.

Another smart move is to join your local chapter of the Society for Human Resource Management (SHRM), which you can find at www.shrm.org. They're the leading organization for recruiters and HR specialists, and they can offer you in-depth advice about everything from hiring to firing.

When you can't know everything . . .

No matter how much you bone up on your company's products and services, you won't be able to answer every question a prospect has. When you can't, turn this to your advantage. You can say, "I don't have the answer to that right now, but I'll research it and get back to you quickly" — thus showing that you're interested and efficient. Or you can say, "I'm not familiar with that aspect of geothermal engineering — can you explain it to me?" This gives your candidate a chance to talk, and gives you a chance to assess how well your prospect communicates and passes on information.

Part II

Sell Yourself! How and Where to Advertise Your Jobs

The 5th Wave   By Rich Tennant

"Okay, so maybe the Internet wasn't the best place to advertise a product that helped computer illiterate people."

In this part . . .

To win at the recruiting game, you need to be better than the competition at finding new prospects and attracting their attention. In this part, we offer advice on writing tempting job descriptions, and tell you where to place those descriptions for maximum effect and minimal expense.

Chapter 5

Writing the Dynamite Job Description

- -

In This Chapter

▶ Understanding the job

▶ Picking an eye-catching job title

▶ Playing up your strong points

▶ Defining your dream candidate

- -

A great job description says, "Hey — we're a great company — come work for us!" It stands out in a crowd. It says, "We're fun," "We pay well," "We admire your talents," "We'll challenge you." It's tempting, persuasive, and welcoming. It attracts stellar applicants, and it's specific enough to dissuade the unqualified.

That sounds like a lot to accomplish with a few dozen words, but it's actually easy once you get the knack. Moreover, a great job description costs no more than a bad one. Thus, if you're clever, you can steal candidates from your competitors at this early stage in your recruiting efforts, without spending an extra penny.

Before You Start: Know What You Want!

Ever had this experience? Your eyes light up as you log in to check your e-mail and watch the resumes roll in. Then you start reading them, and the gleam fades. You wanted experienced Java programmers, but all of your applicants are brand-new grads looking for their first jobs. Or you advertised for medical transcriptionists, and received three resumes from people who misspelled the word "transcriptionist."

The problem, most likely, lies in your job description. Too often, recruiters write descriptions that sound good on paper but don't offer candidates enough information about the skill set and experience necessary for the job. To avoid this situation, sit down with the hiring managers seeking new employees, and find out exactly — *exactly* — what they want. Ask about the following:

- ✔ The day-to-day duties of the job
- ✔ The overall responsibilities involved
- ✔ Whether the employee will work in a team environment or independently
- ✔ Whether the position is contract or permanent
- ✔ Whether the job is full-time or part-time
- ✔ The career path/growth plan for the position
- ✔ The salary range
- ✔ The people with whom the new employee will interact
- ✔ What specific skills are required, and which are preferred but not necessary
- ✔ What technologies/computer systems the employee will be using
- ✔ How much education is required

If your hiring manager uses jargon you can't understand ("What we really need is an NDTA-certified therapist and a special ed teacher who can do discrete-trial behavior mod"), ask for a translation. Still fuzzy? See Chapter 4 for advice on deciphering the lingo of your field.

To gain still more insight, talk to employees who do the job you'll be advertising. Ask them, "What do you need to know to do your job well?" Also, have them describe a typical day, or even tag along with them for a few hours as they work. Often, in the process, you'll identify crucial skills you should include in your description.

As you meet with employees, try to get a feel for the type of applicant you're seeking. Does the position tend to attract college students, "techno-wizards," suit-and-tie business professionals, or talkative and outgoing individuals? Is your typical prospect likely to spend his free time surfing the waves, surfing the Net, or reading up on sine waves in a library? You can use that information later to aim your advertising at your target market.

If the job is new, and no one in your company performs this type of work, you'll need to do some detective work. Talk to other recruiters, or contact a professional organization that can put you in touch with a pro — what recruiters call an *SME,* or *subject matter expert.* Most people find it flattering to be tagged as experts, and they will happily share their wisdom with you.

LINGO

A word about keywords . . .

You can write the best ad in the world, and still miss dozens of your best candidates. How? By failing to include enough keywords. Here's where knowing the lingo of different job positions helps. For example, if you're posting an online job description for Visual Basic programmers, your keywords should include both Visual Basic *and* VB. Trying to hire C++ programmers? List object-oriented programming and OOP as well. Job seekers use a variety of keywords to search for jobs online, and the more inclusive your list is, the more prospects you'll attract.

Be sure to ask the people in the department requesting the hire to give you a list of all relevant keywords if you aren't fluent in the language of their field. Also, check online technical dictionaries (see Chapter 4).

In newspaper and magazine advertising, however, extra words cost more money — so pare your print ads down to the basics. Because readers don't need to search online to find your newspaper or magazine ads, an extensive list of keywords isn't necessary.

Who's Your Ideal Catch?

There's no such thing as a perfect employee, especially in a market where qualified candidates are as rare as needles in haystacks. Conversely, hiring an unqualified employee leads to poor job performance and, all too soon, an open position to fill all over again.

To avoid either scenario, ask your managers to list the skills and qualifications they want, and then go through them point-by-point to determine whether each skill or qualification is required, desired, or marginal to the job. This exercise will help you avoid writing ads that look like this: "Senior programmer needed. Must know C, C++, Visual Basic, Java, SQL Server, HTML, Oracle, COM/DCOM, and ActiveX. Basic cooking skills and black belt in karate preferred." Left to their own devices, many managers will write job qualifications that no person on the planet can fulfill.

Of course, sometimes you need to push managers into listing *more* qualifications, not fewer. If a manager merely asks for a technical writer, for example, find out what word processing and desktop publishing applications the writer should be able to use proficiently, what level of technical expertise the job requires, and what types of writing the candidate will be doing — marketing and promotional materials, user manuals, software installation guides, and so on.

Also, ask if your candidate really needs a college degree. If your prospect is a 25-year-old programmer, that degree translates into real job skills. But if he's a 45-year-old who's been writing code for twenty years, making a degree a requirement may remove a highly trained candidate from your prospect pool.

To maximize your chances of finding qualified candidates, without asking the impossible, ask your managers if they can be flexible. Can you consider years of experience in place of a college degree? Conversely, can training, education, or certification compensate for a lack of experience? If a candidate has experience that could transfer to a new setting or new equipment — for example, if a receptionist candidate has experience with different phone systems than yours — can you train on the job? If so, you'll expand your job pool without compromising on quality.

In addition, decide whether you can relocate applicants. If so, mention this in your job description, and post your description on out-of-state boards and in national newspapers. Also, determine whether you need a full-time, permanent hire, or if a part-time or contract person can fill the bill. If telecommuting is an option, play this up in your job description.

When you write your description, provide separate lists of *required* and *desired* skills if possible. Also, let prospects know if even the required skills are negotiable. You don't want an almost-perfect candidate to avoid you simply because she's lacking a little extra experience or an easily trainable skill.

Once you've defined your job, and the perfect person to fill it, it's time for stage two: writing the job description itself.

What's in a name?

Glance over the pairs of job descriptions shown in Table 5-1. Which one of each pair sounds more challenging, more interesting, or more enticing?

Table 5-1	The Power of Naming
Job Description A	*Job Description B*
clerk	retail salesperson, fashion/clothing department
nurse	critical care RN, leading pediatric hospital
accountant	tax accountant — three day weekends
kitchen help — vegetable prep	assistant to world-famous chef — learn as you cook
secretary	administrative assistant — wear jeans every day!
senior specialist	Java developer — cutting-edge e-commerce project

Analyze this!

One Fortune 500 company uses the following job titles for dozens of the jobs advertised on their Web site, no matter what department the jobs are in: Analyst, Analyst II, Senior Analyst, Associate Analyst, Lead Analyst, Coordinator, Consultant, Director, Manager, Representative, Programmer/Analyst, System Analyst, Technical Specialist.

These job titles tell job seekers next to nothing about what the jobs entail, or what skills are needed. If you were a Visual Basic Developer looking for a new position, would you click on 25 jobs with the title of "Analyst" to see if one of them might involve VB programming? Neither would we.

Clearly, the second description in each pair is the winner. That's because it better describes the job (retail salesperson versus clerk), advertises a major plus of the job (three-day weekends, casual dress, opportunities to learn), or promotes the company's image (world-famous chef, leading pediatric hospital).

Remember as you describe your job that it's just one of hundreds of jobs your prospects will see listed as they scour the boards or the classifieds. If your description jumps out at them, they'll read it first. Otherwise, you'll be lost in the crowd.

But what if writing isn't your thing? Not to panic! If you're having a little trouble writing winning job descriptions, visit www.shrm.org and www.jobdescription.com for tips on what to say and how to say it. Also, check out what your competitors are saying in their job board ads. (But don't use the same job description as other companies; customize it to fit your job and your firm.) Another piece of advice: If you're hiring for a critically important position, check with your company's public relations department. PR people usually are good writers, and they may be able to offer tips on making your job description more enticing.

How much should you say?

In the advertising world, words come with a price tag — and it can be a hefty one. While a 20-line ad in the classifieds may run you several hundred dollars, a full-page ad can set you back tens of thousands of dollars. Ads in trade journals also can cost you a pretty penny. And online ads often have word limits, so even on the Net it's important not to be too wordy.

How do you decide how much to say? Keep three goals in mind: Your ad needs to sell your company, sell the job, and describe the job well enough to attract qualified applicants and deter others. (It also needs to be legal; check out Chapter 21 to find out what you can and can't say.)

Also, consider the type of position you're filling. An executive or director-level job entails a vast amount of responsibility and requires extensive skills, experience, and education. In this case, a few hundred dollars worth of additional words can save thousands of dollars down the line, by helping you attract the right candidate the first time around. If you're hiring for a receptionist or a retail clerk, on the other hand, it's a good idea to keep your job description simple and to the point. And even for an executive position, anything longer than one page is too much. Save something to say for the interview!

No matter how short or long, your ad should say enough to be clear and understandable. In advertising, vague doesn't translate into mysterious and intriguing; it translates into unqualified applicants, or no applicants at all. Among the basics you need to spell out are the following:

- ✔ The job title (see preceding section).

- ✔ Brief info about your company — why a job seeker would want to work for you. (For example, you may want to emphasize highlights such as working with a progressive technology or for a prestigious firm.)

- ✔ Benefits, perks, and other advantages. (For example, "We offer competitive salaries, stock options, and some great benefits and perks including 4 weeks of paid time off, a quarterly education allowance, and a casual work environment.")

- ✔ Overall responsibilities and job focus. (For example, "As project manager, you'll coordinate and oversee the development of cutting-edge B2B e-commerce projects.")

- ✔ Day-to-day duties.

- ✔ Required/desired skills.

- ✔ Educational requirements.

- ✔ If applicable, your willingness to relocate prospects.

- ✔ Contact information. Remember your target market: If you're seeking candidates who don't need computer skills, chances are they may prefer to fax or mail their resumes. It's best to include your e-mail address, fax number, and street address in all ads; this gives the job seekers options, and making it easy for them is the goal.

We recommend drafting your ideal description, and then tailoring it later to fit the word count of your online posting or newspaper advertisement. You can use the full text on your Web site (see Chapter 7).

Making an offer they can't refuse

The following job descriptions show how it's done.

From MSN: tempting text that tells the reader the job is challenging, exciting, and important

Database Administrator

Contribute to the success of the MSN Platform and participate in revolutionizing MSN Technical Operations by integrating and deploying Data Operations as a leveraged discipline. Challenge the breadth of your systems expertise and the depth of your data analysis skills. Join a committed, results-driven team on a mission, who know that systems ultimately live or die by the ability to intelligently manage data. You will provide Database Engineering for the implementation, integration and ongoing technical support of the MSN Platform User Profile Store (UPS), a projected 5TB database system servicing a billion transactions per day. Your desire to improve, evolve or revolutionize the systems and processes you are exposed to will drive our success . . .

From Springfield Hospital in Vermont: selling the location with alluring imagery

Imagine this: air that smells like sunshine, mountains rising from the banks of rivers, villages suddenly appearing as the morning mist parts. Imagine sounds — a churchbell, a cow mooing, children laughing. Now imagine yourself in this picture. Do you like what you see? Then maybe there's a place for you at Springfield Hospital. Nestled on the banks of the Connecticut River in southern Vermont, minutes from Killington and Okemo ski resorts, our 69-bed community hospital is seeking a few good employees to fill our vacant positions . . .

From NetIQ: clearly defining the job and the skillset

Staff Technical Writer

What We Do:

Write, review, maintain, and release product documentation, including online help, user guides, reference manuals, training guides, and marketing materials. Obtain information from developers and product specialists, and on our own. Work independently and as a team to create high-quality, well-respected documentation. Play a vital role in user interface design and the software development process by helping to ensure our products are easy to use and understand. Deliver documentation in paper and in online formats, to the high praise of our customers and partners.

What We're Looking For:

Excellent writing, communication, and organizational skills.

Experience with publishing tools and technologies, including FrameMaker, Microsoft Word, RoboHelp, Adobe Acrobat, HTML, and HTML Help.

Entrepreneurial attitude and enthusiasm.

BS or BA degree in computer science, English, technical communications, or related field.

Experience in writing software documentation.

Experience in presenting technical information to a diverse audience, including self end-users, system administrators, and developers.

Extra Credit For:

Experience with graphics packages or web publishing tools.

Experience in writing API guides or developer reference materials.

Any technical exposure to Microsoft BackOffice technology (SQL Server, Exchange Server, etc.), relational database management, or performance, network, or database monitoring.

Salaries — when to be specific, when to leave wiggle room

If you know your ideal salary or hourly rate, or (better yet) you can offer a range, we suggest saying this in your job description. You'll get a better response, and you'll weed out candidates whose asking price is too high. If there is no set salary range for the job, or your company rules prohibit posting one, be sure to mention that you offer competitive salaries. (Be realistic, however, and know your upper limit.) If your salary is negotiable, say so in your posting; for example: "$25,000 to $35,000, negotiable depending on experience." This may prevent the $37,000 candidate from skipping over your job.

One caution: List salaries or hourly rates in your job descriptions only if it won't ruffle the feathers of current employees ("Hey, wait a minute — that's more than I'm making!")

Focus your sights

Be sure your job description targets the type of candidate you want. Are you looking for a recent college grad? Then describe your work site as modern and cutting edge, and play up the perks likely to appeal to Generation Y (see Chapter 1 for more about perks). Does the type of job you're advertising usually appeal to women? Then emphasize childcare and flex time.

Information technology professionals, engineers, doctors, nurses, and researchers will want to know the details about your work. Instead of simply saying "microbiologist needed;" say, "We're seeking an experienced microbiologist to work in a leading bioengineering laboratory that's at the forefront of pharmaceutical research," and then describe the technologies you use. Rather than saying, "RN for diabetes education," say, "RN needed to head diabetic education program. Working with a skilled team, you will meet with all diabetic patients, offer instructions on insulin use, diet, and exercise, make home visits, and work closely with physicians to coordinate outpatient services that will maximize the quality of life for our diabetic patients." The more skilled your candidate, the more detailed you should be.

If you're hiring cashiers or factory workers, on the other hand, you'll want to emphasize benefits and perks. Because driving a bus or working a cash register for Company Y is more or less the same as doing the same job for Company Z, it's important to identify the other factors that make your workplace different — for example, more vacation time, better salaries, or a medical plan that covers dependents.

Top of their class

For your how-to file, here's a job description that really makes the grade (*with our comments about why the job description works well*).

From JUNOT SYSTEMS: C++ Software Design Engineer

RESPONSIBILITIES (*Provides a detailed description of the job*)

Design and develop object-oriented components for a configurable enterprise application integration (EAI) product in Windows/NT Server using C++.

Work with seasoned software development R&D professionals in designing and developing future products.

Research new technologies, techniques and tools and successfully integrate them into the product development process.

Actively participate in recruiting and building the R&D team, developing and enhancing the R&D department infrastructure.

GROWTH (*Offers information designed to attract high achievers looking for challenging work*)

Develop experience in transaction processing using online and offline capabilities, SAP and/or Windows/NT security and monitoring.

Work with new technologies such as CORBA, XML, and EJB.

Opportunity to work on future products.

Opportunity to move into consulting role, working with our customers to analyze their requirements and configure our product to meet their needs.

QUALIFICATIONS (*Offers a concise list of the skills need for the job*)

Innovative!

Excellent communication and software development skills.

4+ years' software development experience using Object-Oriented techniques using Windows/NT and Visual C++.

Experience in object-oriented modeling, multi-threading, distributed systems, Remote Procedure Call (RPC), and relational databases preferred.

Experience in developing and/or enhancing software products (vs. custom applications) preferred.

Demonstrated ability to work both independently and in an aggressive, small team environment.

Demonstrated experience in all phases of product development.

BENEFITS (*Offers a tempting and extensive list of benefits*)

Major Medical (HMO or PPO)

Dental Care

Vision Service Plan

Life Insurance

Accidental Death and Dismemberment Insurance

Short Term Salary Continuation Plan

Long Term Disability Insurance

Education Assistance

Employee Assistance Program

Dependent Care Spending Plan

Credit Union

Voluntary Term and Universal Life Insurance through Payroll Deduction

401(k) Plan and Trust

Vacation and Perks

Horizons Expansion

What's Next?

Once you perfect your job description, the next question is: What do you do with it? You have a wealth of options, from posting your job on the Internet to advertising it on your Web site, to using the low-tech methods of journal and newspaper advertising. To choose, consider these factors:

- ✔ **What market are you targeting?** College graduates in high-tech fields hang out on the Internet, so hunt for them online. People looking for low-tech or entry-level jobs are more likely to peruse the classifieds. Executives and scientists are trickier to locate: track them down by advertising in specialty journals.

- ✔ **What do your candidates read for fun? Where do they hang out when they're not working?** Your answers may steer you toward creative advertising venues, from video game magazines to movie theaters to sporting events or local festivals (see Chapter 10).

- ✔ **How fast do you need your jobs filled?** Internet, radio, and TV ads often result in instant gratification. Weekly classified ads in newspapers usually pull in responses within days, but you may wait weeks for a response to a journal ad.

- ✔ **Do you have a Web site, or can you create one?** Web site recruiting is fast, efficient, and inexpensive, and should be on your list of musts.

- ✔ **How much money do you have?** Journal and television ads are usually costlier than small newspaper ads. Internet advertising can be very cost effective, and sometimes it's even free. Other forms of recruiting, as we explain later, can range from budget-friendly to extravagant.

In the next three chapters, we offer an in-depth look at your best recruiting options, from Internet job boards and Web site recruiting to print ads, TV and radio spots, and job fairs. In addition, we take a look at some of the more creative advertising approaches that today's companies are using, from blimps to pizza boxes to movie trailers. No matter what your budget or your target market, you'll find something that's right for you.

Chapter 6

Mining the Net: Secrets of Successful Online Recruiting

*O*nce upon a time, job seekers pounded the pavement all day, handing out resumes and filling out endless forms. Now they loll around in bathrobes or blue jeans, watching the soaps and playing fetch with their dogs, while Internet job boards and online resumes do the hard work of job hunting for them. Or, if they're currently working, they let the Net do their job hunting for them while they're busy making money at their current jobs. They love it — and so do employers, with more than 70 percent of companies now recruiting via the Net. It's a revolution you should join, if you want to compete in today's competitive labor market.

Internet recruiting isn't as easy as it sounds, however. Where do you list your jobs? How do you search resume banks? What do other recruiters mean when they talk about *flipping* or *X-raying* Web sites? How do you track down *passive* candidates — those who aren't actively seeking new jobs?

Our recommendation is to start with the simple skills, such as posting to job boards. As you grow more confident at online recruiting, try the more advanced techniques we outline in this chapter for tracking down potential employees on the Web.

How Web-savvy is America?

With computers getting cheaper, Internet connections getting faster, and Americans becoming more computer-literate, we're quickly becoming a nation of Web surfers. It's predicted that 194 million Americans will use the Internet by 2005, and currently 61 percent of the population that's 18 or older has Internet access. For college grads, of course, the numbers are even higher: In 2000, 87 percent of graduating seniors used the Internet to check out employment opportunities. (Sources: Jupiter Research, Mediamark Research, NACE 2000 Graduating Student Survey.)

Placing Job Ads: Why You Need the Net

"We need another radiology tech down here — yesterday."

"Where's the new programmer you promised me?"

"Memo to Human Resources: Help!!!!!!!!"

Does this sound like a typical day in your office? If so, you need the Web — and now. Internet recruiting is a powerful tool that can fill your open positions and make your recruiting stats soar.

One reason is speed. When you need to hit the ground running, job boards are one of the best places to start. You can post a new job in minutes, and start fielding resumes within hours. You can access resumes 24 hours a day, 7 days a week. And you can cancel posts quickly, saving the hassle of responding to applicants for a job that's already filled.

Additionally, most job boards include resume banks that you can search online. This gives you access to a steady supply of prospects, and allows you to screen resumes by searching for keywords rather than wading through stacks of hard copies.

Because they're global, job boards allow you to target candidates from San Francisco to Singapore with a single ad. They're also an excellent way to target hard-to-find employees in unusual fields. And job postings on the Internet attract candidates who are savvy about technology — the very people you want, if your jobs require high-tech know-how.

The price is right, too: Job boards charge anywhere from nothing to several hundred dollars for a posting, while newspaper ads can run you $500 to $50,000. For a quarter of the price of a small print ad, you can run an ad for months on a job board — and job boards let you include in-depth job descriptions, without shelling out extra dollars for those additional words (see Chapter 5). Many smaller commercial sites, and hundreds of nonprofit sites and university or professional boards, are entirely free.

Moreover, Internet boards aren't just for techies any more. Everyone from chefs to chauffeurs is posting resumes online these days, so the job boards are a good bet for most candidates (but not all — see the nearby sidebar, "Think before you post!"). However, with thousands of boards online, and new boards starting up every day, choosing the right ones can be a challenge. Here are some tips on getting the most for your money.

Big or small?

Odds are you've already heard of Monster, Dice, and HotJobs. That's because the "big boys" of the job board world attract the most attention, and the greatest number of job seekers. When you advertise during the Super Bowl, as Monster and HotJobs do, people notice! Monster boasts a database of more than 9 million job seekers, with FlipDog, HotJobs, Dice, HeadHunter, and similar boards posting impressive numbers as well.

Among the big boards that currently are the most popular with recruiters are the following:

- ✔ Monster.com
- ✔ Hotjobs.com
- ✔ Headhunter.net
- ✔ Careerbuilder.com
- ✔ Jobs.com
- ✔ **America's Job Bank** (www.americasjobbank.com)
- ✔ Flipdog.com
- ✔ Net-temps.com
- ✔ Jobtrak.com (college specific)
- ✔ Collegerecruiter.com (college specific)
- ✔ 6figurejobs.com (executive/director level)
- ✔ telecomcareers.com (telecom specific)
- ✔ Computerjobs.com (IT specific)
- ✔ Dice.com (IT specific)

Think before you post!

Before you jump into online recruiting, think about the types of jobs you're offering. Candidates for low-tech positions requiring no computer skills are less likely to be surfing the Web for jobs than IT professionals, salespersons, executives, medical staff, and financial professionals. Post jobs online for the latter, but use newspaper classifieds, in-store signs, and other avenues to attract the former.

Should you join the companies flocking to the big boards? Probably. Among the advantages of posting on larger boards are the following:

- ✔ Exposure — people see you. Many job seekers gravitate toward well-known boards and skip the rest.

- ✔ Big boards let you reach around the country or the world with a single posting.

- ✔ You can have postings for a wide variety of jobs at one convenient site.

However, bigger isn't necessarily better. Among the disadvantages of the larger job boards are these:

- ✔ You'll receive dozens or even hundreds of resumes that don't fit your needs.

- ✔ Most of the time, you'll pay more for big boards than you will for smaller boards.

- ✔ If relocation isn't in your game plan, you'll spend valuable time weeding out responses from candidates who live too far away.

That said, you'll probably want to advertise on at least one or two of the big boards — or more, if you're recruiting for hard-to-fill jobs, trying to fill lots of positions, or hoping to gain exposure. However, you'll also want to add some niche boards to your game plan, in order to reel in specialized candidates.

We list lots of URLs for job boards in this chapter, but don't be surprised if some of these boards vanish by the time you read this book. Internet job boards are highly volatile, with new ones springing up and old ones folding almost daily. So don't be discouraged if the board you're trying to reach is kaput; instead, search the net for the new one that's almost assuredly taken its place.

Narrowing your focus

Targeting job boards is a little like using the zoom feature on a video camera. You can use the big boards to "zoom out," casting a wide net and gaining exposure for your firm, but often pulling in resumes that don't match your needs. Or you can use specialized boards, called *niche boards,* to "zoom in" on candidates more likely to fit your ideal profile. Niche boards, which target a small slice of the job market, allow you to narrow your focus by geography, by skill, or by other factors. In addition, by posting to a variety of niche boards, you increase your exposure and garner more resumes.

Most recruiters use the big boards, but work niche boards aggressively to find highly desirable candidates who may be lost in the sea of big-board job seekers. In deciding which niche boards to use, consider three factors: the skills needed for the jobs you're advertising, the special qualities of the candidates you want to catch, and your location.

Using niche boards to post your job openings

Whatever the specialty, odds are there's a special job board for it. You may not be able to track down a trapeze artist or flugelhorn player — although it's possible — but you'll find boards for everyone from artists (`artjob.org`) to zookeepers (`aza.org`). You can locate niche boards simply by using the right search terms; for example, to locate boards for insurance agents, simply type in **job boards** and **insurance** at your favorite search engine and check out the results. Or join the recruiting forums we mention in Chapter 4 and post a message saying, "Help! Who can point me to boards for insurance agents?" Within 24 hours, you'll be barraged with helpful replies.

As you search for niche boards, be aware that job boards now enable you to zoom in on ever-smaller niches. Here are some examples of how you can catch the right candidates by using ever-more-focused job boards:

✔ Looking for high-tech professionals? Start with boards such as the following:

- `Computerjobs.com`
- `Dice.com`
- `Techies.com`
- `Brainbuzz.com`

And then narrow your search further; for example, if you're seeking Java programmers, try these:

- `javajobs.com`
- `justjavajobs.com`
- `javajobsonline.com`

✔ Looking for engineers? Start with boards such as the following:

- Jobs4Engineers (`www.ajob4engineers.com`)
- `Engineeringjobs.com`
- `Ceweekly.com`
- `Ieee.com`

And then search by category of engineer, for example:

- `chemicalengineer.com`
- `civiljobs.com` (civil engineering)
- `cfd-online.com` (computational fluid dynamics engineering)
- `electricalengineer.com`
- `petroleumengineer.com`
- `spacejobs.com` (aerospace)

✔ Looking for healthcare professionals? Start with general boards such as these:

- `Medimatch.com`
- `Healthcarejobstore.com`
- `Medhunters.com`
- `Medicareer.com`
- `alliedhealthjobs.com`
- `healthdirection.com`

Then narrow your search by category, for example:

- `Aorn.org` (operating room nurses)
- `Rehabquest.com` (occupational therapists)
- `Sportsmedicine.com`
- `ache.org/career.html` (American College of Healthcare Executives)
- `directorofnursingjobs.com` (management positions for nurses)
- PharmacistJobSite.com (`www.pharmacistjobsite.com`)

Using niche boards to pick the right people

Sometimes your firm is seeking more than just a skill set. Perhaps, for example, you're striving for a more diverse workforce. Here again, niche boards can help. The trick is to define the category of employee you're seeking, and determine which niche boards best fit your needs.

Who's on the Web?

No matter what the job, your future employees are just a few computer clicks away! Some examples of niche boards for large and small professions:

- journalismjobs.com (print and electronic media)

- nukeworker.com (nuclear power)

- physicsweb.org (physics)

- biostatisticianjobs.com (biotech)

- awn.com/career/ (cartoonists)

- marketingjobs.com

- teacherjobs.com

- attorneyjobs.com

- museum-employment.com (curators and other museum employees)

Here's an example. Say you're after an executive. You can post your job on sites such as the following:

- Exec-U-Net (bizwiz.com/touch/execunet)

- 6FigureJobs (6figurejobs.com)

- ChiefMonster.com (my.chief.monster.com)

- Careerjournal.com (careerjournal.com)

Now, take this example a step further. Suppose that you're hiring this executive for a firm in a largely minority community, and you want to be sure that you reach out to all candidates, including minority candidates. In addition to posting your job on your usual boards, you also can post on sites such as these:

- The National Society of Hispanic MBAs job board (www.nshmba.org)

- The National Black MBA Association job board (www.bmba.net)

- The Minorities Job Bank (www.minorities-jb.com)

- diversityemployment.com

- iminorities.com

- diversilink.com

By posting your job descriptions on these boards, you'll double your chances of finding a candidate who has the right skill set and can make your company more responsive to your community.

Similarly, if you want to diversify your workplace by reaching more women, seniors, or disabled candidates with your job ads, seek out niche boards for job seekers in these groups.

Using niche boards to attract local candidates

A third plus of job boards is that many are local, allowing you to reach candidates in your own backyard. Again, you can target both geographical location and job skills, to refine your search.

Suppose, for example, that you work for a Baton Rouge hospital that's short on nurses. If you advertise on Monster or on national medical job boards, you'll receive resumes from all over the country. You can narrow your search, however, by posting on Med Job Louisiana (medjoblouisiana.com). Nurses who search this board are likely to be Louisiana residents, and many may live right in your neighborhood. Thus, local boards can save you both time and the money you'd spend on relocation expenses.

Most major cities have job boards and resume banks specific to their area, as well as online versions of newspaper classifieds. To track down these boards, run a computer search or ask the members of a recruiting forum (see Chapter 4) to steer you to them.

Judging the Job Boards

Big boards, little boards, general boards, niche boards — how should you spread your advertising dollars around? Not all job boards produce, and the best way to find out which boards work is by trial and error.

To make this process fairly painless, research the boards before you buy a membership or post a job. Ask for specifics about what each board offers, how many resumes it lists, and how it advertises its site to job seekers. Also, request references. And ask about free trials; most boards, except for some of the biggest, offer them.

In addition, ask if the boards that you're considering can offer these features:

- ✔ *Job wrapping*, in which the job board can automatically import job postings from your company Web site
- ✔ A link to your Web site
- ✔ Productivity tools such as automated search agents and form letters

Take advantage of other people's experience, too. Visit the recruiting forums we discuss in Chapter 4, and ask the forum participants about their experiences, both good and bad, with the boards you're considering. In addition, ask your current employees which job boards they've used, and what they liked or disliked about each one. Also, look for Internet surveys that rank job boards — but be sure you find fairly recent surveys, because job boards make frequent changes to their sites.

Keep costs to a minimum by advertising on any free job boards you find, including the job boards of professional organizations, universities, and alumni groups. Some free boards are great and others aren't, so keep track of the winners and don't waste time on the duds.

Give each board you're considering a test run, by pretending that you're a job seeker and navigating the site. Is it easy to use? Does it offer options for searching, such as keywords, location, and so on? What results do you get when you search? Does the site charge you to post a resume?

Last but not least, find out where your competition is posting. You should post in some of the same areas.

Getting on Board: It's Easy!

After you choose a board, signing up is a snap. Some boards offer an online sign-up option, while others have sales reps who contact you to explain costs and services. In either case, know what you want ahead of time. All major boards, and some minor ones, offer both job postings and resume banks, and most offer you these options:

- ✔ Posting jobs only.
- ✔ Accessing the resume bank only.
- ✔ Using both.

It's pricey to purchase both services if you use lots of boards, so be picky. Pay one or two boards for resume search access, and limit the rest to job posting only.

Many boards allow you to choose between paying for individual postings, or purchasing a membership. The memberships save you money, and give you unlimited access to resume banks, but try a few individual postings first. This allows you to gauge how many resumes a board pulls in, and the type of applicants it attracts.

Contract lengths for job boards vary, with some boards requiring a full yearly membership and others charging monthly fees. Try to negotiate an out-clause, so you can escape from your contract if you're not satisfied within the first 30 or 60 days.

Even the best job boards aren't perfect, so establish a good relationship with your rep, and keep in touch with him. That way, if you encounter problems later on, you'll have a friend in your corner. Also, don't hesitate to complain if a job board fails to live up to its promises.

When you sign up for a board, you'll find easy instructions for posting your jobs. After you've followed them, simply sit back and wait for the resumes to land in your inbox. Don't get too comfortable, however; be sure to work your site hard, by using all of your allotted job postings, and taking full advantage of any free trials you're offered.

Using job board resume banks

Resume banks put thousands of online resumes at your fingertips. With a few keystrokes, you can craft searches that scour these resumes to find exactly the prospects you're seeking.

The major boards usually offer more search options than smaller boards do. For example, in addition to letting you search by skill set, big boards often allow you to search for one or more of the following:

- Candidates with college degrees
- Candidates in specific states and cities
- Candidates with specific salary requirements
- Candidates seeking temporary or part-time work
- Candidates willing to relocate

To search a resume bank, start with the obvious search terms — for example, **accountant** and **Memphis** — and then refine your search if needed. Seeking an accountant with experience in the health industry? Then add terms such as **health** or **hospital**. Want someone with a Master's degree? Then search on **Master's** or **MA**. Play with your key words, so they're not too vague or too exclusive.

Also, try different search terms on different resume banks; we've found that what works on one doesn't always work on the others. Start by reading the searching tips at each resume bank, and then practice until you get a feel for which terms bring results. Many larger resume boards allow you to refine your searches if they return too many resumes, so start with a few broad search terms and then add more if necessary.

Some boards allow you to create *search agents* that will automate your searches so that it isn't necessary to enter your search string on each visit. Whether you use search agents or create your own search strings each time, be sure to search your resume banks regularly — at least once a week, and every day if possible.

When you spot a dynamite resume, make contact immediately (especially if it's for an IT position). Remember, thousands of other recruiters are mining the resume banks at the same time you are!

Keeping score: Do your boards earn their keep?

Some boards flood you with dozens of hot prospects, while others leave you empty-handed. To track which boards work and which don't, create a spreadsheet and list the following to help you know how well your boards are producing:

- ✔ The number of resumes each site helps you track down.

- ✔ The number of qualified job seekers that each site locates for you. A board that generates 10 dynamite resumes a week is a better value than one that sends you 100 mediocre ones.

- ✔ Other strengths and weaknesses. For example, which boards are best for targeting diverse candidates? Which have the best or worst customer service? Which sites are the most efficient, the easiest to post on, the easiest to search, and the easiest to navigate?

Beyond the Boards: Seeking Passive Candidates

In the following sections, we tell you how to master more advanced techniques for finding passive candidates on the Internet. This is trickier than simply posting to the job boards, but for professional recruiters, it's where the action is.

What do we mean by *passive candidates?* They're people who aren't actively hunting for a job, but who might be willing to contemplate a move — either now or in the future. Maybe they're already thinking about looking for new positions. Maybe they're not, but a gentle nudge could set them in motion. In effect, passive candidates are those who have the skills you need — even if they're happy in their current positions, and leaving is the furthest thing from their minds.

To find these passive candidates, you need to sift through both personal and corporate Web pages, scour newsgroups, and use search engines. Then, after you track your passive candidates down, you can use your recruiting skills to convince them to take a look at your company and what you have to offer. Here's how to start.

Step one: Search the newsgroups

Newsgroups are discussion forums where people of similar interests get together to share ideas and information online. There's a newsgroup for almost everyone, from actors to aerospace engineers. In particular, newsgroups are popular with high-tech professionals and high-level employees in biotech and other fields.

To use Google (`http://groups.google.com`) to search for newsgroups that interest the prospects you're targeting, click on Search Discussions. Before you do, however, read up on the rules and etiquette for posting. Also, never — never, never, never — post a job description or other recruiting information in a newsgroup that doesn't specifically allow such posts. (Google specifically lists the newsgroups that are job-related.) Rather, if you spot a person in a newsgroup who seems to have the skills and knowledge that your company needs, e-mail that person separately, using your company's e-mail address. (For more information on using newsgroups, check out *The Internet For Dummies,* published by Hungry Minds, Inc.)

Step two: Use search engines

Whether you're seeking new salsa recipes or tracking down cheap airline tickets, odds are you use search engines almost every day. But did you know that you can use them to hunt for passive job seekers as well? To do so, you'll need to master the basics of Boolean searches.

The word *Boolean* scares some Internet beginners, but you probably use Boolean searching already without even realizing it. For example, you're using a basic Boolean search if you do the following:

- Look for a recipe using **beef and crockpot**.
- Check out car part prices using **Nissan + 02 sensor**.
- Look for information on the new drug you got from your doctor, by searching on **glucophage or metformin**.

Basically, Boolean searching uses words such as AND, OR, NOT, and NEAR, or the symbols + and -, or similar commands to fine-tune searches. Some examples:

- **Java or XML** will find resumes of people with either skill.
- **Java not XML** or **Java - XML** will find resumes that list Java but not XML.
- **Java and XML** or **Java + XML** will find only resumes that list both skills.
- **Java near XML** will find resumes in which these two words occur close together.

> ✔ **Java and (XML or Unix)** will find resumes with Java as well as either XML or Unix.

> ✔ **"senior Java programmer"** (including quotation marks) will find resumes in which all three words appear together.

The more terms you use, the more powerful your search will be. Advanced Boolean searching is beyond the scope of this book, but you'll find plenty of tutorials on the Internet. (In particular, we recommend www.searchenginewatch. com.) Remember that different search engines use different terms, so check the search engine's searching tips and tailor your searches individually. (*Researching Online For Dummies,* published by Hungry Minds, Inc., has loads of valuable tips on finding what you need on the Internet.)

The top search engines for recruiters include Alta Vista, Northern Light, Infoseek, Alltheweb, and Google. Metasearch engines, such as Dogpile and Copernic, search several engines at one time. To do advanced Boolean searches, use the Power Search or Advanced Search options for each engine. Compile a list of keywords ahead of time; for example, if you're searching for a Visual Basic programmer, your keywords can include Visual Basic, VB, developer, programmer, and application. The better your terms, the more luck you'll have.

Step three: Run "title" and "URL" searches

Search engines put a whole world full of prospects within your reach by allowing you to use title or URL commands to search for resumes. Using these terms, you can find any employee, anywhere on the planet, who has a resume posted on the Internet.

For example, to search for resumes of civil engineers, enter this search string in a search engine's advanced search box:

```
(title:resume or url:resume) and "civil engineer"
```

You can refine your search still further by adding an area code, city, or other key words.

Step four: Flip Web sites

Flipping, one of the hottest new skills in recruiting, means looking for resumes or other documents that link to a Web site in which you're interested. For example, if you're looking for technical writers, you may want to flip the Society for Technical Communication. By doing so, you'll be looking for resumes on the Web that link to this organization.

Or suppose you want to hire candidates who work at (or once worked at) NoName Airlines. These people often list the company name, as well as a link to the company, on their resumes. To find them, enter the following search string into the Advanced Search box at one of the major search engines:

```
(title:resume or title:resumes or URL: resume or URL:resumes)
            and link:noname.com
```

Or try:

```
(title:resume or title:resumes or URL: resume or URL:resumes)
            and link:noname.com and "network administrator"
```

Each search engine has different ways to flip and search, and different settings you can select, so check each site for instructions.

Step five: X-ray Web sites

X-raying, which is somewhat similar to flipping, is a technique for viewing all of the pages within one server. When you X-ray, you're peering into normally closed off areas of sites, where you'll often find lists of employees, graduates, board members, or executives. (Think of it as sneaking in the back door of a Web site, and exploring everything linked to the site's home page — employee directories, resumes, and so on. It's not hacking, because the information is readily available, so you don't need to feel guilty about doing it.)

If you're looking for programmers, for example, you may want to X-ray the sites of firms that create computer software. You can also X-ray a college server, to look for names of alumni, or X-ray the server of an organization to look for board members, officers, and general members. For example, to X-ray an organization, you can enter the following into AltaVista's advanced search box (where * is the organization you want to X-ray):

```
host:*.org and "chapter officers"
```

One common search term for X-raying is domain:*.com, with * being the name of the server you want to X-ray. For example:

```
Domain:xyzcorp.com
Domain:yale.edu
```

Again, each search engine has its own setting for X-raying. Check the advanced search section for each engine to see how it's done.

One trick for unearthing useful info when you X-ray: Use search terms such as **Meet the Team** or **Employee Directory,** which sometimes lead you to the e-mails of key employees.

You Too Can Be an Online Recruiting Guru!

Online recruiting is a new game, and you're getting in on the ground floor. That's good news, because it means that even if you're starting from scratch, you can catch up to the pros in just a short time.

You'll find plenty of resources, both on and off the Net, to help you become an online recruiting genius. Check out the newsletters and forums we list in Chapter 4, and consider taking seminars specifically geared to Internet recruiting. The best include those offered by the following:

- ✔ AIRS (Advanced Internet Recruiting Strategies) — even if you can't attend a seminar, check out their homepage, `www.airsdirectory.com`, for information.

- ✔ `RISEway.com`

- ✔ `Recruiting-Online.com`

- ✔ The Breckenridge Group (`www.breckenridgegroup.com`)

- ✔ interbiznet.com (`www.interbiznet.com`)

- ✔ `Monster.com`

And practice, practice, practice. Keep refining your searches, and mastering new techniques such as the tricks we suggest for flipping and X-raying. Each week, try out new search engines and investigate new job boards. Find Web sites on advanced Boolean searching, and get tips on Internet recruiting from the experts on recruiting forums. The better you get at online searching, the more employees you'll "Net"!

What works best?

According to Monster.com, the following online strategies bring in the best resumes:

Job posting sites: 38%

Resume databases: 25%

Internet resume searches: 21%

Company web sites: 15%

Other: 1%

Chapter 7

First Impressions Count: Using Your Web Site to Win Employees

*A*re you putting your Web site to work for you? With a solid design and smart content, you can use your site to paint a picture of your firm as a wonderful place to work. You can reach out to qualified candidates from around town, around the state, around the country, or even around the world. You can also offer easy access to your current job openings and give candidates a choice of convenient ways to contact you.

Clearly, if you don't yet have a Web site, you need to get one — fast. It's equally important, however, to have a *good* Web site. That's because a bad site can actually hurt your image, by frustrating would-be employees and making you look antiquated or incompetent. Luckily, the rules for creating a winning Web site are simple.

Making Your Web Site User-Friendly

Above all, you want your Web site to welcome visitors — and especially visitors who might be interested in opportunities at your company. This sounds simple, yet an astonishing number of firms shell out good money for Web site designs so annoying that they drive job seekers away. How?

Many of these companies go for form over function, hiring artsy Web designers who create fancy but slo-o-o-ow pages that irk users rather than impressing them. They also tend to go overboard on frames, multimedia applications, plug-ins, and other elements that many browsers can't handle. If you're a high-tech company, use these new technologies — they say, "we're modern, smart, and up-to-date" — but be sure they don't stop job seekers in their tracks.

Other companies make the opposite error and hire amateurs ("Hey, Bob's kid needs to design a Web page for a college project. Let's just hire him.") The sites these amateurs create almost always project the counter-productive message, "We're operating on a shoestring."

To avoid either mistake, assign the job to a professional who'll make your site look state-of-the-art, but make your instructions crystal clear: Speed and user-friendliness are your top priorities.

Also, make sure your employment/current jobs section is simple to find. Have an "Employment" or "Career" link on your home page that takes job seekers directly to your employment opportunities, rather than hiding this link in an "About us" or "Who we are" section. Remember the two-click rule: Job seekers should be able to reach your employment section and current job postings with no more than two clicks. When they get there, be sure your online application is easy to complete and your postings are up-to-date. (See "The All-Important Employment Section," later in this chapter.)

Projecting Your Image: Does Your Web Site Say "Wow" or "Zzzzz"?

Your site should be easy to navigate, but equally importantly, it should convey who you are. Do you want your prospects to see you as a cutting-edge leader? Then use Web page technology that makes your site look modern and cool. Are you aiming for friendly and dependable? Then you'll want your site to be warm and welcoming.

The following sections offer advice on using your Web site to say, "Here's who we are — and here's why you'll love us."

Talking up your company culture

Your Web site's content should paint a picture in a viewer's mind. Avoid burying readers in text; instead, use short, eye-catching phrases to describe your products, your goals, and your company culture. Points to play up include the following:

✔ **Your major projects:** Especially cutting-edge products or services that set you apart from the crowd.

✔ **Your atmosphere:** Are you casual? Innovative? Challenging? Exciting? Use your Web site to convey that image to your visitors.

✔ **Your benefits and perks:** If you have a competitive package, list your perks and benefits prominently. If you have a beautiful day-care facility, a fully loaded gym, or an on-site cappuccino bar, use photos to show it off.

✔ **Your training opportunities:** Today's employees want to know more, more, more, especially if they're in the fast-paced IT and health industries. If you offer a good training program, feature it on your site.

✔ **Your charitable activities:** Do you host an annual run to raise money for a women's shelter? Give your employees time off to work for a food bank? Sponsor a children's soccer team? Mention your activities, and also post information and press releases about upcoming events.

Also, impress your visitors with hard facts that show your company in its best light: "Our newest software product was top-rated by *PC Magazine*." "We grossed over 4 million dollars last year." "Our hospital received the highest ranking from JCAHO."

In addition, your Web site design should include photos that enhance your image, such as the following:

✔ Views of your office, if it's attractive.

✔ Photos of your surroundings, if you're in a great area.

✔ Candid shots of employees enjoying your game room, playing on the company softball team, or working in a casual and relaxed environment.

If your budget allows, and your facilities are truly impressive, consider including a virtual tour of your office and surroundings.

Personalizing your site: Bios and beyond

Give your Web site a human face by adding stories about a range of employees from the CEO to the stock clerk. Be sure your profiles help to reflect the culture and image you want to project. Ask your Web site stars to talk about what makes them proud to work for your company, what makes your company a fun or challenging place, what makes their jobs enjoyable, and what makes your company better to work for than your competitors.

Try to pick employees whose stories will pique your prospects' interest — for example, "Bob hiked through India in 1995, rafted down the Amazon last year, and plans to climb Everest some day. That's why he picked our firm — 'The project I'm directing is a challenge, not a daily grind.'" Also, feature a variety of employees — men and women, different ethnic groups, different ages, and different backgrounds.

Employee stories also give you the opportunity to use photos cleverly, sending multiple messages. For example, if you're featuring an emergency room nurse, use two photos: one of her working closely with a doctor, and another of her playing in your hospital's annual touch football game for charity. You'll send several messages: "Our nurses are respected members of the team," and "We have fun when we're not working hard."

One caution, however: Other companies, or outside recruiting firms, may target the employees featured on your Web site and attempt to steal them away. Limit the number of employees you feature by name, and avoid showcasing the most valuable and the most vulnerable. Also, don't use employees' last names, unless it's absolutely necessary.

Also, include bios of your senior management staff on your Web site. Job seekers want to know who's running your company, and what their backgrounds and qualifications are.

Remember, however, that employee information is a double-edged sword: Your bios can attract new employees, but they can also give other recruiters the info they need to attempt to steal these star employees (see Chapter 28). So introduce visitors to a few select employees, but don't publish the names of all your employees on your Web site.

Letting others sing your praises

Did *ComputerWorld* say that your new database product is "a cut above the rest"? Did *Business Week* run a fascinating profile of your CEO? If so, spread the news on your Web site by linking your homepage to a Press Releases or News section. It's more impressive when outsiders praise you than when you praise yourself.

Also consider including testimonials on your Web site (for example, "Your product doubled our productivity in two weeks!" Or "We wouldn't hire any other ad agency — your people are smarter and savvier than anyone else in the business.") Prospective employees want to know that your products or services are highly regarded.

Other features that can impress viewers and make them envision your company as a desirable place to work, include the following:

- ✔ Lists of awards your company has won
- ✔ Lists of recent patents the company has received
- ✔ Lists on which your company appears as an "Employer of Choice"
- ✔ Graphs showing profit growth or increasing stock value

Showcase your people on your Web site

Note how this vignette accomplishes several purposes: It makes XYZ 's jobs sound rewarding, it shows the company culture in a positive light, and it mentions one of the company's charitable activities:

> Six years ago, Jerri didn't have any idea she'd be working for XYZ Corp. In fact, she'd never even heard of us!

> "Back then I was just another worker ant in a drab little cubicle, working at a boring job," she says. Then, serendipitously, Jerri signed up for XYZ's annual Mountain Climb for Charity.

> "I spent the morning hiking with a couple of XYZ employees," she laughs. "And by the time I got back down to the bottom of the mountain, they'd convinced me to call for an interview."

> Jerri called the next week, and within a month she joined the XYZ team as a senior software developer. Is she happy she made the move? "Delighted," she says. "It's the best career decision I ever made. Here, I deal with managers who respect my work and give me the freedom to create a great product. I'm not an ant in a cubicle; I'm a respected member of the team, and management listens to what I have to say. And I like knowing that the medical software we're developing will make people's lives better."

> In addition, Jerri loves XYZ's on-site gym, and her husband enjoys dropping by at lunchtime for a quick game of billiards in the XYZ game room. Oh, and she still participates in the XYZ Mountain Climb every year, with the two employees who sold her on XYZ, Brenda, who's now our assistant director of hardware design, and Gary, our chief network administrator.

Making your jobs sound irresistible

Use your Web site to promote your jobs in terms that will attract qualified prospects. Your creativity isn't limited on your own site, as it is on job boards or in ads, so think of imaginative ways to make your jobs sound tempting. (See Chapter 5 for tips on creating powerful job descriptions.) Also, add positive quotes from your managers: "I look for self-starters who can take a project and run with it," or, "I've continuously found new challenges and opportunities to learn new skills at XYZ Corp."

One more tip: List the skills and qualifications of employees you're likely to be hiring later on, even if you don't have openings right now. It's a good way to recruit qualified candidates for future openings in your company.

Writing for the Web

Does your Web site text catch your readers' eyes, or make them yawn? Here's how to perk up your prose:

- Use descriptive sentences, but don't be wordy.

- Use "you," "we," and "us," rather than "the employee" or "the company."

- Use bullets and short paragraphs, to give readers' eyes a rest.

- Break information down into short, reader-friendly categories.

- Use color and bolding to make important text stand out.

- Use tables, charts, and text boxes to play up your strong points.

- Spell it right! Nothing says "incompetent" like misspellings and grammatical errors. Also, be sure several people with good writing skills proof your Web site before you go live.

- Use active voice. Don't say, "Great reviews were earned by our product;" instead, say, "our product earned great reviews."

- Don't use a big word when a little one will do.

The All-Important Employment Section

You want your prospects to think your Web site looks great. You want them to admire the company image you're projecting. But what you want above all is for them to hit that little button that says "Jobs." Make sure that button is easy to find — and then keep your prospect hooked, by following these rules.

- **Keep it simple:** Offer an application form that asks a minimum of smart, well targeted questions and allows the option of pasting or attaching resumes. Make your form detailed enough to screen out unqualified candidates, but not so long and boring that it'll chase off qualified ones. To find out what works and what doesn't, try completing forms at other companies' sites.

- **Offer options:** Some job seekers come to you with resumes in hand, eager for an interview and a job. Others happen across your Web site and say, "Hmmm. I wonder if I should think about changing jobs. This company looks really interesting." Your job site should appeal to both active and passive job seekers. Offer the option to cut and paste a resume, to attach a resume (as a Word document, for example), to fill out an online application form, or simply to sign up for more information. Make the process as easy as possible for your prospects no matter what stage of job hunting they're in.

✔ **Allow job seekers to send their resumes even if you currently have no open positions:** Some companies also allow candidates to submit resumes for specific positions, even if these positions are currently filled. This provides the firms with a pool of candidates that they can contact as soon as a job opens up.

✔ **Stay current:** Outdated postings create a bad impression. Make it a rule to remove jobs from your Web site postings as soon as they're filled, and to add new job openings as soon as they become available.

✔ **Offer search options:** If you have lots of job openings, it's important to let candidates search by job title, skill set, department, or location (if you have more than one site).

✔ **Make sure your form works:** Have friends or employees "beta test" your application form, using different computers at their homes or the local library. Make sure your pages work with different browsers (that is, both Netscape and Microsoft Internet Explorer).

✔ **Don't waste prospects' time with bad design:** Beware, in particular, the multi-page application form that "nukes" all of your applicants' entries if they make a single mistake. Make sure your candidates can page forward and backward, and make revisions on any page, without losing the data they've entered. (For that matter, a multi-page application form, in and of itself, may drive job seekers away. It's much more effective to give them the option of attaching their resumes. If you do use a form, keep it short.)

✔ **Offer a "New Jobs" button:** This allows repeat visitors to access your most recent job postings quickly and easily.

✔ **Tell them how to reach you:** Be sure that in addition to an e-mail address, your site lists your geographical address and telephone number — as well as a fax number, if you're able to accept faxed applications.

✔ **Publicize your referral program:** If you have a referral program that rewards employees for bringing in new recruits (see Chapter 9), mention this prominently.

✔ **Provide information on internships, too:** If you offer an internship program, make sure it's easy for interested individuals to obtain information about the program and to apply for positions.

✔ **Let them know you're there:** Respond right away to on-line applications. Consider using an auto-responder, which will automatically send out a reply — for example, "Thank you for your interest in XYZ Corp. We're reviewing your application/resume and will contact you soon if your background fits a current opening or if we have an opportunity for you in the future."

✔ **Include a *boss button* (also known as a *bail button*):** Many potential candidates will spot your Web site while they're at work. Encourage them to linger by providing a button that quickly changes the screen from "Jobs at XYZ" to a neutral site. That way, your prospects won't have to fret about a supervisor catching them job hunting.

✔ **Foster a long-term relationship:** Ask interested job seekers to sign up to receive new job postings by e-mail. If possible, tailor your e-mails, so recipients get lists of jobs that suit their specific interests and skill sets. You'll keep your name in your prospects' minds, and collect their e-mail addresses to boot.

Should You Outsource Your Web Site Design?

Perhaps. It's key to get your Web site just right, because it's the first impression many prospects have of your firm. You wouldn't wear a T-shirt and blue jeans to call on a major sales client, and a badly designed Web site creates just as poor an image.

Moreover, unlike a print or online ad, which expires after a few days or weeks, your Web site promotes your company all the time. A good Web site, in addition to advertising your product or service, can attract job seekers day after day, for a fraction of the cost of print or online advertising. Thus, a poorly designed Web site that doesn't work well will actually cost you, sometimes dearly, down the line.

If your company has a Web site developer with talent and experience — and that means experienced in designing *commercial Web sites with employment sections* — then keeping your Web design in-house is a good option. The advantages: It's less expensive than outsourcing, you'll have more control over the design, and it's easier to update and maintain an in-house site.

However, if you don't have a skilled Web designer on your staff, outsourcing can make sense. A company that specializes in Web design can offer greater expertise, greater speed in getting you online, and a team of people experienced in different aspects of Web design — for example, design, content, and marketing.

Hello? Hello? Is anybody there?

You're out there — but does anyone *know* you're out there? Make sure your Web site is listed by as many search engines as possible. For a small fee, you can hire an outside firm to place your site on a large number of search engines.

Also, list your Web site address on your business cards, in your ads, on your stationery, and on your brochures.

LINGO

Sticky + viral = successful

Whether you outsource your site or do it yourself, try to make it *sticky* and *viral*. It sounds icky, we know, like the awful bug your office mates are spreading around. But here's a translation:

A *sticky* site offers lots of interesting features that keep people coming back for more. How can you make your site sticky? Some sites offer free articles by experts on topics of interest to job seekers. Some offer free products or discounts, wallpaper for computer screens, software, or other little goodies. And others offer online mini-courses or host chat rooms where people interested in relevant technologies can share ideas and information.

A *viral* site is one that encourages viewers to pass the site's information on to friends. Make your site viral by including buttons such as "send this job description to a friend" and "send a copy of our newsletter to a friend."

If you outsource your Web site design, choose a firm carefully. Request a portfolio of sites they've created, and visit each one online. Do the sites work? Are they fast? Do they project a clear, positive image? Are the sites accurate reflections of that company's image and culture? Test the functionality and user-friendliness of the sites, too, by pretending that you're a job seeker. Is it easy to find job postings, apply for jobs, or obtain more information?

Also, contact the companies listed in the portfolio, to see if they're pleased with the design company's work. And when you do choose a design firm, be sure that your company holds the copyright to your site. Otherwise, disagreements can become messy and costly.

Whether you choose to outsource your site or keep it in-house, do your research up front so that you'll know what you want. To get a feel for how your site should look, visit leading company Web sites, and see if their designs are worth emulating. Also, find out what the experts and Web site reviewers think of some of the recruitment Web sites out there. For example, www.wetfeet.com offers a Recruitment Web Site of the Week review that tests the navigation, functionality, and user-friendliness of different sites.

Chapter 8

Selling Your Company: The Low-Tech Options

*W*ith all your Internet advertising options, is it ever necessary to step out of the virtual recruiting world and into the real world of newspapers, magazines, radio, and job fairs? Yes, because sometimes the traditional methods of advertising work better than high-tech approaches. And other times, you need both new technology and tried-and-true techniques to find the candidates you seek.

This chapter offers tips and tricks for maximizing your return from traditional advertising techniques, when online recruiting is more than you need, or conversely, not enough to get the job done.

When Job Boards Are Overkill: Using Newspaper Ads

You can pay hundreds of dollars to post ads online for janitors, cashiers, or clerks, but you may be wasting your money. That's because it's often easier to attract entry-level and low-tech employees simply by placing a small ad in your local newspaper's classified section.

Small newspaper classifieds also can be an attractive option for advertising for retail sales positions, receptionists, secretaries, and similar positions.

Smaller newspaper ads are less effective in recruiting experienced programmers, nurses, and other in-demand professionals, however, and they generally won't attract top-management-level candidates. For these positions, consider running large display ads. They're expensive, but they can pull in qualified candidates who supplement job-board searches by skimming the newspaper ads. Display ads can also be worth the money if you need to hire several employees in a short time.

To post effective newspaper ads, you need to know what days (usually either Saturdays or Sundays) the employment ads are featured. These schedules differ from paper to paper and city to city, so check out each paper or regional edition in which you plan to advertise.

Pare your job description down to size for a newspaper ad by reducing it to these basics: an eye-catching job title, a quick description of what the job entails, a line or two about your advantages — good benefits, flexible hours, and so on — and adequate information about how to contact you. If you're buying a display ad and have more room to work with, play up the challenging aspects of the job, opportunities for advancement, competitive salaries, and benefits and perks.

Where should you place your ad? For entry-level or retail positions, target community or regional papers that can attract candidates in your immediate area. If you need more candidates, with more skills, run your ad in larger newspapers that have regional editions. For management positions, consider statewide and out-of-state papers, and think about advertising for executive positions in the *Wall Street Journal* or *Financial Times*. (Table 8-1 gives you a basic idea of what you can expect to pay for newspaper advertising.)

Table 8-1	What's the Tab?
Typical costs for newspaper advertising	
Full page ad in a major metropolitan paper	$40,000 to $100,000
Half page ad in a major metropolitan paper	$30,000 to $50,000
Quarter page ad in a major metropolitan paper	$12,000 to $25,000
Display ad in a metropolitan paper	$500 per inch
Classified ad: 20-word ad, one day	$80 to $160
Pennysaver ad	$12 to $40

When Job Boards Aren't Enough: Advertising in Journals

Passive candidates with top skills won't be scouring the online job boards or looking through newspaper classifieds. They don't have to. You have to go to them, especially if they're currently employed and you hope to lure them away from their current positions. One way to lure them is by advertising in the journals these professionals read. Among the fields in which journal advertising can pull in hard-to-find candidates:

✔ Information technology

✔ Medical and biotech research

✔ Healthcare

✔ Financial services

✔ Engineering

✔ Executive level management

To make the most efficient use of your money, ask current employees in your target job what journals they subscribe to, as well as which journals are considered the most prestigious in their field. (Remember that readers form an image of your corporation based on the types of journals in which you advertise.) Target national or international journals, if you're looking for candidates outside your area, or local journals, if your budget doesn't allow for relocation.

Plan on spending some serious money (hundreds to thousands of dollars) for a large ad in a specialty journal, especially if it's a leading national or international journal. Also, plan on a long lead time, because it may sometimes take weeks for your ad to appear.

If a journal has both a print edition and an online edition, consider advertising in both to maximize your exposure.

Want More Options?

In many cases, posting job descriptions online and/or advertising in newspapers and journals will bring in a good supply of qualified candidates. If you need still more power, however, try these additional advertising avenues.

Radio

Radio ads can be a cost-effective recruiting technique, if you target your market correctly. For example, if your target employees tend to fall into a certain age range — college grads, for example, or Baby Boomers — target music or talk-radio stations accordingly. Ask your current employees what stations they like, and place ads on these stations. And purchase enough ads to ensure that candidates hear your message several times; the key to effective radio advertising is repetition. Other tips:

- Target *drive time,* time slots that occur during peak commuting hours, if you're hoping to recruit currently employed candidates.
- Consider sponsoring a popular regular program to achieve name recognition.

For some companies, TV is also an option. If you like the idea of TV advertising, talk to your marketing department about costs. Remember that with TV, the major cost (if you're advertising on inexpensive cable channels, which is probably your only realistic option) is for up-front production. TV commercials aren't cheap, and it takes hard work to prevent them from looking amateurish. You may be better off getting free TV exposure by offering your employees as guest experts on talk shows, or by sponsoring media-covered events (see Chapter 14).

Job fairs

With all the Internet, print, and electronic advertising that recruiters do in an attempt to attract job seekers, there's still no substitute for meeting people face-to-face. (That's why politicians who spend millions on TV ads still hit the pavement to shake hands and kiss babies.) And while job fairs may not be your idea of entertainment, they can be well worth your while.

Free media coverage: It's easier than you think!

If your advertising budget is too small to allow for radio or TV advertising, or even for large print ads, take advantage of the free coverage you can receive for community activities, charitable events, or special employee accomplishments (see Chapter 14 for more on community activities). To get the most mileage from your contributions to the community, obtain an up-to-date media guide (often available from libraries, or for purchase on the Internet). Media guides list the addresses of television stations, radio stations, and newspapers, as well as contact people for different types of stories. Using this information, you can locate a large number of media outlets, and target your press releases to the right people at each one.

Job fairs can be cost-effective, even if they're not the least expensive form of advertising your jobs. You'll pay several thousand dollars to participate in a fair, but coming away with even one hot prospect who becomes a hire can make the event pay for itself.

In addition, job fairs often provide quick results. The time from hello to hire is shortened if you meet candidates up front and have them complete application forms (or, better yet, schedule them for interviews within the next few days). This eliminates the time lag involved in placing an ad and waiting for candidates to find it and reply.

However, job fairs can have their drawbacks. Too often, recruiters find themselves stuck behind folding tables drinking too many cups of coffee while talking to unqualified candidates all day. How can you avoid this experience? By targeting your fairs wisely, going in prepared, and taking control of the situation when you get there. Our advice:

- **Pick your fairs carefully:** Know who's sponsoring each fair, and research their track records. How long have they hosted fairs? How many? What's the scoop from other recruiters about how good their fairs are? Do their printed materials or Web sites suggest "expert," or "amateur"? Do the fair promoters offer participating companies a resume database of job seekers who attended the fair? Do they advertise widely and intelligently to attract the right candidates?

- **Pick your times carefully, too:** Avoid fairs scheduled for dates that conflict with major holidays or popular community events. (For advice on timing campus job fairs, see Chapter 11.)

- **Pick your market:** If you're seeking IT employees, hit IT-specific job fairs. You'll have more competition, but you'll have more qualified prospects as well.

Job fair strategies

Before you leave for a fair, assemble your team and your materials. Brush up on the specifics of your current job openings, and have a plan for handling your paperwork. Consider bringing a laptop computer, so prospects can log on to your site while you're talking. Block out some free hours in the weeks following the fair, so you can interview prospects.

On the day of the fair, be ready to move fast! If possible, have managers interview candidates on the spot; otherwise, schedule interviews for them. Have application forms on hand for prospects to take with them. Consider assembling your management team at the office during and after the fair, so you can send dynamite candidates directly to interviews. Other companies at the fair will spot your hot prospects too, so your best bet is to out-maneuver them with blinding speed.

Job fair pointers: Tips for standing out in the crowd

Just showing up at a job fair isn't enough. To get your money's worth, you need to attract people to your booth, and you need to wow them when they come. Here are the best ways to make a good impression:

✔ **Keep your booth staffed at all times:** If possible, send at least three or four people to each fair. If you're on your own, ask a fair staff member to hold down the fort when you dash off for bathroom breaks or coffee. And bring some snacks and sodas with you, so you won't need to leave for lunch just when things are getting hot. (Job seekers often come to fairs during their lunch breaks, when they can escape from their current jobs, so the lunch hour often is rush hour.)

✔ **Don't sit behind that table:** Stand in front of your table, where it's easier to say "hi" and get a conversation started.

✔ **Send out scouts:** If there are at least two of you, one of you should leave the booth every hour or so and stroll the floor, handing out brochures to newcomers.

✔ **Project the right image:** Are you a casual company? If so, wear jeans — and maybe a humorous company T-shirt that'll attract attention.

✔ **Be polite:** Make eye contact with the people passing by, and give them a friendly smile. Don't get too wrapped up in conversations with the rest of your booth team, or you'll make prospects uncomfortable about interrupting you. Keep your cell phone calls to a minimum. Treat prospects the same way you'd treat your boss: Be attentive, be courteous, and don't keep them waiting.

✔ **Offer freebies:** Candy, doughnuts, beverages, and balloons attract people to your booth. If you can afford it, hand out company T-shirts or hats — gifts that keep on advertising. If that's out of your price range, give away pens, key chains, mousepads, coffee mugs, or sticky notes with your company name. (Include your phone number, Web site address, and/or e-mail address, too.)

✔ **Treat every candidate with respect — even those who don't meet your current specifications:** Remember that the recent grad who's too inexperienced to work for you now may become an outstanding Java developer in a year or two, and you'll want him to remember you fondly.

✔ **Use job fairs to scope out your competition:** What image are they projecting? What positions are they trying to fill? What are they offering job seekers? How do you compare? What you discover may help you fine-tune your own recruiting efforts.

After the fair, send an e-mail or card to each qualified candidate you met. If you're not interested in them, let them know as politely as possible, rather than avoiding their calls. If you are interested, let them know they'll be hearing from you — and give them a number where they can reach you.

Virtual job fairs

Don't have time to tend a booth? Virtual job fairs may be an option. Today's college students are accustomed to doing everything online, and job fairs are no exception. For a fee, your cyber-host provides you with a virtual booth that connects job seekers to a page with your company info, a list of your job openings, and an online response form. It's not quite the same as meeting candidates in person, but you can do it without leaving your office.

The downside: These fairs are a new concept, and some are disappointing. Check the recruiting forums for inside advice on which to try and which to avoid.

Open houses: Hosting your own job fair

Here's still another variant of the job fair: invite job seekers to an open house at your company. Offer munchies and sodas, and have managers on hand to conduct preliminary interviews. Attract job seekers by advertising your open house in local papers, on the radio, and on the Internet.

Billboards

If zoning rules allow, think about putting up a billboard in front of your firm and using it to advertise job openings. It's an effective way to reach potential employees who live in your area. Or advertise on a billboard along a high-traffic route, or near your chief competitor's location.

Direct mail campaigns

If other advertising avenues bring disappointing results, consider sending out a direct mailing. One Midwestern hospital purchased mailing lists of nurses and sent a mailing to 13,000 in their area, asking: What's important to you? What's your specialty? Would you consider leaving your current job? The hospital received more than a thousand responses, supplying them with a good database of potential candidates.

Getting Your Name Out: Dare to be Different!

There's no limit to how creative you can get when it comes to the hunt for employees. Some of the more unusual approaches companies use include the following:

- ✔ **Advertise in movie theaters:** You can pay to have a brief message included in the lead-ins to films. Costs vary, depending on how many theaters your ad runs in and how long a contract term you sign up for.

- **Survey your employees:** Find out what they do in their spare time and then target your ads to attract your prospects when they're at play. One company we know did this and discovered that many of their employees like jazz and pizza. The company used this information to target their recruiting efforts at local jazz events and concerts, as well as to include fliers about the company in pizza boxes.

- **Take to the skies:** Hire an airplane to fly a banner, or purchase a mini-blimp with "Now Hiring!" emblazoned on it, and fly it over your company.

- **Place ads on the sides of your company cars or trucks:** For a few hundred dollars, you can advertise all day, every day. Or advertise on city buses or in subway stations.

- **Target your customers:** They know you, they like you, and they live in your area. To reach them, try everything from the old-fashioned "help wanted" sign on your window to printing "we're hiring" messages on your bags, cash register receipts, or product ads. Consider printing brochures and placing them on counters or by the front door, or have your employees wear buttons saying, "Ask me about working for XYZ!"

- **Customize your search:** Looking for people-oriented types, such as salespeople or restaurant or club employees? Advertise in entertainment guides, or at local festivals and other community events.

- **Hit the mall:** Ask your local mall how much it costs to place a booth, staffed by a recruiter, inside the mall for several weeks or months. You're likely to meet some good prospects, and you'll get your name in the public eye.

- **Fish for leads:** Pay to sponsor a business-card fish bowl at a bar or restaurant frequented by the types of employees you're seeking. It's an excellent way to collect the phone numbers and e-mail addresses of prospects.

- **Use "apparel ads":** Give your employees lots of free company T-shirts, caps, sweatshirts, and so on — and consider giving away free clothes for family members as well. Be sure to include your Web site address in the clothing design.

Smart Choices Equal Big Rewards

Before you leap into any type of advertising, be prepared. Compare rates, demographics, and each approach's ability to target your most likely candidates. Survey your employees, and find out where they heard about you. And, once you do place ads, keep statistics on which ones generate waves and which don't. Among the stats to chart:

Pink-slip parties can provide hot leads

An idea born in 1999, when the first dot-coms started going under, *pink-slip parties* are now common events in major cities. Promoters invite laid-off workers (and those who fear that they're soon to be laid off) to parties at area restaurants or bars, where they can mingle with potential employers while enjoying drinks and entertainment.

Consider schmoozing at some of these soirees if you're in the market for high tech employees.

In some cities, the parties are well advertised; in others, you need to keep an ear to the grapevine. Check Internet newsgroups, job boards, and business newspapers for ads promoting parties in your area. Parties in large cities can draw 500 or more participants, so they're a good way to meet a large number of prospects in the span of a single happy hour.

✔ How many candidates did this advertising medium bring in?

✔ Of those candidates, how many did we hire?

✔ Of those hires, how many are in hard-to-find categories?

The results of your research will help you add effective advertising venues, eliminate poor producers, and fine-tune your recruiting efforts. And that, in turn, will reward you with a steady stream of hires, for fewer dollars than your less-efficient competitors are spending.

Keep your eyes open!

We recruit candidates everywhere: At grocery stores, restaurants, sporting events, airports, you name it. How do we spot prospects? A person wearing a shirt advertising the JavaOne conference is probably in the IT industry, while someone in an "RNs have a better bedside manner" T-shirt is bound to be a nurse. We also keep an eye out for bumper stickers, parking stickers, and other identity clues.

Once we spot prospects, we look for opportunities to strike up a conversation. ("What did you think of that conference?") Sometimes we wind up with a resume or a referral, and often we start building relationships with people who'll be interested in new jobs in the future.

Part III

Need More Power? Advanced Recruiting Tips

The 5th Wave — By Rich Tennant

"I don't need a recruiting agency to get organized. Programmer resumes are under the PC, resumes for sales reps are under my laptop, and those receptionist applications are under my pager."

In this part . . .

*J*ust as you can't be too rich or too famous, you can't have too many tools in your bag of recruiting tricks. Chapter 9 tells you how to take advantage of one of the most powerful of these tools, the employee referral program — a cost-effective way to double your recruiting power almost overnight.

In Chapter 10, we explain how to entice employees away from other companies (and why you needn't feel guilty when you do). Chapters 11 and 12 offer advice about luring college students, and about widening your sights to include seniors, ex-military employees, and other often-overlooked employee markets. And Chapter 13 tells you when bringing in the big guns — outside recruiting agencies — can save the day.

In addition, we explain how to make a name for yourself in your community by *branding* your company as a great employer, a move that can make candidates flock to your door. We also discuss maximizing your recruiting power by using *down time* — those moments when all of your jobs are filled — to network, refine your database, and plan for future hiring needs.

Chapter 9

Getting Your Employees Involved in the Recruiting Game

In This Chapter

▶ Developing an employee referral plan

▶ Selecting and managing rewards

▶ Promoting your program

▶ Expanding your recruiting team

ou need an army of recruiters to fill your job positions. Your employees need extra spending money. Clearly, it's a match made in heaven.

By creating an employee referral program, in which you offer cash bonuses or other rewards to employees who bring in new recruits, you'll find talented job candidates who may be hard to locate through other sources. In addition, you'll make your referring employees happy — and happy employees are more likely to stay put.

In short, an in-house referral program works on two fronts: recruiting *and* retention. And that's a deal a good recruiter can't pass up!

Why Referred Employees Are Better Employees

Obviously, referral programs bring in additional employees. But there's another bonus: They tend to bring in employees who are a good match for your company. That's because the candidates your employees refer already know about your firm's products and services. They're also likely to be highly qualified, because your current employees don't want to jeopardize their reputations by referring sub-par candidates. And employees brought in through referrals feel a greater sense of loyalty, because of their connection to the employee who referred them.

How Much Should You Offer for Referrals? It Depends

The incentives that companies offer employees for making referrals run the gamut from frugal to fantastic. Even tiny firms can usually afford tickets to concerts and ball games, or gift certificates for shopping sprees or dinners at fancy restaurants. At the other end of the scale, Fortune 500 firms are offering everything from $5,000 bonuses to Caribbean cruises and expensive electronic toys.

How generous can you afford to be with your referral bonuses? Before you answer, consider that employees aren't likely to knock themselves out for a $20 gift certificate or a pair of movie passes. The more serious you are, and the more hard-to-find employees you need, the more seductive your offer should be.

Be aware, too, that you have tough competition in the incentive game. Your top employees probably get frequent calls from recruiting agencies, and those recruiters — in addition to trying to entice your employees away — are offering them generous bonuses for referrals. If you're only offering free movie tickets or spa days, even the most loyal employees will send their friends to outside recruiters instead.

In calculating your bonus amount, be sure to factor in how long your key positions are going unfilled. If job vacancies are hurting your bottom line, a $1,000 referral fee can be a bargain. Also, ask yourself how much you would pay in agency fees to fill these positions.

Remember that a large sum of money paid at one time tends to impress an employee more than a small perk offered on a consistent basis — and the perk won't win you a new hire.

What's it worth to you?

The size of your referral bonuses should depend, of course, on the types of candidates you need. Referrals for high-level, hard-to-fill positions are worth far more than referrals for less-skilled, easier-to-fill jobs. Different companies set dollar amounts for referrals in different ways:

✔ Some companies determine the referral bonus based on a percentage of the first year's base salary for the new hire. For example, if an employee refers a friend and that friend hires on for a $50,000-a-year position, the company pays a referral bonus of two percent of the new hire's salary, or $1,000.

> ✔ Other companies set amounts for each position. In such a company, for example, a referral for an administrative assistant position may pay $250, a referral for a manager $1,000, and a referral for a senior director $2,000.

Do some serious calculations before setting your bonus amounts, but plan on being flexible; if your $1,000 reward doesn't bring in candidates, be prepared to double it (or augment it with additional prizes).

It's crucial not to offend current employees in lower-level positions, by insinuating that their jobs aren't important. Be sensitive to this issue when informing employees about the different levels of bonuses for different positions.

But I can't afford cash!

When it comes to rewards, nothing beats money. But if your cash flow is tight, and monetary prizes are out of the question, offer any incentive you can to encourage employee referrals. Employees enjoy it when their friends come aboard, and sometimes even little rewards encourage them to become volunteer recruiters. Among the relatively inexpensive bonuses you can provide are the following:

✔ Gift certificates to restaurants, stores, or spas

✔ TVs, stereos, Palm Pilots, or other electronic "toys"

✔ Luggage

✔ Watches

✔ Maid service

✔ Extra paid time off

✔ Passes to movies, sporting events, or amusement parks

✔ Golf days

✔ Car washes

✔ Special parking spots

✔ Gift baskets

✔ A month of free lunches in the company cafeteria

✔ Contests — offer a small bonus for each successful referral, and enter your employee recruiters into a raffle for one big prize (for example, a cruise). Or give the employee who refers the most new hires during each quarter a new computer or laptop.

Oh, baby!

Among the incentives that companies offered in recent years in order to pull in employee referrals:

✔ BabyCenter, a San Francisco firm, brought in new recruits by offering its existing employees $2,000 and a bottle of Dom Perignon for each successful referral.

✔ Freddie Mac recently offered a $27,000 dream vacation to anywhere in the world — plus 5 extra vacation days — to the winner of a company-wide employee referral contest.

✔ Canadian firm Nortel offered $2,000 for referrals for optical Internet positions, and then entered referring employees into a $100,000 drawing.

✔ Texas Instruments recently premiered a "Texas Two-Step" referral program that paid cash bonuses and entered employees into a drawing for a Ford Explorer.

If you offer non-cash prizes, try to provide a menu of prizes to choose from. That way, a golfer can pick a day on the green, a gourmet can select a restaurant gift certificate, and a working parent can enjoy maid service for a month. The more you gear your program toward your employees' interests, the harder they'll work for you.

Let Everyone Play the Referral Game

No matter what you offer as a bonus, make sure all employees are eligible to earn rewards. A universal referral bonus program is important for company morale, and it makes good sense as well, because even an entry-level employee may be related to, be friends with, or live next door to the computer programmer or healthcare professional you're seeking.

Money isn't everything

Although cash and other rewards will be your biggest draws, let employees know that referrals benefit them in other ways as well. Explain that filling job openings will reduce stress, heavy workloads, and overtime, and will help your company grow and become more productive.

And remind them that higher productivity translates into higher profits, and the potential for higher salaries and more valuable stock options. In addition, point out that they'll enjoy working with friends and colleagues they already know and like.

Throw a party!

You've heard of birthday parties, graduation parties, and wedding parties, but here's a new idea: a resume party.

To gain admission, an employee must bring the resume of a friend, family member, neighbor, or former co-worker who's qualified for one of your positions — or the resume of a candidate who has a skill set your company often needs or will need in the near future. In return, you provide food, drinks, entertainment, and a fun evening — and any employee bringing a winning resume that results in a hire receives a bonus through your referral program. It's a good way to motivate fun-loving employees who may not make the effort to drop resumes by the HR office.

Moreover, bonuses mean more to employees on small salaries than they do to those who make comfortable incomes. Thus, your clerks and receptionists are just as likely to work hard to find prospects for you as are higher-paid employees.

To create plenty of winners, offer small prizes instantly for any referrals — even those that don't result in hires down the road. Hand out movie passes or $10 or $20 gift certificates each time your employees refer a qualified candidate (be sure you carefully define what you mean by *qualified*) and you'll keep them interested. And consider offering a prize to the person who refers the largest number of qualified prospects, even if not one of them gets hired. (An alternative: Each time employees make referrals, whether the referrals pan out or not, enter them into a drawing for a larger prize, such as a jet ski, an all-expenses-paid vacation, or a big-screen TV.) One caution, however: If you find yourself inundated with unqualified referrals, spell out your requirements more carefully and make sure that your employees understand the rules.

Also, offer bonuses for *every* successful referral that an employee makes — not just the first one. (In fact, consider increasing the bonus for each additional successful referral, in order to keep your top producers highly motivated.) In addition, consider offering small "anniversary" rewards to employee recruiters, at the end of each year that the referred employees complete. It won't cost much, and it'll motivate your top employee recruiters to keep up the good work.

To keep your employees on your recruiting team, respond fast to referrals. Pay referral bonuses quickly, too, so employees know their efforts will pay off immediately.

Work Out the Details of Your Referral Program

Before you start a referral program, put your plan on paper and have your higher-ups approve every aspect of it. Hammer out the details in advance, so misunderstandings don't arise, and make sure your employees get clear instructions in writing. Some issues to address ahead of time include the following:

✔ **How will you pay rewards?** In general, companies offer large cash bonuses only if the employee hires on and stays with the company for a specified amount of time. Some companies pay half of the referral fee when hiring an employee, and the other half after the new employee completes a 3-month or 6-month probationary period. No matter what system you use, be sure employees clearly understand the ground rules.

✔ **How will you ensure that the right employees receive the prizes?** For example, what will you do if two different employees send you the same referral by office mail on the same day? Be sure you have a foolproof system — for example, time-stamping employee referrals (also see the e-mail tip in the following paragraph), or splitting the finder's fee if two employees make the same referral in the same day.

✔ **How will you track referrals?** Mistakes can result in your company paying an agency fee for a candidate and then discovering that an internal employee referred the same person weeks earlier. If this happens, you're out the agency fees, and your angry employee is out hundreds or even thousands of dollars — not a pretty scenario! To avoid such sticky situations, document and automate your referral process. Use an applicant tracking system (see Chapter 16) to keep data on all candidates referred by employees, and the dates of the referrals. Encourage employees to send referrals by e-mail, so you'll have a computerized record of the time and date they arrive. And maintain long-term records of employee referrals, because the prospect you don't hire today may be the candidate you need in 6 months — and the employee who referred him should earn the referral bonus at that point.

A few more tips for avoiding problems when you implement a referral program:

✔ Be sure to explain clearly that you want employees to bring in *people they know or people whose skill sets they know are valuable to your company* — not strangers whose resumes they grab off the job boards. They don't need to bring in Mom, Dad, or Cousin Sally, but the person they refer should at least be an acquaintance. One exception is the *field recruiting* referrals we discuss later in this chapter.

✔ Make it clear, too, that referrals must be relevant to the company and appropriate for your open positions — or at least for positions likely to open up in the near future.

✔ Promote your program, but not to the extent that employees spend more time looking for new hires than they spend doing their jobs. This can be a real issue for lower paid employees, for whom large cash rewards are especially tempting.

✔ If an agency sends you candidates, don't ask these candidates for referrals during the interview process. This is unfair to the candidates, because they're not yet employees and can't collect referral bonuses. (It's also unfair to the agency, which by rights should receive these referrals.)

✔ Don't let referrals trump diversity. Keep track of your diversity statistics and make sure your referral program isn't counter-productive.

Advertise Your Referral Program

You want every employee on your recruiting team, even the ones who don't work in areas where you need new hires the most. After all, the kid who busses the tables in the company cafeteria may live next door to a great Web designer or play basketball with the respiratory therapist you're desperate to recruit. So motivate everyone from payroll clerks to programmers to join your recruiting campaign, by advertising your referral program and giving all of your employees the recruiting tools they need to follow through.

Start by publicizing your program at every occasion. Feature it in your company newsletters, tell new employees about your program during their orientation, include fliers with paychecks, and put up posters in break rooms and other locations. Send out company-wide e-mails, post information about the program on your Web site or intranet, and mention it prominently in your employee handbook.

Give your program even more visibility by handing out awards to your referral champions during company events (one major company gives out its prizes at ice cream socials) — and make sure top management officials present the prizes, to impress your employees with the importance of the program. If you offer a special award for the employee who brings in the most referrals, announce the winner at a party. Post news about your top employee recruiters on bulletin boards, display their pictures on your Web site, and feature them in your company newsletter. Give them special parking places, flowers, and other little extra perks if you can.

In addition, provide all of your employees with up-to-date information about your jobs and benefits. Also, if you have a graphic artist on staff, ask about designing *virtual postcards* that employees can send to prospects. (These are pre-designed e-mail cards your employees can personalize and send to friends or relatives. They're much like the virtual holiday cards available on the

Internet, but they include information about your company and a "thought you might be interested in one of our jobs" message that can be updated regularly.) Each time a qualified candidate returns a virtual postcard, give the referring employee a small bonus — even if the candidate doesn't hire on. Or equip your employees with business cards with your firm's phone number, e-mail address, and a message — for example, "We're always looking for great people to join our team. To find out more, log onto our website at XYZCorp.com."

To ensure that your employees refer people with the right qualifications, use your Web site and company bulletin boards to post specific, up-to-date information about your job openings. Offer clear-cut instructions for making referrals, and provide hints about where employees can find candidates; for example, encourage them to mention openings to college friends, neighbors, and members of clubs and organizations to which they belong. Encourage them to refer passive candidates (those who aren't actively looking, but might be interested) as well as active job seekers. And be sure employees have a single point of contact in your human resources or recruiting department, in case they need information or assistance.

Make Your Employees "Field Scouts"

If you have a highly motivated staff that really wants to help solve your hiring problems, consider sending them out as "talent scouts." Ask your employees to visit their favorite stores or other businesses that deal with the public and try to spot high performers. (One big advantage of this recruiting technique: Your employees can evaluate the real-life, on-the-job performance of prospective hires.)

Reward your scouts either by paying them by the hour for their searches, or paying them a reasonable reward for any good resumes you garner through their efforts. Then pay them a larger reward for any actual hires that result from their efforts.

Instruct your staff to be tactful when they act as field scouts. You don't want them to offend the management or staff at other businesses by interrupting work or interfering with customer transactions. Instead, suggest that your scouts get their message across quickly, politely, and in a low-key manner — for example, "Hi, I really like the way you handle your customers. If you're ever interested in working for us, we'd love to talk with you. Here's my card."

Also, encourage your employees to pass on the names of helpful people they meet over the phone, such as customer relations reps or technical assistance personnel.

An etiquette tip

Keep your referring employees in the loop! Let them know the status of their referrals, whether their candidates are being considered, being interviewed, or receiving offers. Your employees will feel more like part of the team if you involve them in the hiring process.

Sometimes, of course, your employee referrals won't result in hires. When this happens, tell the referring employees how much you appreciate their referrals, and explain (tactfully) why the matches didn't work out. Encourage the employees to keep making referrals, so they won't be dissuaded by a single failure.

It's especially important to exercise tact and be positive if you need to say no to a candidate who's a relative or close friend of the referring employee. Be sure to explain your decision in terms that are positive and complimentary to the referred candidate, so you don't create hurt feelings.

Put your managers to work

To add more octane to your referral program, give additional bonuses to managers whose employees bring in the most new recruits. (You'll need to adjust for the number of employees in each department.) Or host contests to see which department can generate the most referrals over a six-month or one-year period. Reward the winners with public accolades, as well as special perks — good parking spaces, free lunches, or extra days off.

Spread the wealth

In addition to enlisting your employees as recruiters, consider expanding your referral program to include other people who interact with your company. Among the contacts who can provide you with valuable leads are the following:

- ✔ Your customers
- ✔ Your vendors
- ✔ Your volunteers, if you work for a hospital or similar organization

Remember that your vendors and volunteers, like your employees, know your company and can send you candidates who fit in with your needs and your culture. While you don't want to pay these "outsiders" as much as your employees, make your rewards tempting enough to get their attention. The more interest you generate in your referral program, the larger your team of recruiters will grow — and the shorter your list of unfilled jobs will be.

Measure your results

By now, you know our mantra: Always watch your stats! It's as true for referral programs as for any other aspect of recruiting. Is your referral program bringing in lots of candidates? And are those candidates well qualified? Are your employees happy with the amount of their bonuses? But not so happy that they're ignoring their own jobs and focusing on recruiting? Are your agency fees or advertising costs going down? Keep an eye on your program's results, and make sure you're getting the results you want. And keep promoting your referral program, until it's second nature for your employees to say to friends and family, "Hey, you should take a look at my company!"

Chapter 10

Who's Hiring the People You Need — and How Can You Turn the Tables?

In This Chapter

▶ Sourcing candidates from your competition

▶ Knowing the ground rules

▶ Using an agency when you can't source directly

*Y*ears ago your mother told you, "Never steal." But then, Mom probably didn't work as a recruiter. If other companies are scooping up your best employees on a regular basis, the only way you'll survive is to lure away their employees as well.

With unemployment low in spite of economic fluctuations, and almost all of the qualified employees already working, you can't staff all of your positions with unemployed job seekers — especially if you're recruiting IT candidates, engineers, or healthcare professionals. There simply aren't enough qualified, out-of-work people to fill your slots.

That means, obviously, that you have to go after people who already have jobs. And that means enticing them away from other companies. (Think of it as "trading." After all, those other companies are taking *your* employees, too.)

But Is Hiring from Other Companies Ethical?

Technically, every time you place an employment ad, you're trying to lure an employee away from another employer — because, as we just noted, almost all of your new hires will be leaving another job. In this chapter, however, we'll look at more proactive ways to persuade other companies' employees to join your firm.

And yes, we hear your mom's voice whispering in your ear: "Is that the way I raised you?" But in reality, enticing employees away from other companies — as long as you do it the right way — benefits everyone. (Really!) Here's why.

- **They'd leave anyway.** You won't succeed in luring employees away from a company that's giving them everything they want. If they make a move, it means they weren't perfectly happy to begin with; otherwise, they wouldn't have considered your offer. In today's job market, a dissatisfied employee will eventually leave for another firm — and it might as well be yours.

- **Employees naturally move onward and upward.** Remember your first job mowing lawns, delivering newspapers, or babysitting? Clearly, you've moved up in the world since then. Similarly, employees working their way up in the job market often need to change companies, because the internal ladder in any company has limited room for climbers. If your potential employee's company is chock-full of managers, and he's management material, and you need a manager... then you're doing both yourself and him a favor. And, as we noted in the previous point, he'd leave anyway, no matter who enticed him away.

In short, the employees you lure away will leave a so-so job for a better one. They'll most likely improve their chances of moving up, getting more training, and tackling challenging and rewarding projects — and they'll probably get a better salary and/or benefits as well. And the companies who lose employees to you will merely lose an employee who would be shopping around anyway. So tell Mom it's okay.

Okay, How Do I Recruit from Other Companies?

Now that your conscience is clear, you can look at the nuts and bolts of sourcing job candidates from other companies. Clearly, you can't walk in the front door of your competitor with a bullhorn and announce, "Tired of working here? Then follow me!" Equally clearly, however, you can't just sit back and hope that your competitor's employees show up on your doorstep one day. Other companies are actively recruiting them right now, and you'll miss out if you aren't doing the same.

To start, find out who's employing the candidates you're after. If you follow our advice about researching your competition in Chapter 1, you'll have a good feel for your competitors. But which of them have the outstanding employees you're seeking — and how can you locate those employees? Here are some tips.

- ✔ **Make a list of your top employees.** Where did they work before they came to you? If you find a consistent pattern, such as several of your employees coming from the same competitor, this competitor is doing a good job of selecting top candidates and training them to be even better. (In short, they're doing much of your work for you.) Put them high on your list.

- ✔ **Keep an eye on newspaper columns about company promotions.** The people who get these promotions are top performers, and you want them. Contact them six months to a year after their promotions, to find out if they're ready for a move.

- ✔ **Tell new hires immediately about your employee referral program.** Many new employees jump at the chance to bring a friend into the company, and to earn some extra spending money in the process.

- ✔ **Focus both on your top-performing competitors and on competitors who are (financially speaking) at death's doorstep.** In the case of the hot companies, the reason is obvious: They're successful in large part because they have outstanding employees. But failing companies may be on the rocks due to a lack of funding or a weak management team, and most have some excellent employees you can grab. These employees often have an inkling that trouble lies ahead, and smart ones will be ready to make a move before their ship sinks. Be ready for them by scouring the news for reports about layoffs, drops in stock prices, or other trouble signs.

  Advanced Internet Recruitment Strategies (AIRS), at www.airsdirectory.com, publishes a weekly outplacement, mergers, and IPO report that can clue you in on your competitors' shake-ups and shakeouts. Other good resources include www.business.com, local newspapers and business journals, and — in the case of IT firms — magazines such as *ComputerWorld* and *InfoWeek*.

- ✔ **Go on the hunt.** Spend time at public places (such as restaurants, happy hours, sporting events, and local festivals) where your competitors' employees are likely to hang out. Advertise your company on Web sites that these employees are likely to visit. Also, place ads in magazines and newspapers that they're likely to read, and advertise on a billboard that's close to your competitor. See Chapters 8 and 14 for more ideas.

✔ **Work the Web.** Use the tricks you can find in Chapter 6 to locate the names of employees listed on company Web sites. In particular, search Internet resume banks for resumes containing the name of the company whose employees you're seeking. (For example, if you'd like to contact employees at NoName Airlines, go to Monster.com and search resumes using the keyword **noname**.) You're likely to turn up past or current employees you can contact — and they, in turn, may point you to other prospects.

Following up with prospects

Compile a list of the best prospects you hear about through the grapevine or through your research. If you're lucky enough to garner home phone numbers or e-mail addresses, contact your prospects directly at home. (See Chapter 16 for tips.) If not, call them at work.

If you do call prospects at the office, tell the truth about who you are and why you're calling. We know recruiters who pretend to be salespeople, conference organizers, or even technical support people. This is unethical, and it doesn't work well either. (Do you want your prospect's first impression of you to be, "Wow, what a slime ball"?) Instead, be upfront and rely on your recruiting skills to entice your prospect to look at your company and what you have to offer.

No trespassing!

Be assertive in seeking out competitors' employees, but end your efforts at your competitor's front door. Otherwise, your actions may do more harm than good.

An example: One company we know (we'll call them Company A) has an office across the street from a competitor, Company B. In an effort to lure employees to cross the road and sign on with them, Company A once put recruiting fliers on every car in the parking lot of Company B. Needless to say, this created bad blood and, in the long run, probably chased away Company B's employees instead of tempting them to make a move.

Another example of poor recruiting involves rolling billboards — that is, job advertising on trucks, cars, and buses. Many companies use rolling billboards effectively and ethically, but

others misuse them by parking their signs in front of competitors' offices. Needless to say, this draws attention — but it also draws the wrath of other firms and creates an image of the offending firm as underhanded. In one example, Company A parked a large truck outside the front door of a competitor, Company B, with a billboard on the side saying, "Tired of working 60 hours a week? Check out our company," and listing a Web site address. Not surprisingly, the move generated more bad publicity than job prospects.

To avoid unpleasantness, stay off your competitors' property and recruit in public places. Trespassing isn't likely to win you many friends, and it can jeopardize your reputation or even lead to minor legal trouble.

Because most people are uncomfortable talking to a recruiter during work hours, keep your message brief and to the point. Ask your prospects if it's a good time for them to talk or listen; if they say yes, quickly describe your jobs and your company's strong points. Give them your phone number, e-mail address, and Web site address, and ask if you can call or e-mail them at home. Be sure to get their phone numbers and e-mail addresses before you hang up!

When you talk to your prospects, choose your words carefully. Don't badmouth your prospect's current employer; instead, take a more subtle approach. Emphasize your company's strong points, selecting areas in which you know your competitor is weak. (For example, play up your training programs if your competitor doesn't offer free training.) The key is to answer the question, "What do you have to offer that I'm not already getting?" — not to trash your competition.

If the people you call aren't interested, don't push. (However, follow up with them in a month or two to find out if their situation has changed. Also, if you have a chance, ask them for referrals.) When you encounter hot prospects, follow up by offering to call again or to meet with them as soon as possible.

Some recruiters find it awkward to contact passive candidates, but a good percentage of these candidates are ready to think about changing jobs. Some just need a gentle nudge, and it's your job to provide it.

Using agencies to outsource

It's time-consuming to track down candidates employed by your competitors, and approaching them can be tricky. Thus, you may want to consider outsourcing this task to an agency.

Recruiting agencies use sophisticated Web search techniques and have extensive databases of candidates and far-reaching contacts, making it easier for them to reach the candidates who aren't actively saying, "I'm interested." Also, using an agency provides a buffer between you and your competitor, and that may make both you and your candidate more comfortable. (For more on outsourcing, see Chapter 13.)

Competitor or friend?

Does your firm have partnerships or agreements with other companies? If so, find out if this prevents you from hiring employees away from them. (In this situation, you may still be able to use an agency to contact their employees.) Tread carefully, or you may wind up in trouble with the management at both companies.

Chapter 11

Grabbing the Grads

• •

In This Chapter

▶ Selecting schools

▶ Making contacts

▶ Staking out job fairs

▶ Posting on college job sites

▶ On-campus recruiting: pizza parties and beyond

• •

*E*ach year, millions of college grads bid a fond farewell to their alma maters and head off to look for jobs. As a recruiter, your job may include steering a steady stream of these new grads straight to your company's front door.

College recruiting is well worth your time and effort, because it's an opportunity to establish long-term relationships that can pay off, year after year, with new hires who are eager, highly trained, and not already employed by someone else. In addition, a successful college recruiting program can save you money, because it costs about half as much to hire a new graduate as it costs to hire away an employee who's already working at another company. Grads are typically inexpensive to relocate, because it's simpler to move a guitar, a computer, and a collection of textbooks than it is to pack up a family and a four-bedroom house.

However, attracting top graduates takes hard work. The market for grads is competitive, and if you're looking for candidates in high-demand fields, you'll be up against the biggest companies in the nation. You can still win at this battle, however, if you plan an effective college recruiting strategy. The keys to this strategy should include the following:

✔ Picking the right schools

✔ Networking with key people on campus

✔ Locating students and grads through university and alumni associations

> ✔ Attending campus job fairs and other recruiting events
>
> ✔ Establishing a permanent on-campus presence

This chapter helps you hit the ground running with your graduate recruiting program.

Creating an A+ Campus Recruiting Strategy

As you recruit at colleges and universities, remember to keep three goals in mind: Signing up active job seekers, establishing a presence that makes you attractive both to active prospects and to passive students, and fostering long-term relationships with administrative officials, faculty members, and student organizations. As you select the activities and events you'll use in your campus recruiting efforts, ask yourself the following questions:

✔ Does this activity enhance our image — for example, by showing that we're caring and involved in our community, or that we're an exciting place to work?

✔ Does this activity directly help students or faculty members and thus generate positive feelings toward us?

✔ Does this activity give us substantial name recognition?

✔ Will this activity help cement our relationship with key administrative personnel?

By designing a well-rounded recruiting plan that will "sell" your company to interested students and create widespread name recognition on campus, you'll help provide for both your current and future recruiting needs — and you'll earn high grades from your managers as a result.

Which Schools Should You Target?

Obviously, if you're in or near a university town, put your local "U" on your list of schools to cultivate. However, don't stop there. Consider recruiting at community colleges in your area, as well as at local trade schools and private colleges. Focus, of course, on schools that offer strong programs in the skills your company needs; it's better to pick a few schools with outstanding reputations and skilled candidates than to spread yourself too thin with too many schools.

Demand for grads skyrockets

Nearly one-fifth of new job offers in the near future will go to new college graduates, according to a survey by the National Association of Colleges and Employers (NACE). College recruiting is now jumping by 23 percent yearly, with the heaviest campus recruiting being done by these groups:

✔ Product manufacturers in the fields of computers and electronics, scientific equipment makers, and chemical companies

✔ Service providers including consulting companies, accounting firms, insurance companies, merchandisers, and computer systems design firms.

In addition, NACE says, more than a third of employers say they plan to hire international students, primarily in engineering and computing fields.

Use your time effectively by focusing on the schools most likely to bring you qualified candidates. Before contacting for-profit trade schools and colleges, for example, do your homework. Find out if these schools are accredited, and use the Internet to find out how good their reputations are. Some for-profit schools, especially in the high-tech field, have reputations so sterling that their graduates should head your list of prospects. Others are fly-by-night diploma mills unlikely to be worth your while.

If you're recruiting in very high-demand fields, such as computer programming and medicine, it's a must to recruit at all the major colleges within your state. In fact, you'll probably need to extend your reach to selected colleges nationwide. How far afield you should go depends, of course, on your budget, the size of your company, and your time constraints. If possible, at least identify the university that's most renowned for graduating people highly skilled in your company's line of work. (For example, if you're recruiting top-of-the-line scientists and high-tech people, consider targeting Stanford. If you're recruiting experts in agriculture or food science, think about recruiting at Purdue.) Also, consider schools and training centers that offer certification programs — for example, Microsoft Certified Systems Engineer (MCSE) certification.

To find information on the best schools for each field, check resources such as *U.S. News & World Report's* annual Best Colleges survey, which is available online, and the National Association of Colleges and Employers (NACE) at www.naceweb.org. Also, ask your employees which schools are the most noted in their fields. And check out each college's promotional literature, campus newspapers, and Web site.

...rly!

...ompanies hit campus in the spring, just before graduation. If ...hen to make your move, however, the best grads will be car-...-bird companies that start recruiting as soon as school starts. ...r December, many of the best students already have contracts

To avoid being left in the dust, contact campuses as early as possible and sign up for recruiting activities. Generally, you'll want to sign up during the summer for fall recruiting activities, begin your employee recruiting efforts in early fall, and initiate your internship recruiting efforts (more on this later) in late fall or early spring. Most schools can provide recruiting calendars months in advance.

In addition, start immediately (no matter what time of year it is) to network with people and organizations at the schools you're targeting. The best college recruiters know that every day is recruiting day on campus.

Start with the career center

All colleges and universities have staff members in charge of helping students enter the job market. These *career centers,* as they're usually called, post job listings, offer career counseling, and organize many on-campus activities. They also work closely with companies like yours, and they're your most valuable contacts on campus.

Thus, you want to begin your recruiting efforts by contacting the staff at each school's career center and setting up a meeting. (We recommend taking them to lunch.) Find out what works best for them. How should you submit your job openings? What are their deadlines? Let them know, too, exactly what types of candidates you're seeking. Invite them to tour your company, and talk about internships or other ways in which your company can assist them. And, of course, get information on job fairs and other activities.

Recruit your in-house alumni

Look through your personnel files. Did any of your current employees graduate from the schools where you plan to recruit? If so, these employees can play a major role in making your efforts a success by identifying key contacts and giving you an "in." For example, a staff chemist who's still friends with her old chemistry professor may be willing to put in a good word for you. Or a physician who graduated from the local med school may be willing to put in

a call to the department head, giving the schoo
you. Recent grads are the best employees to ap
familiar with current campus activities, organiz

Also ask alumni employees if they're willing to p
other on-campus activities, making sure that the
time off, or other compensation for their efforts

Meet the profs

Get more mileage from your campus recruiting efforts by using alumni employees to point you toward influential professors. If these employees are willing,
ask them to make an initial contact on your behalf. Teachers are flattered when
former students remember them, so you'll get off on the right foot. But be careful to contact profs at convenient times — not during midterms or finals. Also,
many professors prefer to be approached by e-mail rather than by phone; you
can usually find their e-mail addresses at the schools' Web sites.

If your employees can't point you to specific professors, ask the Career Services department, or contact the deans of the departments in which you're
interested. Once you find the professors you want to contact, find out a little
about them:

- What do they teach?
- How long have they been teaching?
- Are they active in any civic organizations? Passionate about any causes?
- Have they authored books or articles?

You can generally locate this information at the school's Web site or through
other resources on the Internet. The more you know up front, the better an
impression you'll make — and the better you'll be able to gauge how you and
the faculty members can strike up a mutually beneficial relationship.

When you contact professors, offer to help them by providing employees as
guest speakers, or by supplying equipment, financing, or staff support for
classroom research projects. If you can build a long-term relationship that
benefits your targeted professors and departments and creates a positive
image of your company, you're likely to generate leads for years to come.

Many colleges and universities have *industrial advisory boards.* Volunteering a
member of your company to serve on these boards is another excellent way
to make contacts with professors and make a name for your company on
campus.

Grading the grads

When experienced candidates apply for jobs, you look at their track records. New grads, however, usually don't *have* track records. So how can you tell if they can do the job? You can start, of course, by looking at their grades — but a 4.0 grade point average doesn't guarantee that your candidates can handle workplace pressure, get along well with other employees, or translate school learning into on-the-job skills. We offer some additional information that can help you choose your grads wisely:

✔ **Are they motivated?** Students who participate in training programs, campus organizations, student government, internships, and volunteer work often have the energy, enthusiasm, and self-starter characteristics that add up to job success.

✔ **Are they mature?** Look for clues that your candidates are grown-up enough to function well in an adult workplace and mature enough to handle full-time work commitments. Also, if you'll be relocating your candidates, try to judge whether or not they're independent enough to adjust to being on their own in a new city.

✔ **Can they think critically?** Ask your prospects logic-based questions. For example, think of a common problem that arises at your workplace and ask how they'd solve it. (This type of interviewing is called *behavior-based interviewing,* and it's very effective for assessing candidates with little or no work experience.)

✔ **How good are their verbal and writing skills?** Your candidates should be able to speak well, especially if they'll be meeting with your clients. If their jobs involve written communication, they should be able to write clearly and effectively.

Go "club hopping"

Most campuses have dozens of specialized student organizations, ranging from computer clubs to political groups. The students who participate in these extra-curricular activities are likely to be the type you're seeking: energetic, intelligent, and involved.

To establish a positive relationship with student organizations, offer to participate in their fund-raising and charitable events by providing funding, equipment, food and beverages, or advertising. Also, offer to provide guest speakers for meetings or to host meetings at your company site. Develop working relationships with the officers of student organizations, as they are the decision-makers. Again, employees who belonged to campus groups during their student days can help you get a warm welcome.

When you contact student organizations, be sure to include alumni groups. We talk in Chapter 6 about reaching these groups through the Internet; in addition, contact them by phone or mail, or through their Web sites. Advertise in their newsletters or on their Web sites, offer to help with campus activities, and build a network of contacts who'll be willing to refer new candidates to you.

Planning Your Job Fair Strategy

One of the principal campus recruiting opportunities, of course, is the job fair. We cover job fairs in Chapter 8, but you'll want to fine-tune your approach a little for the college crowd.

Before attending a campus job fair, identify the job openings that match the skill levels of the young prospects you're seeking and provide this information to your contacts in the career services office. Often they can make your job easier by identifying students most likely to be interested in your positions. Also, send information packets and lists of your jobs to the heads of the departments whose students you're targeting.

When picking the team you'll send to the fair, try to select a diverse group of people who are well versed in the habits, interests, and technology of the 20-something crowd. Also, bring along one or two employees who are alumni of the school if possible. On the day of the fair, skip the suits and go for business-casual work dress instead, unless your company has a mandatory dress code. Students used to going to class in shorts and sandals tend to shy away from recruiters who give the impression, "We're stuffy and you'll need to wear a tie." (Again, however, check with the career center. At some job fairs, students are required to dress in suits, ties, and other business attire — and in those cases, you should dress up, too.)

Offer some giveaways at your recruiting booth, and encourage your team to be outgoing. Many students won't be assertive enough to walk up to your booth and ask questions, so you'll frequently need to take the lead in starting conversations. Be sure, too, that you have a good system for tracking the resumes you receive, and for recording information about particularly great candidates.

Host a pre-fair party

Here's an opportunity to hire grads out from under the noses of companies that wait until the day of a job fair to recruit on campus. A few weeks in advance of a fair, host an informal get-together. Provide plenty of food and drinks; pizza is always good, but a creative menu — for example, a luau — is even better. Give students a chance to meet with some of your most personable and interesting employees, to ask questions, and to view information about your products or services. Consider taking your best prospects out to dinner after the party, as a way of showing that you're interested in hiring them.

To maximize your results, send e-mail invitations beforehand to your most promising prospects (the career center can probably give you leads) and place ads in campus papers. Also ask the Career Services staff to publicize your event. Use student organizations to advertise your party, too.

When you find hot prospects, give them a step-by-step explanation of the hiring process. Many college grads haven't looked for jobs before, and they're nervous because they don't know what to expect. Encourage them to ask questions — "Who will I talk to?" "What should I wear?" "What will they ask?" And if they follow through and begin the hiring process, keep them in the loop with calls or e-mails so that they won't wonder what's happening.

Keeping the "Undecideds" in Your Sights

In Chapter 6, we talk about passive candidates — individuals who aren't actively seeking employment, but who may agree to take a look at your company if you give them a nudge. Passive candidates on campus are an even harder breed to attract, because they're busy nailing 4.0 GPAs, chairing campus clubs, and enjoying campus life. Some aren't even thinking about jobs yet. Others aren't worried about job hunting, because they know all the top companies want them.

You won't catch these candidates by throwing company parties or attending job fairs. Instead, set them up for future recruiting efforts by making them aware of your existence. It's important to make an impression on them early on, while they're still freshmen or sophomores, so they have time to learn the skills they'll need if they decide to work for you.

How do you attract the attention of passive candidates? By achieving name recognition — and, equally important, by creating a positive image. Earlier in this chapter ("Go 'club hopping'"), we talk about providing speakers and hosting meetings, but that's just a beginning. If you have the time and the budget, also consider these recognition-building activities:

- ✔ Hosting fun off-campus events that college students love to attend, such as concerts or street fairs.

- ✔ Participating in community charities popular with students, such as Habitat for Humanity, or in activities that help the university itself.

   The Houston company, EnForm, for example, assists the University of Houston in updating the school's Web design and computer curriculum. The company reaps two rewards from this good deed: students recognize the company name, and the school produces more high-tech grads with the skills that the company needs.

- ✔ Sponsoring grants or scholarships. If you offer scholarships, consider offering several modest ones rather than one large one. The reason for this is obvious: You'll make more potential prospects happy. And, of course, be sure to offer scholarships or grants in the fields in which your company specializes.

Targeting Older Students

These days, colleges cater to students of all ages. It's common to find 30-year-olds, 40-year-olds, and 50-year-olds training in fields as diverse as computer programming, law, and medical technology. In fact, adults over the age of 25 now make up half of overall higher education enrollments, and adults over 40 account for more than 11 percent of all college students. Moreover, these older students have the added advantage of valuable life experience. In addition, studies show the following:

- Older students (defined as over 25) have higher grade point averages than younger students.
- Older students are even more motivated than younger students.
- Older students have a strong internal drive for new knowledge — making them ideal employees.

You can reach these students through the same avenues as their younger peers. In addition, contact the Adult Education Departments at the campuses you visit, and let them know you're interested in meeting with students of all ages. Also, check to see if any of the campuses you visit have clubs or organizations specifically for older students.

Establishing an Internship Program

Every young person knows that famous Catch-22: Employers want experience, but you can't gain experience until you work for someone. One solution, for both them and your company, is an internship program.

If you have part-time positions going unfilled, think about contacting public and private universities in your area and offering internships. In some cases, you can obtain an intern absolutely free. But even if you need to pay (and you usually will), the price will be right. That's because interns are willing to work for a reduced rate in exchange for the following:

- The on-the-job training they'll be getting
- The chance to say on their resume, "I held a job at XYZ Corp," and to use you as a reference.
- The chance to work at a job that fits in with their school schedules. (This is an advantage for you, too, if you're seeking people to work evenings or weekends.)

For your part, you get inexpensive help and, more importantly, the chance to convert your interns into long-term employees. Interns often make great permanent hires, because they already know the job and your corporate culture. In addition, interns who enjoy working at your company will spread the word about you, aiding in your campus recruiting efforts. That's why even short-term internships, or internships that don't really reduce your workload, can be profitable in the long run.

In addition to contacting schools, you can list your company on WetFeet.com, InternJobs.com, Internweb.com, and other Internet boards that list internship positions. Following are some of the different types of internships you can offer:

- ✔ **Cooperative education internships (co-ops):** Students get credit for working in jobs related to their majors.

- ✔ **Field experience internships:** Students conduct research such as helping a hospital's infection control nurse track data on *e. coli* rates among patients or helping an over-worked HR employee set up a database to track resumes.

- ✔ **Practicums:** Individuals or groups of students work on projects, often for a one-semester period, under the supervision of a manager or a faculty advisor.

- ✔ **Service learning:** Assisting in community service projects such as school reading programs.

- ✔ **Externships:** Short (usually 1-week to 3-week) periods during which the intern *shadows* a professional to learn more about the job. While externships won't solve your immediate hiring problems, they'll help you make friends with young people interested in your firm's line of work, which can translate into hires down the line.

If you decide to use interns, encourage their loyalty by making them part of your corporate family. Provide them with mentors who can show them the ropes and make them feel welcome, and give them decent work areas with phones, computers, and other necessary equipment. If you use several interns, host parties or other special events for them — and be sure to invite them to all of your company's other social activities as well. Celebrate their birthdays, invite them to lunch, and always treat them with the same respect as you treat other employees. Also offer them the opportunity to participate in company training programs, and keep them informed about any permanent job openings that match their skills.

Avoid using interns simply to type meeting minutes, make sandwich runs, or stuff mailers — a guaranteed way to lose their interest. Instead, give them challenging assignments that match their areas of interest. If possible, put them in charge of small projects, so they can stretch their leadership wings.

How popular are internships?

Today's students understand that interning is a great way to gain entry to the professional world. According to a survey by WetFeet.com, 53 percent of undergraduate seniors and 64 percent of second-year MBAs participated in internships in the summer of 2000.

However, signing on an intern doesn't guarantee that your trainee will opt to stay with you.

The same survey found that almost half of interns who received an offer of employment from the companies at which they interned turned down those offers. So offer interns what they want: training and experience, a network of professional contacts, and a decent salary— and throw some fun in the mix.

Using the Net to Get the Younger Set

Many colleges now offer their own job boards. Check the Web sites of colleges and universities in your area to see if they offer this service. And, if you're recruiting for difficult-to-fill positions and can pay for relocation, check the Web sites of out-of-town and out-of-state schools as well.

In addition, check out Internet boards designed to hook up new grads and employers. Here are a few:

- ✔ JobTrak (www.jobtrak.com)
- ✔ BrassRing Campus (www.brassringcampus.com)
- ✔ CollegeRecruiter (www.collegerecruiter.com)
- ✔ Collegejournal (www.collegejournal.com)
- ✔ CollegeHire (www.collegehire.com)
- ✔ College Grad Job Hunter (www.collegegrad.com)
- ✔ Peterson's Education Center (www.petersons.com/career)
- ✔ CampusCareerCenter (www.campuscareercenter.com)
- ✔ JobPostings (www.jobpostings.net)
- ✔ JobDirect (www.jobdirect.com)
- ✔ CareerPlanit (www.careerplanit.com)

For more information on using the Internet to recruit students, see Chapter 7.

Give grads a warm welcome on your Web site

Use your Web site to attract college students by including a "just for grads" section that plays up the aspects of your company that appeal the most to young men and women. Emphasize your challenging jobs, your charity work, your lifestyle perks (for example, casual dress or free food), your salaries and stock options, and anything that's fun about your company culture. Provide a schedule of your college recruiting events on your Web site, and offer an e-mail address for students who want to ask questions about these events.

Also, consider including short career aptitude tests with such questions as, "Are you cut out to be a programmer?" or "Is a career in medicine right for you?" Provide information, too, about the training your jobs require. If possible, give students the opportunity to sign up for an e-mailed company newsletter directed specifically at the college crowd. And encourage students to e-mail you directly if they have questions or want to learn more about your company.

Once you design your "grads" page, recruit a focus group of college students to test it and make suggestions. Among the questions to ask: What image does our site project? Is it easy to use? Would it attract you, or create a negative impression? When your site is ready to go, be sure to include your Internet address in all on-campus recruiting materials.

For general information on setting up a Web site, see Chapter 7.

Chapter 12

Tapping Untapped Resources in a Tight Labor Market

*Y*ou're desperate. You're posting jobs on every high-powered job board on the Internet. You're running display ads in the newspapers. You're paying big employee referral bonuses, offering great salaries and benefits, hitting every job fair you can schedule, and even flying a "Work for Us!" blimp over your office. And you still have vacant positions.

Is it time to throw in the towel? No way! Instead, it's time to start thinking outside the box. Thousands of highly qualified candidates are being overlooked at this very moment simply because few employers are smart enough to court them. Tap into this market, and you'll suddenly find your recruiting horizons expanding exponentially.

This chapter tells you about some of these job seekers, and how you can target them.

Senior Citizens

As a group, they're highly educated and literate. They don't worry as much about fancy perks or fringe benefits. Instead, they worry about showing up on time, being courteous, and doing a good job. And they're often less interested in big salaries than in feeling needed.

"Seasoned" employees show their worth

Amfac Parks & Resorts actively recruits seniors to fill seasonal positions at national parks. "Having lived through busts as well as booms, seniors have solid work ethics, and there's just no substitute for experience," says Julie McCluskie, director of human resources for Amfac.

The Days Inn frequently hires older employees as reservations agents. Compared to younger employees, the company finds, seniors take the same amount of time to train, they have lower turnover rates, and they are more likely to complete a call with a successful reservation.

Who are these ideal employees? They're senior citizens, and as the Boomers age into their 60s, businesses will be hiring more and more of them — especially since new regulations allow people age 65 to 69 to earn unlimited outside income without losing Social Security benefits.

To attract employees over 65, recruit at senior centers (often populated by the most active, energetic, and talented seniors) and other locations frequented by seniors in your area. In addition, contact the National Council on the Aging's Maturity Works program (www.maturityworks.org), the American Association for Retired Persons (www.aarp.com), or Experience Works (www.experienceworks.org), a senior staffing agency hosted by the non-profit Green Thumb. All three organizations can help match senior employees with jobs. You can also advertise your jobs at these sites:

- ✔ The Senior Job Bank (www.seniorjobbank.org), which is free for employers
- ✔ The Senior Staff (www.srstaff.com), which has a special section for high-tech employees

To interest seniors, offer perks and benefits that attract them (see Chapter 1). And train, train, train, so your over-65 employees will feel comfortable around your computer- and Internet-savvy younger staff.

Seniors are often ideal for part-time job slots, because many who've tired of the 9-to-5 grind still aren't ready to retire from the work world. Increasing numbers of these seniors are looking for a few hours a day of challenging work — what the HR industry calls *phased retirement*. Because they have fewer family obligations, these seniors can frequently work flexible hours, nights, or weekends.

FACTS & FIGURES

The graying of America's workforce

Count on your job pool getting older, not younger, in the near future. The median age in this country grew from 28 in 1970 to 35 today, and will increase to 40 by the year 2010. By 2006, workers age 34 and younger will make up only 36 percent of the U.S. workforce.

Wise companies, noting both the growing population of seniors interested in working and the too-small numbers of job candidates in general — and particularly in high tech areas — are taking active steps to cultivate seniors. Recently, for example, Microsoft donated training materials to be used in a government-sponsored program to train seniors for high tech jobs.

Moreover, as companies hire more seniors, they're discovering that employing older workers pays off. A survey by the Society for Human Resource Management and the AARP found that 77 percent of employers found older employees to be more reliable than younger employees, and 77 percent also said that older employees showed a higher level of commitment to the employers than their younger counterparts.

High School Students

When you think of hiring teen employees, don't just think of fast food jobs. In 1998, companies employed 22,000 kids between the ages of 16 and 19 to work as computer programmers or other computer specialists — and that number will only grow.

Today's teens are weaned on PlayStation and computer games, and by the time they're 16, many can troubleshoot a server, design a Web site, or even program in Java. "Technology changes so quickly that it's almost a full-time job keeping up, but the only people who really have the time to play with new technology are people in high school," says Ron Schmelzer, founder of the computer firm ChannelWave.

Think about hiring some of these whiz kids for part-time or seasonal jobs, or offering them internships. To target them, advertise at malls, school sporting events, video game stores, concerts, and restaurants that high schoolers frequent.

Part-Timers

If you're having trouble filling a key full-time position, ask yourself the following: Can this job be done by two part-time employees? If so, you'll vastly expand your pool of applicants. With millions of young parents in today's workforce, many women and increasing numbers of men are seeking jobs that allow them to spend time with their children. Retirees, too, often prefer part-time to full-time work, and college students appreciate employers who can schedule around their class times.

Moreover, many part-timers eventually seek full-time work as their circumstances change — for example, as their children go off to school. Thus, the employee you hire part-time today may reward your flexibility a few years from now by signing on as a full-timer.

To encourage this kind of loyalty, be sure your company treats part-timers with the same respect it offers full-time employees. Keep part-timers in mind for advancement opportunities, offer them benefits if possible, and be sure to include them in company activities. Your employees should see part-time work as a stepping stone, not as a dead end.

Also, if your position is full-time, don't hire a part-timer and expect her to get the job done. Hire two part-timers and split the responsibilities. Surveys show that many part-time employees quit because they're pressured into doing impossible amounts of work, so be sure your assignments are realistic.

What jobs are suitable for part-timers? *Any* job, from entry-level to management positions, that

- Can be performed in less than 40 hours per week, or
- Can be structured so that two or more people can perform the job's responsibilities.

   Among good careers for part-timers: technical writing, human resources and recruiting, and many medical and clerical jobs. Don't rule out any position, however, without considering whether or not a part-timer could handle the job.

Military Employees

In today's tight labor market, the military is finding it hard to keep recruits for a lifetime. That's bad news for the armed forces, but it's good news for you, because many departing sailors and soldiers are highly trained in technical skills. They also tend to be disciplined, motivated, and hard working. Another plus, if you're seeking to diversify your work force: Because the military actively promotes diversity, many ex-military job seekers are women and minorities.

Remember when interviewing ex-military candidates that you're not allowed to ask about the status of their military discharges unless this information has a direct bearing on the job.

Relocating ex-military employees can be simple, too. When military person-nel transition to civilian life, it's the military's job to pay their relocation expenses either back home or to a community about the same distance away. (And no matter where an ex-soldier or ex-sailor is moving, the military pays the big up-front costs of packing.) Thus, it can be nearly free to relocate an ex-military employee from almost anywhere in the world.

Where can you find ex-military job seekers? Check out specialized Internet sites, such as the following:

- ✔ DoD Job Search (`dod.jobsearch.org`)
- ✔ Military.com (`www.military.com`)
- ✔ Jobs for Ex-Military (`www.jobsforexmilitary.com`)
- ✔ Transition Assistance Online (`www.taonline.com`)
- ✔ VetJobs.com
- ✔ Operation Transition (`www.dmdc.osd.mil/ot`)
- ✔ Corporate Gray Online (`www.greentogray.com`)
- ✔ The Destiny Group (`www.destinygrp.com`)

While you're thinking about recruiting ex-military employees, also think about attracting prospects currently serving in the National Guard. These men and women often worry about mentioning their service during job interviews, fear-ing that companies might consider it a drawback. By making it clear that you welcome reservists, you'll attract their applications and earn a good reputation in your local reservist community. If possible, make it company policy to pay reservists' salaries (minus what they earn from reserve duty) when they're on active duty, and publicize this benefit in your recruiting packet. It won't cost you much, and it's likely to expand your pool of highly motivated and well-trained prospects.

Employees with Disabilities

Publicize your jobs to groups for the disabled, and you're likely to discover talented job seekers willing to go the extra mile to prove that they're every bit as capable as your other employees.

To find highly skilled candidates with disabilities, network with schools such as Gallaudet University (a premier university for deaf students). Also contact local organizations for the disabled and visit Internet job boards for disabled job seekers — for example, JobAccess (`www.jobaccess.org`), and the job board of the National Business and Disability Council (`www.business-disability.com`). In addition, if you have jobs that are appropriate, consider contacting organizations for the developmentally disabled. Most programs for mentally disabled employees now provide free on-site job coaches, who will train disabled employees and ensure that your jobs are performed quickly and correctly. Contact your local chapter of the Association for Retarded Citizens (ARC) for additional information.

Company Alumni

People leave your company for many different reasons. Some retire. Some leave because they're starting a family and want to spend more time at home. Others take jobs that offer more money, bigger benefits, or more challenging work.

It's a mistake, however, to consider these employees as history. Instead, consider them as "alumni" of your company. Keep their names on file and contact them occasionally to see if they'd like to return, either permanently or on a single-project basis, or if they know anyone else who'd be right for your company.

Also, keep your alumni connected by inviting them to picnics, holiday parties, and other company events. If you have a newsletter, mail it to your former employees so that they can stay up-to-date on your company's activities. Ask managers to occasionally call their favorite ex-employees, if possible, and invite them to lunch. And if you have the resources, start an official alumni program and offer your former employees their own newsletter and activities. (Some companies provide an alumni Web site, and others allow alumni the use of some office equipment and research facilities.)

Why cultivate ex-employees? Often, especially in today's volatile market, employees who leave companies for better jobs realize they should have stayed — but many are too embarrassed to call up their former employers and say, "Do you still want me?" By checking with former employees occasionally, you'll make it easier for them to be what recruiters call *boomerangs* — employees who leave, thinking the grass is greener on the other side, and then fly back to their original employers when they discover that it isn't. Circumstances change for other ex-employees, as well. Parents who quit to be full-time moms or dads may start thinking about returning to work when their children enter preschool. Retirees may grow bored and long for the hustle and bustle of the workplace. Catch these former employees at the right time and you may convert them back into current employees who are already knowledgeable about your work and your company culture.

Reaping the rewards of an alumni program

The accounting firm of Ernst & Young has offered an alumni program for nearly a decade, and currently reaches out to former employees in the United States, Canada, and Latin America.

In the last quarter of 2000, 23 percent of hires at the manager level throughout the firm were "boomerangs," and the company hopes to increase this number to 50 percent.

In addition, a returning employee is a valuable retention tool. In effect, when you hire back an employee, you're sending other employees a message: "We're so much better than the competition that the people who leave us want to come back." But be careful not to anger the loyal employees who didn't jump ship, and avoid rehiring an employee who's unlikely to be loyal the second time around. Some questions to ask yourself, when you consider rehiring an employee, include these:

✔ **Did the employee learn any new skills, or earn a degree, while he or she was gone?** In that case, a salary raise or new title may be justified. If not, giving your returning employee additional money or benefits may offend the employees who stayed.

✔ **Do the issues that made the employee leave still exist?** An employee who left because of a lack of advancement opportunities, for example, is likely to leave again if the situation hasn't changed. And if your employee left for money reasons, he's not likely to be loyal the second time around if your salaries haven't increased.

Think Inclusive

As you review your job openings, avoid limiting yourself to preconceived ideas about which candidates will fit your needs. Instead, make it a point to ask yourself the following questions. Can this job be done by a senior citizen — or, conversely, by a high school or college student? Could we train an intern (see Chapter 11) to do the work? Does the job really require a college degree, or could military training be equally useful? Can we increase our pool of qualified candidates by tapping organizations for the disabled? Does the job need to be full-time, or can it be divvied up into two part-time positions? As you expand your sights, you'll attract more and more outstanding job candidates that other recruiters overlook — and, as a bonus, your workplace will be a far more diverse and interesting place to work.

Chapter 13

Calling in the Pros: When It's Time to Use a Recruiting Agency

Remember the tale of Hercules and the many-headed Hydra? Each time Hercules chopped one of the Hydra's heads, two new ones grew in its place. If you're a recruiter whose hiring needs are surpassing your ability to find qualified candidates, you know just how Hercules felt: Every time you find a new employee, two more positions open up.

If this is a temporary problem, you can probably solve it by doubling your recruiting efforts and telling your hiring managers to be patient. But if you're experiencing chronic problems meeting your staffing needs, and especially if the problems are growing worse, it's a smart move to call in the pros. This chapter shows you the way.

When Do You Need an Agency?

As we note in Chapter 3, not every company needs an agency — and there's no point in paying agency fees if you can solve your problems simply by beefing up your in-house hiring efforts. But in many situations, an outside agency can save you significant money by finding high-quality candidates quickly — thus increasing your productivity and, in turn, your bottom line.

How do you know when to go it alone, and when to hire an agency? Ask yourself these questions:

- ✔ How many open positions do you currently have?

- ✔ How soon do you need to fill these positions?

- ✔ How many in-house recruiters/staff do you have, and can they handle the workload by themselves?

- ✔ Do you have openings for positions that require very specific or hard-to-find skill sets, or for senior-level positions (executive, vice president, or director level) — and, if so, do you have little or no experience in recruiting for these type of positions?

- ✔ Are your vacancies for key positions? If so, is leaving them unfilled seriously affecting your productivity, or otherwise negatively affecting your business?

- ✔ How much does it cost you to let these positions go unfilled?

- ✔ Are your current employees experiencing burnout due to overwork — and are you in danger of increased turnover, and even more vacancies, as a result?

- ✔ Are you losing customers and revenue because of your vacant positions?

- ✔ Is your database of candidates, or your network of contacts, too small for you to locate enough good prospects?

If the answers show that your hiring crunch is hurting your firm's morale, productivity, and profits, and that you don't have the in-house resources to solve the problem, then it's time to think about bringing in an agency to help out.

You'll discover, most likely, that your top competitors are doing the same thing. Most high-tech and medical companies, in particular, simply can't locate enough good candidates through in-house recruiting alone. Companies undergoing quick growth and expansion also have trouble playing catch-up without calling in reinforcements. And firms seeking top-level employees almost invariably hire agencies, because CEOs and other senior-level candidates usually don't check out "help wanted" ads or post their resumes on Internet job boards. Instead, they rely on a network of contacts — and agencies know how to reach those contacts.

What Should You Look for When Selecting an Agency?

When you're buried under a blizzard of job requisitions, and the hiring managers are howling at your door, it's tempting to pick up the Yellow Pages, dial the number of the first agency you spot, and yell, "Help!" It's also tempting to say "yes" to any agency that contacts you by phone to solicit your business. But different recruiting agencies have different strengths, so it's crucial to do your homework and choose only the agencies that can best meet your needs.

Matching your agency to your employees

To begin, look for an agency that specializes in recruiting the category of candidate you're trying to attract. You'll find agencies with expertise in many different aspects of recruiting, from those that recruit high-tech professionals, engineers, administrative personnel, or healthcare employees, to those that conduct executive searches.

You'll also find agencies that do it all; but beware, these agencies may not have as much expertise, or as extensive a database, as a specialized agency will.

Your choice depends, too, on whether you need permanent employees, temporary/contract employees, or a combination. Some agencies handle both, as well as contract-to-hire positions. (These are positions in which employees hire on as contract workers, with the company offering permanent employment at the end of the contract period if the relationship is mutually satisfactory.) Others handle only permanent placements because they aren't set up to administer payroll and benefits for temp or contract workers. If you use an agency to fill contract or temp positions, ask for proof that they carry workers compensation, general liability, and professional liability insurance.

Asking around for references

Hop on the recruiting and human resources forums we discuss in Chapter 4 and ask for advice about selecting an agency that's right for you. Solicit recommendations from other companies, too, and check with your own hiring managers and employees to see if they're familiar with any good agencies. When you participate in job fairs, visit the booths of the agencies that attend and evaluate their services and professionalism.

Once you narrow your choices, investigate the agencies you're thinking of hiring just as carefully as you'd investigate a potential employee. Check their references and schedule face-to-face meetings with reps from each agency you're thinking of using. This is important, because the agencies you select will represent your company to candidates. They should be knowledgeable and professional and project an image that reflects well on your company. Give the representative of each agency a tour of your firm and explain your culture, benefits, work environment, and job openings to make sure that you and the agency are on the same page.

As you interview agencies, don't focus solely on nationwide agencies with branches in every major city. While these large agencies are generally good, smaller local agencies often have an in-depth understanding of the local market and the local candidate pool. In addition, the "little guys" are often more willing to negotiate on fees and may be more responsive to your needs.

Getting it in writing

Before you give an agency any job orders, sign a fee agreement. Read this agreement carefully, and be sure it includes all of the terms you've agreed on. The agreement should spell out what the agency's fees are, how you will pay them, and the procedures for sending and interviewing candidates. In addition, it should include the agency's guarantee policy. (Most agencies guarantee a placement for a certain amount of time, usually 60 or 90 days.) The agreement should also specify the following:

- ✔ If the agency will conduct reference checks and background checks.
- ✔ If the agency will conduct both phone screens and preliminary in-person interviews.

Your agreement should include a clause stating that the agency will not solicit employees from your company for a specified amount of time (usually one year), as well as a guarantee that the company will keep all information about your business and products confidential.

Even after you sign the agreement, continue to exercise caution. Don't give a new agency all of your company information, such as organizational charts, employee directories, and so on. Instead, give them only the information they need to market your company to candidates. The vast majority of recruiters are highly ethical and professional, but a few unscrupulous agencies will use your data to recruit employees away from you, or will give your information to other agencies that will try to lure away your employees — so keep everything on a "need to know" basis at first. Once you build a strong relationship with an agency, you can feel safe in divulging additional information.

How Much Should You Pay?

It depends. For a permanent position, you usually pay the agency a percentage of the employee's first year's base salary. For example, if you agree to pay a 25 percent fee for a full-time placement, and the agency finds a candidate that you hire for an annual salary of $60,000, you pay the agency a $15,000 fee.

The percentage that you and the agency agree on may range from 20 to 35 percent, depending on the jobs you're trying to fill. In general, agencies charge more to fill high-tech and other in-demand positions than for placements in jobs where candidates are fairly easy to find.

If possible, negotiate rates with the agency. Some will agree to negotiate and others won't, but it never hurts to try. In addition, ask if the agency will offer a discount if you pay invoices quickly — for example, upon receipt, or within two weeks. However, remember that you get what you pay for. You want your agency to send you the best resumes, and send them quickly — and that won't happen if you're paying a substantially lower rate than your competition.

Other issues to determine when you make arrangements with an agency are the following:

Should you pay a percentage or a flat fee?

Agencies usually charge a percentage, but some are willing to negotiate a flat fee. However, paying an agency a low flat fee may give the agency some incentive to send great candidates to a competitor who's paying a percentage. While agencies work hard for all of their clients, agency recruiters often make a good part of their income from commissions — so naturally they may be inclined to submit their best candidates to the companies paying the largest fees.

Should you ask for a volume discount, and should you offer exclusives?

An agency that's placing a large number of candidates for your company may be willing to consider a volume discount, to ensure that they remain one of your favorites. They're most likely to agree if you do one or both of the following:

✔ Agree to give them a large number of job orders, or, better yet,

✔ Offer to give them an exclusive on filling a large volume of orders within a specified time. (For example, you may agree to give the agency 20 positions to fill, and specify that you won't open these positions to other agencies for 2 weeks.)

The drawback to offering an agency an exclusive is that you may miss out on great candidates fielded by other agencies. That's usually outweighed by the fact that the agency will work extra-hard to find the perfect candidates for your jobs, in return for your loyalty. Also, you'll be building a strong relationship with the agency, which can pay off handsomely in the long run. An agency that's granted an exclusive will get to know your company well and will develop good instincts for selecting candidates who fit your needs. They'll also submit their best candidates to you first and work quickly to fill your positions as soon as they open.

A word of warning, however: Offer an exclusive only if the agency has proven itself and you know you can trust its staff.

Should You Hire on a Retainer or a Contingency Basis?

There's one more choice to make when deciding which agencies you'll hire and how you'll pay them. That's the choice between retained and contingency-based agencies, each of which has its pros and cons.

The retained agency

If you hire a retained agency, you pay the agency a fee before they actually fill your position. The agency is then *on retainer* to find the employee you need within a specified period of time, such as 90 days. Usually you pay a third of the fee up front, another third after 30 days, and the final third between 60 and 90 days. In general, the fee is based on the candidate's annual salary, but it may also include a percentage of the candidate's total package, including salary, stock options, and bonus.

Traditionally, companies use retained search agencies to fill key executive jobs such as chief executive officer, chief financial officer, or vice president. That's because finding qualified candidates for these jobs takes a great deal of time and research.

Among the pros of using a retained agency are the following:

 ✔ Retained search agencies usually have strong networks of well-connected individuals who can lead them to strong candidates.

- ✔ These agencies usually employ research specialists to conduct online and cold-calling research and to target specific companies that harbor the talent you need.

- ✔ Retained search agencies usually work on a small number of searches at one time, so you have their full attention.

The cons of using a retained agency include the following:

- ✔ It can be risky. You're paying for work that hasn't been done yet, and if the agency can't fill the position, you're still out the money.

- ✔ The agency has an exclusive, so if you find an outstanding candidate through another source, you still have to pay the retained agency's fee.

To make using a retained agency less risky, insist on receiving weekly or bi-monthly progress reports so that you can judge whether or not the agency is pursuing candidates with vigor.

The contingency agency

Contingency-based agencies don't get paid unless they find a candidate that you hire. In general, companies use contingency-based agencies for most of their recruiting needs and call in retained agencies only for executive-level positions.

Pros of using a contingency-based agency include these:

- ✔ You're not tied exclusively to one agency.

- ✔ There's no risk of paying fees and winding up empty-handed.

- ✔ Contingency agencies earn fees only if they produce, so they're highly motivated to provide strong candidates for your positions.

- ✔ If you open your positions to several agencies at the same time, the agencies will race against each other to find good candidates quickly.

- ✔ Contingency agencies that specialize in niche markets — for example, medical or IT candidates — are highly knowledgeable about their areas and have extensive networks of contacts and potential candidates.

- ✔ Contingency agencies often pay referral bonuses to individuals who provide them with leads that translate into hires. This increases your chances of locating a good candidate.

TIP

Can contingency agencies handle executive searches?

Retained agencies often specialize in executive searches, which take time, research, and a vast network of connections. But don't rule out using a contingency-based agency if you're looking for a new CEO or Vice President of Marketing, because some contingency agencies are very good at this type of search and have a solid network of contacts to lead them to high-level candidates.

If you don't like the idea of paying a retained agency up-front for a search that may prove fruitless, contact contingency-based agencies and ask them what experience they have in conducting executive searches, what techniques they use, and what top-level executives they've placed.

However, there are a few cons:

- ✔ A contingency-based agency doesn't need to fill your position. In fact, it doesn't need to make any effort at all on your behalf. If the agency finds another company that pays more and has more job openings, it's likely to concentrate on that company's needs rather than yours. (To avoid this problem, consider offering exclusives, as we discuss earlier in this chapter.)

- ✔ If you use too many agencies, keeping submittals straight can be a nightmare. Sometimes two agencies submit the same candidate, leading to a battle over which agency submitted the candidate first.

To avoid problems, make sure that you have a system for documenting when a resume comes in and which agency sent it. It's best to have resumes e-mailed, so the dates and times are automatically recorded.

Also, work with a single person at each agency, so you won't be pestered by dozens of calls from different recruiters. And limit the number of resumes each agency sends, as well as specifying that candidates be pre-screened and pre-qualified, to ensure that agencies send you only their top-notch applicants.

What Results Should You Expect?

A good agency will present you with qualified candidates as quickly as possible. They will screen resumes carefully to ensure that they're sending talented people who match your company's culture. They'll ask candidates in-depth questions, spot red flags, and weed out weak candidates so you won't have to.

Be a little patient at first, however, because it takes a new agency a little time to learn about your company and your needs. A good agency will catch on quickly, while a bad one will continue to send unqualified candidates.

Another good test of a recruiting agency is how well they treat their candidates. Ask each agency-referred candidate that you hire questions about that agency, "What did you think of the agency? Were they efficient? Fair? Ethical? Responsive? Courteous?" Complaints may indicate that other good candidates are slipping away, due to dissatisfaction with the agency's practices.

Also, watch out for unethical or unprofessional behavior by an agency. This may include actions such as the following:

- Sending a high volume of resumes of unqualified, unscreened candidates who don't match your job descriptions. (We like to call this "resume spamming.")

- Sending resumes of candidates who never authorized the agencies to submit their names to your company.

- "Placing and pulling" — that is, sending you candidates at the same time that they're hiring employees away from you. If this occurs, end your relationship with the agency immediately, because they're doing you more harm than good.

Listen to the pros!

Once you find a recruiting agency that you value and trust, listen to the agency's feedback (even if it's not always positive). Agencies work with a wide range of candidates, companies, and industries, and know the market value of specific skill sets and the salaries you should offer for each. They also can point out non-monetary reasons for why candidates turn down your job offers — for example, if your benefits aren't competitive or your hiring process is too slow.

In addition, because agencies work with many companies, they're an excellent source of ideas for the following:

- Enhancing your retention, morale-building, and team-building efforts.

- Developing orientation and referral programs.

- Improving your campus recruiting strategies.

- Developing diversity programs.

And because they receive feedback from the contract and permanent employees they place, agencies can tactfully pass on information about your company's problem areas.

While you may occasionally encounter an unethical agency, don't let that dissuade you from calling in professional help when you need it. The vast majority of professional agency recruiters are highly ethical and professional, and extremely motivated to help their clients succeed. An outstanding agency can prevent disaster when staffing needs escalate out of control, locate great candidates at a time when they all seem to be taken, and vastly improve your productivity and your profits. So keep your options open, and call on recruiting agencies whenever you find yourself in a serious hiring bind — but insist on using only the best.

Chapter 14

Making Your Presence Known: Sponsorship, Advertising, and Other Tricks

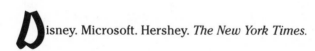

isney. Microsoft. Hershey. *The New York Times.*

Some lucky companies have no trouble keeping their names in the public eye, which gives them a huge advantage in the recruiting game. But if you work for a podiatry clinic, a legal firm, or a local drug store, it's harder to make your company name a household one.

Does that matter? Yes, because job seekers gravitate toward companies they know and like. By making a name for yourself in your community, you'll achieve the following:

- ✔ Let prospects know you exist.
- ✔ Promote the positive image you want to project.
- ✔ Persuade potential hires that you have great jobs.
- ✔ Make your current employees feel good about working for your firm.

It's savvy to focus a significant part of your time and effort on making your company well known and well liked by the public. Recruiters sometimes call this effort *branding*. If your company manufactures a product, you're probably already familiar with the term, but in this case, recruiters are talking about marketing a company itself, rather than its products.

There are dozens of ways, large and small, to make a name for your company. We talk about some of them in Chapter 11 where we discuss college recruiting, and the same techniques apply to establishing a presence in your city or state — or, if you're a larger company, across the country or even around the world.

We recommend three great ways to create name recognition and "good vibes" for your company:

- ✔ Be active in charitable activities and other events.
- ✔ Create a positive, unified message that runs throughout your advertising and promotional materials.
- ✔ Aim for *employer of choice* status.

This chapter takes a look at how you can make a good name for yourself and your company.

Becoming a Community Asset

One of the best and fastest ways to build a great reputation is to support charitable activities that make your community a better place to live. You can do this by donating one or more of the following:

- ✔ Money
- ✔ Materials and equipment
- ✔ Staff expertise
- ✔ Staff time and labor
- ✔ Additional services such as advertising, printing, or mailing

Making the most of your good deeds

When you participate in a charity event, do more than simply donate money and lend your name to the activity. If possible, have a booth or area where representatives from your company can hand out company materials, and recruiters can provide information on your current job openings. Also, offer refreshments and give out prizes — freebies always make a good impression! And consider giving your staff time off in exchange for volunteering at the events you sponsor. Ask them to wear company shirts, buttons, or caps if they work the events. (To maximize active participation by your staff, consider sponsoring "family friendly" charity events where both employees and their children can volunteer.)

It's a win-win approach, because you'll create a positive image for your company — an image likely to translate into new hires who'll more than make up for your expenses — and local charities will benefit from your generosity.

If you're a small operation (for example, a "mom and pop" grocery) and have a fairly easy time recruiting employees close to home, then focus on inexpensive methods of branding. These include the following:

✔ Sponsoring a Little League team or soccer team.

✔ Co-sponsoring inexpensive local charity events and toy drives.

✔ Giving your employees paid time off to tutor in local schools, deliver meals for Meals on Wheels, or do volunteer work for shelters or food banks.

✔ Sponsoring individual employees when they participate in charity events. (A tip: Ask them to wear company T-shirts or buttons, so others will know that you sponsored them.)

✔ Making generous one-time donations to local citizens when tough times (floods, earthquakes, hurricanes, and so on) occur, and donating employee time to help in these situations.

✔ Matching employee contributions to charities.

None of these efforts is very expensive, and all will increase your company's name recognition and show your local community that you're a friendly neighbor who cares about its needs.

Of course, if you work for a larger firm, or you're recruiting in a tough market — healthcare or information technology, for example — it'll take more of an investment to create the image you desire. Among the activities you can participate in are the following:

✔ **Sponsor or co-sponsor a large annual charity event,** such as a golf tournament, 10-K run, or holiday ball. If possible, have the event named after your company. (And don't feel guilty about doing so, because everyone comes out a winner if you gain good publicity and your charity gains extra funds for its efforts. This is not a time to be humble!)

✔ **Adopt a local school.** With your company supplying the funding, your employees can paint and repair classrooms, purchase and plant trees, provide library books and playground equipment, and volunteer in after-school tutoring and sports programs.

✔ **Participate in regular events that will keep your name in the news.** A good example: The Bashas' grocery chain in Arizona sponsors an annual golf classic — and also participates in a yearly "register tapes for education" program, an annual food drive for the needy, and monthly health screenings at store sites.

Motorola makes a difference

Motorola is legendary around the world for lending a helping hand to worthy causes. The company's hundreds of charitable activities include the following:

✔ Endowing a professorship in Community Revitalization at Arizona State University.

✔ Supporting Whizz-Kidz, a British charity for disabled children, by providing thousands of dollars for electric wheelchairs and other supplies.

✔ Co-sponsoring the national Black Enterprise/Pepsi Golf and Tennis challenge.

✔ Helping to build playgrounds for children in low-income neighborhoods.

✔ Supporting tutoring projects and programs to fight domestic abuse.

In addition, the Motorola Foundation offers a grants program to support the favorite charities of their employees.

Also, consider the image you wish to present, and plan activities accordingly. Do you want your community to see you as a cutting-edge research firm? Then sponsor college research activities (see Chapter 11), host national seminars on your company's area of expertise, assist in developing curricula for your local universities, and offer your employees as conference speakers or as guest experts who can be consulted by local or national media. Do you want your community to associate your company with fun and creativity? Then sponsor entertaining charitable events, such as film festivals or Mardi Gras parties. Be sure your activities are a good match for your company culture and the image you hope to project.

Also, make sure the activities you choose are likely to attract people with the talents you need. In Chapter 8, we mention how one company surveyed its employees, found out that many liked jazz, and began hosting jazz concerts in order to attract job candidates. Use a similar approach in targeting your own community efforts, for example:

✔ If you're recruiting for a sporting goods store, host a bike race or a run so that you can attract people already interested in, and knowledgeable about, some aspects of sports.

✔ IT candidates tend to like science fiction, so if you're looking for high-tech employees, help sponsor a sci-fi movie premiere for a charity and set up a booth outside the event. Or participate in the opening of a Star Wars exhibit at a local museum, and use the event to publicize your firm.

Good will is good business!

Statistics show that philanthropy pays off for corporations. Recent studies report the following:

✔ Seventy-six percent of Americans say they'd be likely, if offered two similar jobs, to accept the offer of a company that participates in charitable activities over the offer of a company that doesn't.

✔ Of Americans planning to change jobs in the near future, 90 percent say they're likely to choose a company that supports charitable causes.

Eighty-two percent of companies say they participate in social causes as part of a strategy to establish themselves as preferred employers.

To maximize the benefits of your participation in a community activity, take out an ad in your local paper after the event, thanking your employees for their participation. You'll make the newspaper's readers aware of your good deed, and highlight the fact that you appreciate the people who work for your company. Also, if you have a company area that's open to the public, create a volunteer recognition wall, clearly visible to your customers or clients, where you post the names and pictures of the employees who volunteer in your community efforts.

For more information on volunteer projects that can benefit both your community and your company, contact the following agencies:

✔ The Points of Light Foundation (www.pointsoflight.org)

✔ Business for Social Responsibility (www.bsr.org)

✔ The Boston College Center for Corporate Citizenship (www.bc.edu/cccr)

Advertising

In addition to sponsoring events, you can make a name for your company through advertising. By placing ads on job boards and Web sites that your prospects are likely to visit, you'll make a good impression on candidates who might not otherwise hear about you. This is probably the job of your advertising department; if so, meet with them to ensure that recruitment advertising is being done in the right places at the right times. Again, it's critical to target your efforts toward the candidates you're most interested in attracting.

Get more mileage from your perks!

If your company offers outstanding employees the use of a company sports car or boat as a perk, advertise your company name and Web site address on it. An example: Tonic Software, in Austin, offers a company Hummer, proudly displaying the firm's name and contact information, for its Employees of the Month.

If you can't afford a company car, give your employees free T-shirts, sweatshirts, and caps with your company's name and Web address prominently displayed.

Among the branding issues to address in your advertising are the following:

- ✔ Do your ads project the right image? For example, if you're a high-tech company, do your Internet ads use modern and stylish graphics that tell viewers, "We're on the cutting edge of technology"?

- ✔ Are your ads targeted to attract a diverse workforce? Do your advertising graphics show people of both genders, a variety of ethnic backgrounds, and a range of ages?

- ✔ Does your advertising clearly distinguish you from your competitors?

Remember, too, that the advertising venues you select say as much about your company as the content of your ads. For instance, if you advertise in a local newspaper for seniors, you're saying, "Our company thinks senior employees are particularly valuable," and if you advertise in a New Age magazine, you're saying, "We're looking for free-thinking, creative people."

Creating an Image

If you want people to know who you are, it's crucial to create a consistent, positive company image. From your Web site to your business cards, every tool you use should present a unified, appealing message about your company. This is usually the responsibility of a company's advertising or PR department, but as a recruiter, you should have a strong voice in the process.

How do you project the message you want to send? Start by examining all of the materials you use to publicize your company and recruit employees. What do these materials say about your company? Do they present a unified and positive message, or are they a hodge-podge of unrelated materials? Are they new and catchy, or old and out-of-date? Be careful, as you review your materials, not to be too sentimental. Even if your logo has served you for years, it's probably time to refurbish it. (After all, even Betty Crocker gets a new hairdo every few years.)

If it's time for a corporate face-lift, encourage your company to hire a professional firm to devise a promotional package that communicates the image you want to portray to your public, and especially to your prospective employees. Ask this firm to design a logo and/or slogan that can be used on all of your materials, including the following:

✓ Your advertising

✓ Your business cards and letterhead

✓ Your employee materials

✓ Your print, radio, TV, and/or Internet advertisements

✓ Your Web site

✓ Your company T-shirts and mugs

If your company can't afford a complete image makeover right now, focus first on your Web site (see Chapter 7 for advice on designing your site). Unless you do major television and print advertising, your Web site is the most important of all your recruiting, marketing, and branding tools.

Aiming for Employer of Choice Status

One excellent way to achieve name recognition is to become what's known as an *Employer of Choice,* often abbreviated as *EOC.*

What's an EOC? Strictly defined, it's a company that earns a slot on a "Top Employers" list because it's recognized as being an outstanding place to work. (Depending on your company's size and geographic range, you can shoot for getting your name on national lists, or on lists in state or local publications.) More loosely defined, an EOC is a company that's frequently featured in local newspaper or magazine articles as an excellent workplace.

Becoming recognized as an outstanding employer isn't easy, because you need to earn that reputation by creating the most employee-friendly environment possible. (See Chapters 1 and 26.) In addition to providing generous salaries, benefits, and perks, you'll need to create a company culture that consistently cultivates, supports, and motivates your employees.

If you've already succeeded at these goals, the next step is to tell the media why you're special. Build relationships with local newspapers, business journals, industry trade journals, and radio and TV producers, and make them aware of your company's employee-friendly culture. If you have a public relations department, ask for their help in making the right media contacts.

Reporters and producers will generally ignore self-serving press releases. Instead, offer them valuable information and provide them with story ideas, such as the following:

- ✔ Do you offer special benefits for Baby Boomer employees caring for aging parents? Then host a conference on long-term care for caregiver employees. In your press release about the event, note that your own company provides elder care services and flex time.

- ✔ If you provide a special package of benefits and perks geared toward working mothers — onsite daycare, lactation rooms, flex time, "bring your baby to work" options — make contact with your local newspaper's feature editor and discuss the idea of doing an article on "mom-friendly" workplaces.

Making contacts with the media takes time, so be patient. Remember that reporters and producers receive lots of press releases and story ideas each day, and it may take a while to get their attention. Be polite, be patient, and be persistent, and your efforts are likely to pay off in good publicity and new hires — and, if you're really lucky, they may pay off some day in a slot on someone's "Employer of Choice" list.

Chapter 15

Staying Ahead of the Curve

● ●

In This Chapter

▶ Recruiting 24/7 — even when you *don't* need employees

▶ Keeping your Web site fresh

▶ Keeping your database current

▶ Making new contacts

▶ Honing your skills

▶ Planning for future needs

● ●

Experiencing a little slack time? Congratulations — now get to work! While it's tempting to put your feet on your desk and take a break when your jobs are all filled, slow times are prime recruiting periods. That's because you can use these periods to track down high-quality prospects, building a talent pool in preparation for the next time hiring gets tight. In addition, you can take the time to update your recruiting resources. Among the assignments to put on your list for quiet times are these:

✔ Clean up your database.

✔ Refresh your Web site.

✔ Update your skills and learn new technologies.

Here are our best tips for using your downtime to prepare for the next hiring rush.

Keep Making Those Calls!

Even if you have no current job openings, don't stop looking for great prospects — and when you spot them, give them a call. Explain that you're looking for top talent so that you'll be prepared for the next hiring boom; most of them will be flattered, and you'll have money in the bank in the form of a database of potential hires who already know and like you.

Also, use some of your spare time to touch base with key contacts. Often, you may feel like you're too busy to keep in touch with colleagues and current candidates in your databases. Now's the time to drop them a line, give them a call, or even invite them out to lunch. Keep your relationships strong during slow times, and they'll pay off during brisk hiring periods. It's especially important to keep in contact with high-level candidates, as well as those with in-demand skills.

In addition, consider expanding your outreach efforts by starting a company newsletter and inviting potential candidates to sign up to receive the newsletter by e-mail. This will keep prospects updated on your company news, and keep your name fresh in their minds. And begin an alumni program for former employees, or expand your existing alumni outreach efforts (see Chapter 12).

Make Your Web Site "State of the Art"

When you have extra time and a little extra money in your budget, it's the perfect opportunity to take a critical look at your Web site. Even the best site can be improved, and Internet technology and styles change so quickly that today's stellar Web site can look outdated within a year. Moreover, you want people to return again and again to your Web site — and they won't, if it always looks the same.

See Chapter 7 for ideas on Web site design, and make it your resolution to add at least one or two new features to your site each year. Keep your company news up-to-date, too, adding any recent press releases, media articles, or information about upcoming events.

Also, keep your "Jobs" section active even if you have no current open positions. Encourage visitors to send their resumes or fill out application forms if they're interested in future jobs, and follow up on these leads. In addition, post information about the skill sets you frequently need. Your work will pay off later, when the job orders start flooding in.

If all of your positions are filled, don't simply post the standard "Sorry — there are no current openings" message on your Jobs page. Instead, post a message like this: "Looking for an exciting and challenging career with one of America's fastest-growing companies? Then look into joining the XYZCorp team! Although we have no openings today, our employment needs change frequently, so we encourage you to send us your resume. As soon as positions that match your skills become open, we'll contact you."

Do Some Spring Cleaning . . . of Your Database

Is your database filled with unqualified candidates, or candidates who've left the state, or candidates who don't match your company's needs? If so, this is a perfect time to clear out the clutter. (Think of this as the equivalent of cleaning out your garage. It's a chore you dread, but aren't you glad when it's done?) Take several days to edit candidate profiles, document new information, and delete unqualified prospects.

When you weed out unwanted resumes and outdated contacts, you'll create an efficient, powerful database that will save you time and money. You'll also be helping other recruiters in your company, who might not be familiar with the same candidates you know, by providing them with accurate information.

Schmooze, Schmooze, Schmooze

One cardinal rule for slow times is, Get out! Out of the office, that is. Join recruiting groups, business groups, and other organizations where you can make new contacts. Also, go to the places where your candidates hang out: restaurants, festivals, concerts, theater events, industry conferences and seminars, user group meetings, sporting events. Although you can connect with candidates through ads and Internet job boards, you'll make many of your best connections out in the real world.

Slow times are also good times to sponsor charitable events that will increase public awareness about your company (see Chapter 14). You'll have more time to devote to planning and publicizing events than you would during hiring crunches.

Plan Ahead

Talk to your supervisors and hiring managers about their plans for the near future. Will your company be Web-enabling all of your applications in the near future? Then you'll soon need a flock of developers, programmers, and other IT people. Or will you need a half-dozen sales engineers in a few months? If you identify a future need, start focusing on finding candidates right now by researching for what you're likely to need:

✔ Investigate the Web sites, job boards, and resume banks where you're likely to find these individuals.

✔ Check out user groups or professional groups likely to attract them.

✔ Find out what journals and newspapers they read.

✔ Determine which companies currently employ people with the skills you'll need, and devise strategies for recruiting them away from these companies.

By doing this detective work in advance, you'll cut days or even weeks off the hiring process later on.

Stay on Top of Your Game

Recruiting is a dynamic profession, and the skills you need to be successful are changing every day. To keep up, you need to be aware of the latest recruiting trends, tools, and services. When you have a little free time, ask yourself the following questions:

✔ Am I using the best job boards?

✔ Am I using the best online search techniques?

✔ Is my database technology state-of-the-art, or sadly out of date?

✔ Do I fully understand what my company does, what it will be doing in the near future, and the job skills our employees need?

✔ Am I up to speed on the latest recruiting techniques?

✔ Am I knowledgeable about marketing and advertising?

✔ Are my verbal and written communication skills top-notch, or could they use some work?

If you spot gaps in your skills or knowledge, learn more by participating in recruiting forums and subscribing to recruiting magazines and newsletters. Attend seminars, and join recruiting associations in your area (see Chapter 4 for information on excellent resources). Consider taking marketing or communications classes at your local college or university. Read up on your industry and learn more about your products or services. For a smart recruiter, continuing education is a part of the job description.

Here's to Your Future!

What will your future hiring needs be? Economic booms and cool-downs may keep you guessing, but statistics show that it's likely to be an employee's market for years or maybe even decades to come.

Thus, it's smart to do what the experts in our field do: Keep recruiting, even during the quiet times. Meet with your management team and try to predict future needs. Fine-tune your Web site and your database. Make new friends through professional recruiting organizations. Continue to scour the Internet and other sources for great candidates. Check out new job boards, new applicant tracking systems, and other tools that can make your efforts more efficient. Analyze your college recruiting strategies, and touch base with campus contacts. Review your employee referral program and your employee retention strategies to ensure that they're working for you. Use these rare islands of peace to become even better at your job, and you'll set yourself up for success when the next hiring flurry hits.

Create a "downturn" strategy

Economic ups and downs can leave recruiters desperate for employees one month and flooded with applications the next. In such roller-coaster times, it's important to be able to switch gears quickly. With the advice in this book, you know what to do in an employee-hungry market; in addition, here's some advice for adjusting your strategy if the economy takes a turn for the worse and eager prospects start piling up:

✔ **Be sure your applicant tracking system is up to the task.** In Chapter 16, we offer tips for purchasing software to track your applicants. It's especially crucial to have an efficient system during economic downturns, when a deluge of resumes — many from unqualified applicants — can easily overwhelm you. If you're using antiquated software, upgrade it before you're swamped by a torrent of desperate job seekers.

✔ **Keep an eye on layoffs, but be cautious.** Always focus on the quality of your candidates, rather than on their ready availability. However, don't stereotype all laid-off workers as less desirable; in large-scale layoffs, both high performers and slackers get the ax. To determine the quality of recent-laid-off job seekers, interview them extensively, and check their references carefully.

✔ **Cut your least productive recruiting efforts.** When employees are scarce, you need a broad range of recruiting tools. During economic slowdowns, however, you should focus primarily on the techniques most likely to bring in high-quality candidates. In addition, slow economic times often translate into smaller recruiting budgets. So make a list of every recruiting tool you currently use — Internet advertising, job fairs, newspaper or radio or TV ads, and so on — and redefine your strategy to focus on the approaches with the best cost-per-hire ratios.

✔ **Continue to treat all applicants with respect.** It's tempting, when job seekers are beating down your door, to be brusque with candidates who don't meet your current needs. But, as the economic ups and downs of years past prove, you never know what's going to happen tomorrow — and the nurse or network administrator you don't want now could be the employee that you covet in the near future. So be positive, polite, and kind to all of your applicants during "employer's market" periods, and they'll remember you fondly when the economy — and your hiring needs — change.

Part IV
The Nibble: How to Hook a Hot Prospect

The 5th Wave   By Rich Tennant

"The next part of your employment test is designed to determine your sense of humor."

In this part . . .

Your hard work is finally paying off, and dozens of hot prospects are sending you their resumes. Now comes an equally important challenge: deciding which of these candidates to hire.

It's not easy to tell a super-achiever from an under-achiever, and picking the right person requires smart decisions in every step of the hiring process. In this section, we walk you through that process, step by step, from your first encounter (Chapter 16), to the all-important step of resume screening (Chapter 17), and the different stages of interviewing (Chapters 18 through 22).

Chapter 16

"I'm Interested in Your Position...": Making First Contact

● ●

In This Chapter

▶ Helping your candidates reach you

▶ Making the first call

▶ Organizing your candidate data

● ●

*L*ike a good angler, after you've cast plenty of tempting bait on the water — Internet job postings, print ads, referral bonuses, and cold calls to passive candidates — you're getting your reward, in the form of tentative nibbles from interested job candidates. During this pre-interview phase, you have three important tasks: Creating a smooth path for job seekers who want to contact you, responding quickly when they do, and organizing the information they send so that you can quickly and efficiently select the best candidates to interview.

Keeping the Communication Lines Open

When a hot prospect wants to reach you, keep in mind this cardinal rule: *Make it easy.* Analyze the types of job seekers you're trying to attract, and make sure you provide the most convenient methods for those individuals to contact your company.

If you're hiring high-tech professionals, it's a must to provide them with an e-mail address. In fact, with more and more people becoming computer-literate, we recommend offering an e-mail option for all job seekers. If you're seeking applicants for manufacturing, delivery, food preparation and service, or janitorial positions, you should also provide a fax number and mailing address for candidates who lack access to computers. In general, your best bet is simply to provide all three options — e-mail, fax, and "snail mail" — for all applicants.

It's a smart idea to establish a separate e-mail address dedicated solely to receiving resumes — for example, our firm might select jobs@ triadresources.com, resumes@triadresources.com, or careers@ triadresources.com. Use your unique e-mail address on all of your job postings, as well as on your company Web site. If possible, set up an auto-responder for your e-mail address, so candidates will immediately know that you received their resume and you will contact them if you're interested. Give some thought to your auto-responder message, making it positive and encouraging, because it's the first impression your candidate will receive. Also, make sure you don't make any grammatical or spelling errors.

Sample auto-responder messages

A well-crafted e-mail auto-responder message can keep your candidate hooked until you're able to reach her in person. Here are some examples:

1. "Thank you for sending us your resume. We are always seeking top-notch talent to work on our exciting and challenging projects. Our staff will personally review your resume, and contact you within 2 weeks if we have open positions that match your interests and skills. If no current openings exist, we will keep your resume in our active file for one year. Again, thanks for contacting XYZCorp — we appreciate your interest!"

2. "Thank you for your interest in exploring a career with XYZCorp. We're excited that you'd like to join our team. We will be reviewing your resume, and if we have an appropriate opening, we will contact you within 2 weeks. If not, we will keep your resume in our resource file for one year, and notify you if any positions arise that meet your qualifications. You can also call our job hotline anytime at 1-800-555-1234 to hear about new job openings. If you'd like to know more about us, please visit our Web site at xyzcorp.com."

3. And for agency recruiters, here's a sample from our own firm:

"Thank you for sending your resume.

"It will be forwarded to the recruiter responsible for this opportunity. This recruiter will contact you directly should your background match the requirements for this position. We will also consider you for other positions that match your skills and experience. In the meantime, please feel free to review other openings by visiting our website at http://www.triadresources. com. If you know someone who you think would be a good fit for any of our posted job openings, please feel free to let them know about the opportunity."

Be careful not to write a "downer" message — for example, "We regret that we cannot respond to your e-mail personally." Make every statement positive and project a winning image.

If your candidate mails a resume, and doesn't include an e-mail address, se... a reply by regular mail. Follow the same rules as for an e-mail response: Be quick, be positive, and make sure your letter doesn't contain any typos.

Also, be sure to respond quickly to any "I'm-not-sure-I'm-interested" prospects who want more information about your company. Answer these individuals' questions thoroughly and courteously, and offer to put them in touch with an employee who can serve as a friendly and informative contact.

Contacting Hot Prospects by E-Mail or Phone

Check your e-mail, fax, and office mail regularly, and be sure to respond quickly (preferably within 72 hours) to the most promising candidates. Waiting even a few hours can cost you a candidate in today's high-pressure hiring market, so don't let the competition get the jump on you.

When a candidate provides you with an e-mail address, follow up your auto-responder message with a personal e-mail as soon as possible. If you have a phone number, call right away. If you get an answering machine, leave a friendly, professional message that informs and attracts him.

Use your e-mail and/or phone message to accomplish the following:

- ✔ Identify yourself and your company clearly.
- ✔ Explain why you're calling.
- ✔ Offer tempting details about your job opening.
- ✔ Create a sense of urgency.
- ✔ Provide your contact information.

Ask yourself this question: If this job seeker gets ten calls or e-mails today, what will make mine stand out? Be brief, but take time to tell him what's special about your company. (For example: "We just received major funding for an exciting long-term project, and we need some real pros to head up our development team. I'm looking at your resume, and with your strong aerospace background, I think you'd be perfect. We have great benefits, too — *Fortune* just rated us one of the top 100 companies to work for.")

If you're leaving a message, give the prospect your phone number and e-mail address, and tell him that he can reach you either during or after work hours. If you have both an office number and a cell phone number, leave both.

g a phone message, speak slowly and clearly, and repeat your
ber to make sure it's understandable. Also, sound friendly, inter-
upbeat, even if it's the end of a long, exhausting day. You'd be sur-
much your tone of voice matters; a recruiter who sounds tired,
cold can turn a prospect off instantly.

ndidate doesn't call back, call him again in a day or so to let him
u're seriously interested — especially if he's a hot prospect. We
high-level technology candidates, and several have told us that they
only return calls from recruiters who contact them at least twice, and leave
detailed messages. Once you do reach your prospect, find out if he's interested and available and, if so, set up a phone screen (see Chapter 18).

Getting Organized: Making Sense of the Resume Pile

If your recruiting efforts are successful, you may find that you have a new
problem: tons of e-mailed, faxed, and mailed resumes to screen — and too
little time. In fact, you may wish, as your recruiting demands grow and grow,
for a superhuman assistant capable of zipping through incoming resumes,
sorting out qualified and unqualified applicants, and creating a searchable
database — all at lightning speed. If so, there's good news: You can buy one!
It's a computer application called the *applicant tracking system,* or *ATS*.

What does an applicant tracking system do?

Put simply, an applicant tracking system (ATS) is a computer-based system
for automating the recruiting process from start to finish. Dozens of companies offer ATS software, and packages vary in price depending on how many
bells and whistles you need. ATS systems aren't inexpensive — most cost
thousands of dollars — but they're often cost-effective, because they free
your recruiters from many administrative tasks and give them more time to
network and talk to candidates. Among the services ATS programs can provide are the following:

✔ Scanning or importing resumes and creating a searchable database of
candidates.

✔ Posting job orders from the ATS to your Web site and to Internet job
boards.

✔ Matching candidates with current job openings.

✔ Automatically sending e-mails to candidates when jo▨ their skill sets.

✔ Automatically responding by e-mail to candidates who sen▨

✔ Ranking candidates according to skills, experience, or other cr▨

✔ Tracking candidates' histories — for example, the jobs they applie▨ and the dates they were interviewed.

✔ Tracking employee referrals and references.

✔ Tracking job orders.

✔ Generating reports and letters.

✔ Scheduling and tracking interviews, and performing "daily planner" functions.

✔ Cross-referencing and indexing candidate/job information, to save time and prevent duplications.

How much power do you need?

If you're a small company or your recruiting needs are simple, an ATS that provides all of these features may be out of your price range. If so, decide which features you need and which you can live without. Then contact a variety of ATS providers and find out if they can provide the functions you need at a price you can afford. As you interview each sales rep, be sure to ask the following:

✔ How many users does this ATS allow? Can they use the system simultaneously?

✔ How does the price compare to the prices of competing products? If the system is more expensive, what extra features will you get for your money?

✔ How much technical support is available, and how much does it cost? What hours is customer service available?

✔ What installation fees are involved? What maintenance fees are involved? Are there any other fees?

✔ Are upgrades free?

✔ Is training available? Is it free?

✔ Is the ATS customizable?

✔ Will the system be capable of meeting your company's growth and future needs?

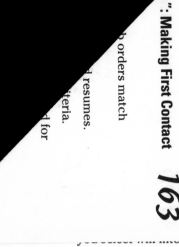

'll need to make is whether to buy and maintain
your ATS from an *application service provider*
software for you and make your data available
n-house technical staff to keep your system up
ter to subscribe to an ASP and let its staff do the
inies prefer to keep their sensitive data on-site.
s accessible, while you may experience delays
to reach your data at all, if your Internet

ror to find the right ATS for your company, and
several ATS providers and asking for advice on
ee Chapter 4) before making your decision. Be
ouse technical staff, too, to ensure that the ATS
you select will integrate well with your other computer technology. If your
budget allows, consider purchasing the Electronic Recruiting Exchange's
research review of 38 ATS systems, available at `erexchange.com`.

In addition, ask the ATS representatives how long their companies have been
manufacturing their systems. You want to select a product with a track record
that suggests that it'll be around for at least several more years. Request references of satisfied customers too, and call these companies to ask for their
opinions on the ATS, the company's customer service, the training provided,
and so on. And when you choose an ATS provider, ask if you can have a free
demo period to see if the product meets your needs.

Inexpensive alternatives

Is an expensive "store-bought" ATS more than you need? If so, consider creating your own tracking system. If your hiring needs are simple, or your budget
simply won't allow for an ATS right now, ask a consultant how much it will cost
to set up a system using software applications you either own or can purchase
inexpensively. At a minimum, your system should include these features:

- ✔ Automated e-mail responses to candidates.
- ✔ A database in which candidates' contact information, qualifications,
  experience, and education can be listed.
- ✔ A system for tracking employee referrals.
- ✔ A system for tracking hires and no-hires.

If you're thinking of opting for an inexpensive homegrown system, however,
analyze your choice carefully to make sure you're really saving money. An
ATS that pre-screens your resumes can save ten or more hours of staff time
per week, which adds up to a lot of cash over the course of a year.

Disorganization equals disaster

Which system you need — ATS, ASP, or a simple "do-it-yourself" system — depends on the size of your company, the technological expertise of your staff, and your recruiting needs. Start with the basics if necessary, but be sure to choose a system that can grow to meet your needs.

Also, be prepared to invest some dollars and some time in setting up your system. A good ATS will work round-the-clock for you, and turn your office chaos into an efficient and streamlined system, so don't skimp on this critical piece of recruiting technology.

Chapter 17

Is Your Applicant Qualified? Top Techniques for Resume Screening

In This Chapter

▶ Spotting your candidate's strong points and flaws

▶ Bad resume, good candidate?

▶ Is your candidate qualified for a different job?

▶ Which resumes to keep, which to throw away

▶ When a resume is necessary, and when it isn't

*W*hat a difference a few days can make! One week you're in despair, thinking that no one will ever apply for your open position, and the next week you're staring at a dozen candidates' resumes and thinking, "How on earth will we ever pick one?"

Needless to say, all recruiters prefer the second scenario. However, selecting the best candidates from a pile of resumes is every bit as challenging as locating those candidates in the first place. And making the right decisions is critical, because you usually don't have the time or resources to interview every candidate — and yet you can't afford to let a great one slip away.

Resume screening is both an art and a science, and the longer you do it, the better your instincts will be. However, even if you're a beginner, you can become a confident screener by using the "Good Signs" and "Bad Signs" lists in this chapter. But before you start sorting resumes into "yes" and "no" piles, you need to do your homework.

First, be sure you understand enough about your company and your industry to select candidates for your position wisely (see Chapter 4 for advice on this topic). Next, decide exactly who your ideal candidate is.

Defining Perfect — and Almost Perfect

To pick Mr. or Ms. Right, you have to know who you're looking for — and to do that, you need to define both the job requirements and the type of person who will flourish in your work environment. Begin by listing the following:

- ✔ Which skills your candidates must possess, and which are a plus but not required.

- ✔ How much experience is necessary.

- ✔ What employment background is preferred.

- ✔ What the minimum educational requirements are.

In a tight labor market, of course, you may need to be flexible and train new employees in some skills. Thus, your next step should be to make two lists:

- ✔ List One: The ideal candidate.

- ✔ List Two: A good, solid, acceptable candidate, with all of the required skills and the ability to quickly learn other skills. (This is the person you'll want, if you don't find your dream candidate.)

Now, refine your criteria further by analyzing the job you're trying to fill.

- ✔ Is it an ideal position for an individual contributor, or will success be measured by team goals?

- ✔ Will the job demand interaction with the public?

- ✔ Does it require frequent, rapid problem solving, or is it repetitive work that may bore an employee who seeks a challenging career?

- ✔ Does the position require on-the-job training, or mastery of continually changing technologies?

- ✔ Will your employee need to handle multiple projects, or concentrate on a single task?

- ✔ What's the career path for this job, and will it better suit a rising star or an employee who's content staying in the same position for a long time?

Keep your answers in mind as you search your resumes looking for perfect or nearly-perfect candidates.

The "Good Signs" List

After you've defined your ideal (or close-to-ideal) candidate, you're ready to start looking for superstars in your stack of resumes. Begin, of course, with the basics: A good resume includes a list of the places your candidate has worked and the dates she worked there; data about the candidate's relevant skills; specific information about her education and training; and solid, descriptive, to-the-point descriptions of her job duties at each position.

Skim the resume for the basic qualifications a candidate must possess to be in the running for your position. If your candidate can't meet your minimum requirements — a degree in mathematics or two years of experience, for example — then place the resume aside. (However, before completely disregarding a resume that doesn't fit, stop and ask yourself this question: Is this candidate qualified for any other jobs in our company? Always keep the big picture in mind!)

If your candidate possesses the basic qualifications for your job, it's time to read her resume more carefully. Look for these additional clues that she's a good candidate:

- ✔ **Successful patterns:** Looking for someone with drive, initiative, and talent? A candidate whose resume shows career progression — say, from administrative assistant to assistant manager to manager — is likely to be highly skilled and motivated. An upward path is an especially good indicator if your open position is a logical next step in your applicant's progress.

    Not all great candidates, however, need to have a track record of promotions. If you're seeking an employee who's satisfied performing a specific job, and who isn't looking to become a supervisor or department head, look for a pattern of success that doesn't necessarily involve promotions. (For example, a candidate who's held three long-term programming jobs, and done well at each, may be a good producer partly because he *doesn't* want to move into management.) But in this case, a candidate's record should reveal other evidence of success — raises, achievement awards, exemplary reviews, a mastery of relevant job skills, and so on.

- ✔ **Specific accomplishments:** A good candidate offers concrete evidence of his talents — for example, "In this position, I was solely responsible for selling $2 million worth of computer hardware." Look for specific actions ("implemented an order-entry and processing system with Oracle") and specific results ("which dramatically improved my company's Web-based sales and service"). If your candidate is a recent grad, look for accomplishments related to college projects, internships, or summer jobs.

✔ **A seamless job history:** Most good candidates list an unbroken series of previous jobs. Where breaks occur, good candidates spell out the reasons — for example, "I took six months off following this job in order to pursue research for my later-published book on East Indian culture."

✔ **Adaptability:** Today's technology changes so fast that almost any employee needs to be a life-long learner. That's especially true, of course, for high-tech and medical employees — but it's also true for receptionists, billing clerks, repair people, and anyone else whose work involves computers or machinery. How can you tell if a candidate is a quick learner? Look for the new skills she's acquired in each job she's held. Also, check to see if she keeps her skills up-to-date by taking educational courses or attending workshops or seminars.

✔ **Extra effort:** A candidate who lists training courses, seminars, and advanced certifications that are above and beyond the basic requirements of his work is likely to be highly motivated, energetic, and capable of constant learning and growth.

✔ **Impressive references:** An applicant who's proud of her past achievements isn't afraid to give you the references to prove it. She'll generally provide you with a thorough list of her former bosses or supervisors, along with adequate contact information to ensure that you can reach them.

TIP

Watch the wording!

As you check a candidate's credentials, read the resume's language carefully. Sometimes a single word or phrase can signify a big difference in skills or experience. Here are some examples:

✔ Does your applicant say "attended college," or "graduated from college"?

✔ Does the resume say "qualified as a candidate for a Master's degree," or "received a Master's degree"?

✔ Does the candidate say that she "sat for a certification examination," or does she say that she "earned a certification"?

If the wording of the resume isn't clear, make a note and ask for clarification during the job interview.

The "Bad Signs" List

Most job candidates won't spell out their weaknesses. Instead, they'll try to hide them. That's why you need to read between the lines to determine what a job seeker's resume really says, and, equally importantly, what it *doesn't* say. Among the red flags a careful resume reading can uncover are the following:

- **Missing months or years:** Does your candidate say she worked for Hospital A from 1995 to 1997 and then at Hospital B from 1999 to the present? If so, what was she doing in 1998? She probably has a good explanation, but she could also be hiding the fact that she worked briefly at another job where she got fired or received bad reviews.

  Also, watch for non-specific dates, such as a candidate who says that her first job ended in 1992 and her next job began in 1993. She could be concealing nearly two years of unemployment (from the beginning of '92 to the end of '93). It pays to find out.

- **Intermittent periods of "self-employment":** Past self-employment can be a plus; many high achievers run their own businesses for a while and then decide they want a change. (And more than a few outstanding high-tech employees entered the dot-com market during its heyday and discovered the hard way that they weren't cut out to be business owners.) But a job hunter who lists two or three periods of self-employment between jobs may be covering for periods of unemployment, or hiding jobs that went badly.

- **Job-hopping:** Even in an age of rampant job-switching, a candidate who's held five full-time, permanent jobs in 4 years should raise your suspicions. She may have a good reason — for example, she may have been unlucky enough to sign on with a couple of dot-coms that died on the vine. On the other hand, it's possible that she's difficult to satisfy, uncertain about her career choice, or too quick to switch jobs any time another tempting offer comes along. Carefully review her reasons for leaving each job, if these reasons are listed. If not, make a note to check her references carefully, and to explore this area thoroughly if you choose to interview her.

- **Inconsistencies:** Does your applicant's history reveal any strange or questionable turns? For example, did he receive an advanced degree in engineering and then switch for several years to a career in bartending? Do the jobs he's held seem unlikely for a candidate with the education and training he claims to have? If so, question him, and his references, carefully.

- **Brief, sketchy employment descriptions:** If your applicant worked at his last company for 8 years, but his description of that job is only two sentences long, it's logical to wonder what he was *doing* all that time. Find out.

✔ **A "laundry list" of skills, with no specifics:** Candidates sometimes succumb to the urge to inflate their qualifications by listing skills that they don't really possess, or haven't mastered. For example, a programmer who lists "Java skills," without being more specific, may have little more experience than helping his kids design a Web site using a little basic Java code. If you come across a "laundry list" resume, don't automatically dismiss it, but make a note to question the candidate closely about how and where he applied each skill on the job.

Also, watch for words intended to disguise a candidate's lack of hands-on experience with a technology. Among suspicious words: "worked in an environment where this technology was used," "am familiar with," "am acquainted with." Again, ask for specifics.

✔ **Skill "inflation":** No one wants to say "answered the phones" if they can say "interfaced with customers" or "handled inquiries from our customer base." But don't be fooled by fancy language. If you choose to interview a candidate whose resume is full of fancy phrases, pin down the candidate by asking: "In what way did you interface with customers?"

✔ **Getting too personal:** This is usually a minor failing. However, an excess of non-job-related info ("married, two lovely children, non-smoker") can be distracting. Ignore it, and focus on job skills instead.

✔ **"Jack of all trades" syndrome:** The candidate for your tech-writing job is only 30 years old, but he's already worked in advertising, public relations, magazine writing, and graphic design. Is he a Superman? Possibly, but it's just as likely that he hasn't yet found his niche, and there's a good chance that he'll move on to yet another career in a few months. Be extra-careful in checking out his skills, as well as his interest in his current career choice.

✔ **"My last company went under":** If your employee says he previously worked for a now-defunct firm, ask for references from that company. Also, check to see if the firm is really out of business, by looking it up in the phone book or on the Internet. If the firm can't be tracked down, ask to see pay stubs or some other record of employment. Your candidate is probably telling the truth, but he may be trying to conceal a bad job history.

Make a checklist

As you review a candidate's resume, make mental notes about the facts that need to be checked. In particular, you'll want to verify the following:

✔ Degrees

✔ Certifications

✔ Special licensing

✔ Previous employment and dates of employment

✔ References

The Diamond in the Rough: Is There a Good Candidate behind That Bad Resume?

"In recognition of my performance at this firm," the resume says, "I received the very first employee-of-the-month plague."

Your immediate reaction: This candidate isn't too bright. He's sent you a resume containing a significant typographical error, and you're ready to set his resume aside. But wait!

Often, smart and qualified applicants are rejected not because they lack the skills for the job, but simply because they don't present themselves well on paper. So before tossing out a resume with several typographical errors, give it a second look. Ask yourself these questions:

✔ **Does the resume reflect an impressive job history?** If so, the employee's strengths may be far more relevant than a typo.

✔ **Are the mistakes in the resume relevant to the job for which you're hiring?** Obviously, you don't want to hire a librarian or technical writer who can't spot the typos in his own resume. But most programmers don't need to be spelling-bee champs to do an excellent job. Many outstanding technical employees are strong analytical thinkers who are far better at troubleshooting code or setting up servers than they are at proofreading resumes.

A poorly formatted resume, or a resume that's lacking important information, is also likely to wind up in the circular file. Again, however, you may find a gem if you're willing to look past these errors and analyze your candidate's strong points. Among the flaws that could distract you from a good catch are these:

✔ **Is the resume too skimpy?** If the candidate looks strong otherwise, call and ask for more details or an expanded resume.

✔ **Is the resume wordy or boring?** If so, simply skim the candidate's most recent history and see if he has the skills you need.

✔ **Are you reacting to real problems in the resume, or to minor irritants such as odd fonts or hard-to-read formatting?** If it's the latter, try to look past the resume's appearance and focus on its content.

Remember that not everyone is a "paper" person, and that some candidates with iffy resumes shine when you meet them face-to-face. If a candidate's experience and credentials are strong, don't let a few typos, poor formatting, or a too-short or too-wordy resume prejudice your selection.

TIP

What a resume won't tell you

Resumes are valuable tools, but they have their limits. For one thing, many resumes are written by professional resume writers, and don't reflect your candidate's verbal or communication skills. For another, resumes won't tell you anything about an applicant's interpersonal skills, personality, or charisma. And most resumes focus primarily on a few key job duties, while face-to-face interviews can bring out additional information about your candidates' overall responsibilities and capabilities. That's why you should never hire on the basis of a resume alone.

Also, realize that people who are already employed and working hard may not have time to create flawless resumes. A quickly thrown-together resume can indicate that your prospect is busy doing more important tasks.

Is Your Applicant Qualified for a Different Job?

You're looking for an office manager. Steve applies for the job, but his resume reveals that he doesn't have the experience or skill set you require. However, it also reveals that he's a real go-getter, with outstanding computer skills.

Rather than simply telling Steve. "Sorry," stop for a minute and run through your mental list of open positions. Would Steve be a valuable addition to your billing department? Could he fill your open administrative assistant position? If so, contact him and ask if he'd be interested in interviewing for either of these positions. Or, if Steve's skills don't match any of your current needs, tell him you're impressed with his background and would like to keep his resume on file and contact him for future openings more in line with his abilities.

To ensure that a great candidate for a different job doesn't slip away, keep informed about all of your current openings and the skills these jobs require. Also, stay on top of your company's future growth plans and anticipated hiring needs, so you'll know which candidates might solve your recruiting problems a few months down the line.

Which Resumes to Keep, Which to Toss

Even if a resume isn't a match for your current openings, you may want to save it. However, if you keep every resume that crosses your desk, you'll wind up with a cluttered database or file cabinet. So keep these rules in mind as you create "keep it/toss it" piles:

- ✔ Keep all resumes of candidates who meet your skill set and education requirements.

- ✔ Keep resumes that *don't* meet your current needs if you think your company's future needs will change, making these candidates' skill sets relevant.

- ✔ Eliminate any resumes that appear dishonest or contain too many red flags.

- ✔ Eliminate resumes from candidates who don't meet the minimal skills requirements for any of your positions, *except*....

- ✔ Consider keeping the resumes of outstanding college grads with good GPAs and some internship experience, even if these candidates don't yet have sufficient experience for your current positions. In a year or two, they may acquire that experience, and turn out to be just the candidates you need.

If you can't decide whether or not a resume is a keeper, save it. With qualified candidates scarce, it's better to be safe than sorry. Also, whether you use an electronic resume scanning or importing system (see Chapter 16) or simply keep hard copies of resumes, be sure to have a good system for filing, finding, and cross-referencing the resumes you keep.

Is your job description doing the job?

If you receive too many resumes from unqualified candidates, take a second look at your job description, because it may not be sending the right message. Analyze the problem: Are your candidates inexperienced? Do they lack the skills you need? Check to see if you've adequately defined the candidate you're seeking, and, if not, write your ad more clearly.

Also, if many of your candidates have unrealistic expectations, evaluate your ad to see if it's misleading. While you want your salary, benefits, and job challenges to sound tempting, you don't want to lure candidates with promises you can't keep.

Do You Need a Resume, or Merely an Application?

Resumes are often unnecessary for entry-level positions. You'll save time and effort by having stock clerks, beginning machinists, and similar employees fill out application forms instead. Make sure you post your application on your Web site, so that applicants who don't have resumes can apply for your jobs online.

For any positions that require experience, education, training, and/or specialized skills, however, a resume is a must. Resumes can offer insight into a candidate's communication and organizational skills, and sometimes provide crucial information that's not included on your application. In addition, they give you an opportunity to compare your candidates' resumes with the information they list on the application form, which can sometimes help you spot untruths or inconsistencies.

Keep Up!

Set aside time every day to screen incoming resumes. If you're screening for a key position, or you're receiving a large volume of resumes, screen more often than that. Remember: If you don't call hot prospects right away, other companies will — and they may grab the best candidates right out from under your nose.

Chapter 18

Narrowing the Field: The Phone Screen

. . . .

. . . .

*I*f you're lucky enough to receive several outstanding resumes in response to your recruiting efforts, congratulations! Now it's time for your next big challenge: Picking the finalists from your promising group of candidates.

The first step in this process — think of it as the semi-finals — is the phone screen. The phone screen is a handy tool for identifying stellar candidates, weeding out candidates who clearly don't meet your criteria, and judging your prospects' expectations and interest level. By screening your candidates effectively, you cut down on the time your team spends conducting formal interviews, while ensuring that every deserving candidate receives consideration.

In addition, the phone screen gives you a chance to sell your job opportunity and your company to potential employees. If a candidate isn't sure about working for your company, you can use this telephone encounter to generate enthusiasm and play up your strong points.

The steps to a successful phone screening include the following:

✔ Preparing before the call.

✔ Asking the right questions, and making the right impression, when you call.

✔ Setting the stage for an interview, if your candidate proves to be qualified.

In this chapter, we explain how to handle each of these steps like an expert.

Before You Call . . .

During a phone screen, time is critical. Typically you have only about 20 to 30 minutes to collect a large amount of information, so be prepared! Gather these facts ahead of time:

✔ How did you obtain the candidate's resume? Was it in a response to an Internet job posting? Did a current employee make the referral? Did a friend simply pass on the prospect's name and number?

✔ If your candidate is applying for a specific job, which job is it? What other openings do you have that might be a good match for this candidate?

✔ If you have your candidate's resume in hand, what points in the resume need clarification?

✔ How hard is this position to fill? How many other candidates do you have? Your answers can give you an idea as to how selective you can be as you screen.

Next, decide whether you should conduct the phone screen yourself or assign the job to the hiring manager. If the position is very technical, the hiring manager is probably the best choice, because she has the expertise needed to evaluate the candidate's skills. Otherwise, ask the hiring manager to provide you with several key questions that will allow you to determine your candidate's skill level.

If you plan to conduct the phone screen yourself, make a list of the questions you want to ask. (Don't count on your memory, because it's embarrassing to have to call a candidate back several times and say, "I forgot to ask . . .") Avoid going overboard on questions; remember that your goal is simply to pre-qualify the candidate for a later, more in-depth interview. Also, leave room for flexibility, because most phone screens take unplanned but informative turns. However, make your list of topics thorough and specific enough to ensure that you answer the ultimate question: "Should we bring this candidate in for a face-to-face meeting?"

Making the Call

Try to schedule your phone screen in advance, by phone or by e-mail. It's best to call when your candidate is at home, free from work interruptions, and able to talk freely. Take notes as you talk, so you'll remember key points later when you talk to hiring managers or compare candidates' qualifications.

As you talk with your candidate, ask probing questions about skills, training, education, and job history. Don't limit yourself to yes/no questions; instead, ask open-ended queries that will reveal your candidate's depth of knowledge and experience. For example:

Don't ask: *"Have you used Visual Basic version 6.0?"*

Instead, say: *"In what capacity did you use Visual Basic 6.0 on a recent project?"*

Or you can say: *"Tell me about an application you developed recently using Visual Basic 6.0."*

Ask your candidate to describe the duties and responsibilities of her current job, her relationship with supervisors and team members, and her most significant achievements. Also ask broad questions, such as the following:

"What are you looking for in a new position?"

"What do you consider your strongest asset?"

Finding Out If Your Candidate Is Looking Hard — or Hardly Looking

Here's a scenario that's all too familiar to many recruiters: You interview a candidate, everyone loves him, you draw up the paperwork and draft an offer letter, and then your candidate says, "I'm not really sure I'm ready to leave my current job."

Not all job hunters are really hunting. Some, for example, are just assessing their current market value so that they can ask their current employers for raises. Thus, it's vital to accurately assess your prospect's interest level. This will help you decide these key issues:

✔ Whether or not to interview the candidate.

✔ How fast you'll need to move, if you're interested.

✔ How strong an offer you should be prepared to make.

Good questions for discovering just how serious your candidate is about your job opening include the following:

✔ Are you currently employed?

✔ If so, what do you like and dislike about your current job? Why are you considering leaving?

- ✔ What are you seeking in a new position that you can't achieve in your current position?

- ✔ If you are not currently employed, why did you leave your last job?

- ✔ How long have you been looking for a new position?

- ✔ Do you have interviews scheduled with other companies? Do you have any offers on the table?

- ✔ What is your current salary?

- ✔ What are your benefits (vacation days, perks, insurance, and so on)?

- ✔ What interests you about this position?

- ✔ Where do you see yourself long-term?

- ✔ How soon could you interview with us? How soon could you begin a new position?

If the answers to these questions confirm that your prospect is indeed interested in pursuing a new position, determine how fast you need to move to catch her. For example, a prospect whose dot-com just went under is often desperate to find a new position fast, while a candidate who's simply shopping around will usually be pickier. If your candidate falls into the "I-need-a-job-now" category, she may be easier to recruit — but you'll have to move fast. If she's in the "shopping around" category, speed is less critical but a strong offer is more important.

As you question your candidate, be careful — as in every stage of the hiring process — not to ask illegal questions. We discuss taboo topics in depth in Chapter 21, but some of these topics are particularly likely to arise during phone screens. The less-formal nature of a phone screen, often conducted when the employee is at home with noisy kids or an interrupting spouse in the background, makes it easy to slip and ask personal questions. So remember: Don't ask your candidate if he's married or has children; and don't ask any questions pertaining to race, ethnic background, nationality, religion, age, or disability. If your candidate brings up these topics himself, tread carefully. (For example, if a female candidate asks, "What maternity benefits do you offer?" you can answer the question, but don't ask in return, "Are you planning to have a baby soon?")

Knowing When to Listen

Silence can be a powerful tool, so don't do too much of the talking during your phone screen. Instead, encourage your candidate to talk freely, and let your interview range beyond your pre-set questions. Also, give her plenty of opportunity to ask her own questions. It's as important for her to evaluate your job and your firm as it is for you to evaluate her.

As your candidate talks, listen carefully for information about her strengths and weaknesses. Among the clues you can uncover are the following:

- ✔ Does the information your candidate offers over the phone match the information on her resume?

- ✔ Does your candidate seem confident? Proud of her accomplishments?

- ✔ Does the candidate seem enthusiastic about the work your company does?

- ✔ Does your candidate answer questions quickly and straightforwardly, or does she hesitate, sound evasive, or change the topic?

- ✔ Does your candidate give you specific and credible information about reasons for leaving jobs, gaps in employment, and so on?

- ✔ Does your candidate offer specific information about her accomplishments, or is she vague and hard to pin down?

- ✔ Does your candidate use the phone screen to bad-mouth her current employer? (This can be a tricky area, because some candidates really *are* working for bad companies and wish to explain their reasons for wanting to leave. However, a candidate who spends most of the phone interview harping on the evils of her current employer may be a chronic complainer.)

- ✔ Does the candidate offer what seems to be proprietary information?

- ✔ If you're considering your candidate for a position that involves meeting face-to-face with your clients, is she articulate and able to communicate effectively?

By listening carefully, you can often pick up valuable information that you won't discover on a resume. One caution, however: Your candidate is likely to be spending hours each day in interviews, and may be tired or stressed. Allow for that possibility as you assess her personality and her enthusiasm.

Be understanding, too, if she needs to put you on hold to handle a ringing doorbell, a barking dog, or a fussy child; it can be difficult for even the most professional job seeker to keep real life from interfering during a phone screen.

Selling Your Job

Use the phone screen to generate excitement about your company and your job opening, especially if your candidate sounds like a good match for the position. Listen for his "hot buttons." Is he interested in generous vacation time? Flex hours? A shorter commute? Better insurance? A higher salary? If your job offers any of these advantages, be sure to emphasize them.

However, be honest about what your company can offer, because one purpose of the phone screen is to weed out candidates who have expectations your company can't meet. For example, be candid about the amount of travel or overtime the job requires, and about opportunities for advancement.

Playing with the Numbers

If you aren't sure whether your candidate's salary expectations are in line with what your position pays, the telephone interview can provide an opportunity to sound him out.

For example, you can say, "The company's looking at something in the range of $70,000 to $80,000," and get your prospect's response. If he says he's expecting more, and you know your company is willing to better the offer you've mentioned, say, "The salary may be negotiable, depending on experience. I think that's a real possibility." If your prospect's desired salary is clearly too high, on the other hand, reply with, "That's probably higher than they're able to go — are you still interested, if $80,000 is as much as they can offer?"

Also, discuss bonuses, stock options, and other elements of your package. If your salary is $80,000, but quarterly bonuses and stock options bring it closer to $90,000, explain this to your candidate. And, conversely, clarify his expectations; if he says he needs $90,000, is he talking about salary alone, or salary plus commissions, bonuses, stocks, and so on? Be sure you're both on the same page when you discuss money matters.

Don't set the salary in stone at this stage, but do determine whether or not your prospect's expectations are consistent with the salary range for the position. You're looking for a ballpark figure, not a set amount, and your primary purpose is to avoid big surprises later on.

Moving to the Next Stage

If your candidate clearly doesn't meet your needs, thank her for her time and explain why she's not a match for your job. ("I'm sorry, we didn't realize that Visual Basic isn't your area of expertise — but thanks so much for talking with us, and we'll keep your resume on file in case we need programmers with your experience in C++.") If you're not sure whether she fits the bill, simply thank her for her time and tell her courteously that you'll be getting back to her as soon as possible. Be sure to follow through on this promise, even if you decide that you're not interested in interviewing her.

If your candidate passes with flying colors, however, keep the interview process rolling. Find out when she's available, and schedule the next interview phase quickly. (If possible, set a time during the phone interview.) Once you set up the face-to-face interview, provide the candidate with the following information:

- ✔ The names and titles of the people who will be interviewing her.
- ✔ The time and date of the interview.
- ✔ How to reach your facility, and where to park.

Send your candidate an e-mail confirming this information, or tell her by phone. Also, provide her with the phone number and e-mail address of a contact person at the company, in case she has questions or needs to re-schedule. Another time-saver: Mail your candidate an application form, or direct her to an online form (see Chapter 7 for more information). As always, speed, and sensitivity to your candidate's needs, should be your top priorities.

Chapter 19

The Application: Writing It Right

Recruiting changes every day, but one recruiting tool — the job application — will never go out of style. That's because this form lightens your workload by providing basic information in a consistent format that makes it easy to compare candidates' qualifications. In addition, your application offers important legal protection in the event of a lawsuit.

But while a well-designed application can make your recruiting process more efficient, a poorly designed one can waste your candidate's time, fail to ask vital questions, or even cause legal problems for your firm. Thus, it's a good idea to evaluate your current form, and redesign it if necessary, to ensure that it makes the grade. First, however, you need to know the functions a good application serves.

Why You Need an Application

If you're recruiting for high-level positions, an application can't replace a resume, which offers in-depth and personalized information about your candidate. However, as a supplement to the resume, the application accomplishes several goals including the following:

✔ It saves time and effort.

✔ It helps weed out unsuitable applicants.

✔ It can uncover *resume fudging*.

✔ It can protect you against employees who charge discrimination or unfair hiring practices.

The following sections offer a quick overview of each of these functions.

The application as a time-saver

All applicants, including those with resumes, should fill out an application. That's because the application standardizes the format and location of your applicants' information, making it faster and easier to skim through and find key points. It's also a good way to make sure that candidates provide all of the data you need to judge their skills and experience.

The application as a selection tool

The application makes it easier for you to objectively weigh candidates' assets and weaknesses. While a cleverly worded resume can convey a misleading impression that one applicant is more skilled than another, the application condenses information into a more objective format.

In addition, the application can point out employee strengths and weaknesses. When reviewing forms, weigh these factors:

- ✔ **Does your candidate have good writing skills?** While resumes are sometimes prepared by hired professionals, an application filled out on the spot has to be completed by the applicant himself. Thus, it can serve as a measure of your applicant's grasp of spelling and grammar.

- ✔ **Does your candidate's application match the information on the resume?** Inconsistencies may indicate that your applicant is fibbing about work dates, degrees, or other information. Any mismatch between a resume and the responses on an application should be investigated carefully. (This is why your application should not allow the option of simply attaching a resume without filling out the application.)

- ✔ **Can your candidate follow directions?** The application can serve as a quick test of your candidate's ability to read, understand, and follow instructions.

The application as legal protection

Because your application asks each applicant to provide similar information in a standardized format, it's a more objective hiring tool than is an interview. Also, you can use your application to inform applicants that you are an equal opportunity employer, to obtain their permission to check references, and to tell applicants if they will be required to take drug tests or participate in other screenings as a condition of hiring.

In addition, your application asks candidates to sign a statement verifying that the information they supply is truthful. This can protect you later, if you discover that your employee lied on the application.

It's crucial, of course, to ensure that your application itself is legal. See Chapter 21 for do's and don'ts, and be sure to have your application reviewed by an attorney. It's especially important to review your applications if they're several years old, because changing laws have made formerly legal questions taboo. (A brief review of the application no-no's: Do NOT ask about marital status, number of children, maiden name, age or date of birth, or date of graduation. Also, do NOT ask any health-related questions.)

The application as a recruiting tool

The references that candidates list on their applications can lead you to referrals. Keep this in mind as you design your application, and don't skimp on the number of spaces you include for references. Also, be sure to ask for the e-mail addresses of references, as well as for telephone numbers and addresses.

In addition, use your application to ask your candidates if they'd like to provide e-mail addresses so that you can send updates on job openings that match their skills. It's a good way to keep in touch with excellent candidates, even if you don't hire them for your current openings.

Designing Your Application: Keep It Smart, Keep It Simple

The first step in designing your application is to recognize that you may need more than one version. The form you use to hire an entry-level machinist should be different than the version you give a top-level programmer or a managerial candidate; otherwise, you'll waste both their time and yours. Thus, it makes sense to have either several different applications or a master application with customized secondary pages.

Questions that can be customized for different positions include the following:

✔ **Skill sets:** For example, the version of your application intended for clerical staff may ask which phone systems they've mastered, the version for machinists may ask if they know how to use vertical milling machines, and the version for programmers may ask if they know Oracle or Java.

✔ **Experience:** An application for managers or high-tech employees should ask for extensive information about past projects and educational experience, whereas an application for entry-level factory workers requires different types of information.

✔ **Travel requirements:** Include questions such as "Are you willing to travel?" "What percent of the time are you willing to travel?" and "Are you willing to travel outside the country?" only in applications for positions that include travel requirements.

✔ **Transportation:** Ask about candidates' means of transportation only if providing transportation is a requirement for the job. If your job requires driving skills, you may ask if the candidate possesses a valid license, but do not ask on your application for the candidate's license number.

Every application, no matter what position it's for, should ask for this basic information:

✔ Names of previous employers and exact dates of employment

✔ Detailed list of duties/responsibilities at each job

✔ Reasons for leaving previous jobs

✔ Salary and compensation (including bonuses) at each job

✔ Supervisors' names and contact numbers

✔ References with contact information

✔ Educational history

✔ Date the applicant is able to start if hired

✔ Desired salary

✔ Skills rating section

Give 'em room!

How many times have you been confronted by a form that says, "List your work experience," and then leaves a space so tiny that you can't write more than two dozen words? A key rule, violated by almost every application, is to make your answer spaces big enough that your applicants can answer the questions fully and clearly. Avoid tiny boxes and short lines that give your applicants writer's cramp and deprive you of essential information.

Make your application attractive

Your application is one of the first interfaces between your candidate and your company. So avoid tacky photocopied forms, and invest a little money in designing a form that looks professional.

In Chapter 14, we discuss the importance of employer *branding* — that is, creating a consistent and positive image of your company. Your application can contribute to creating this professional image. If you have room, add an attractive logo at the top and include your company motto if you have one. Proof your application carefully to make sure there are no typographical errors or grammatical slips that reflect negatively on your company's competence.

One more tip: Provide a clipboard so that your candidates can fill out their forms without difficulty. (While this may seem obvious, the occasional candidate is still forced to awkwardly fill out a form using a chair seat or another candidate's back!) Offer a pen, too, in case your candidate left home without one.

Stick to basic — and legal — questions

You want your application to be thorough, but you don't want to ask unnecessary questions — and you don't want to leave yourself open for legal problems. Review your form, and ask yourself the following:

- ✔ Does every question relate specifically to job skills?
- ✔ Do the questions relate to job skills needed by this specific *category* of employee?
- ✔ Could any of these questions be interpreted as discriminatory to women, minorities, disabled employees, or older employees?

Keep your application as short as possible, without cutting out crucial questions. When designing your form, consider having your hiring managers serve as guinea pigs by filling out the forms themselves, and reporting back on any problem areas. Ask them to ensure you cover all necessary skills, and to eliminate irrelevant questions. And, again, review Chapter 21 for information on the questions you can't legally ask.

It's tempting to allow additional space for applicants to write in comments, but be cautious. One advantage of your application, as we note at the beginning of the chapter, is that it's standardized. If you include a "free-form" space where candidates can say anything, they may mention personal information such as religion or ethnic background. This can come back to haunt you if an applicant later claims that he was denied employment because of discrimination. If you allow a space for candidates to make comments, specify that these comments should be limited specifically to job-related qualifications.

Put it online

If you have a Web site, it's a good idea to put your application online. Also, offer to mail or e-mail the application to applicants scheduled to come in for an interview. This will save time, and keep the hiring process moving smoothly. (On the down side, it's easy for an employee to conceal poor writing skills by having another person fill out an online application. Also, a candidate who fills out an application at home will find it easier to make his resume and application sound consistent, even if he's fudging his answers, because he'll have more time to compare the two documents. However, the time saved by putting your application online usually outweighs the importance of these disadvantages.)

Sample application

To get ideas for applications for specific jobs, check the online forms posted by companies in your field and analyze their strengths and weaknesses. You can also find good examples of generic forms on free recruiting, human resources, and small business Web sites.

Following is a good generic form you can use as a starting point. Of course, you'll want to customize the questions on your own application — and you'll want to have an attorney review your application to ensure that it complies with both state and federal laws.

APPLICATION

[*Your company's name, address, telephone number, e-mail address, and logo*]

Date _____

Name _____

Present address _____ How long at this address? _____

Telephone number _____

E-mail address _____

Social Security Number _____ If under 18, please list your age _____

Position for which you are applying _____

Desired salary _____

Applying for: ___ full-time ___ part-time ___ full- or part-time

Days/hours you are available to work: _____ Monday _____ Tuesday _____ Wednesday _____ Thursday _____ Friday _____ Saturday _____ Sunday

Can you work nights? _____

Are you willing to travel? _____ If yes, what percentage of the time would you be willing to travel? _____

When could you begin work? _____

Education:

High School:

    Name _____

    Location _____

    Number of years completed _____

College/University:

    Name _____

    Location _____

    Number of years completed _____ Major and degree _____

Professional, business, or trade school:

    Name _____

    Location _____

    Number of years completed _____ Major and degree _____

Work Experience:

Please list your most recent jobs held:

    Name of Employer _____

    Address _____ Phone Number _____

    Your job title _____

    Name of last supervisor _____

    Supervisor's telephone number _____
    May we contact this supervisor? Yes _____ No _____

    Employment dates _____ Salary _____

    Duties, skills, advancements, or promotions related to this position: _____

    _____

    Reason for leaving _____

    May we contact your current employer? ___ yes ___ no

    [*Repeat 3-4 times*]

Job Skills [*Note: This section will vary depending upon the position. For this sample application, we're assuming the candidate is applying for a clerical position.*]:

    Typing ___ yes ___ no ___ words per minute

    Computer ___ yes ___ no ___ Mac ___ PC

Please list all relevant software applications you are skilled at using, including version numbers and the months or years of experience you have in using each:

Program_____ months or years of experience_____

Program_____ months or years of experience_____

Program_____ months or years of experience_____

Program_____ months or years of experience_____

Program_____ months or years of experience_____

Please list the office equipment you are experienced in using (phone systems, fax, postage meters, etc.)

_____

_____

_____

Additional skills:

_____

_____

Please list at least two references, other than relatives or previous employers. You may list more if desired.

Name _____

Position _____

Company _____

Address _____

Phone _____

E-mail address _____

Name _____

Position _____

Company _____

Address _____

Phone _____

E-mail address _____

Have you ever been convicted of a felony? ___ yes ___ no

If yes, please provide date(s), type of conviction(s), and sentence. _____

If you are hired, can you provide written evidence that you are authorized to work in the United States? _____ yes _____ no

Application Waiver

I authorize investigation of all statements made in this application. I hereby give the company permission to contact previous employers (unless indicated otherwise), schools, references, and others, and release the company and any individuals/firms it contacts from any liability as a result of these contacts.

I understand that the company requires pre-employment drug testing, as well as testing after employment. I understand that consent to and compliance with this policy is a condition of employment, and that future employment is contingent upon successfully passing these tests.

I understand that the company may, as part of its routine screening process, request from a consumer reporting agency an investigative consumer report including information as to my credit records and general reputation. Upon written request from me, the company will provide me with information concerning the nature and scope of any such report it requests, as required by the Fair Credit Reporting Act.

I understand that my employment with the company shall be probationary for a period of 90 days. (For applications in "employment at will" states, add: I also understand that the company follows an "employment at will" policy and may terminate my employment at any time, for any reason, consistent with federal and state laws.)

I understand that federal law prohibits the employment of unauthorized aliens, and that all individuals hired by the company must provide proof of identity and employment authorization.

I certify that all the statements I have made on this form, and other information provided by me in the process of applying for this position, are true. I am aware that the misrepresentation or omission of facts on this form is cause for dismissal at any time and without notice.

Signature _____ Date _____

This company is an equal employment opportunity employer. It is our policy to make employment decisions without regard to race, color, religion, sex, sexual orientation, national origin, citizenship, age, veteran status, or disability. Your opportunity for employment with this company depends solely on your qualifications.

Chapter 20

The Interview

*I*nterviewing is a high-stakes game, and your reputation is on the line. Pick the right employees when you interview, and you'll be a hero as profits, morale, and productivity soar. Pick the wrong ones, and you're in for trouble — lost money, complaining managers, and, before long, yet more vacancies to fill. That's why it pays to hone your interview skills, using the tips we pass on in this chapter.

In some cases, of course, the "hire/don't hire" decision is an easy one. One group of executives, asked to describe their strangest interviews, told of the following:

> ✔ A candidate who showed up in a swimsuit.
>
> ✔ An interviewee who ordered a pizza to be delivered during his interview.
>
> ✔ A candidate who, when asked to bring two references, showed up with a couple of friends in tow.

Needless to say, none of these candidates wound up with job offers! Neither did the candidate who called our office to ask if she could bring her bird to the interview, or the candidate who called us to cancel his interview because his pet snake had a fever. (True stories — really!)

Most of the time, however, it takes hard work to uncover the strengths that make a candidate a winner, or the weaknesses that can spell trouble. There's no magic formula for the perfect job interview, because interviewing isn't a science. Instead, it's part common sense, part intuition, and part sheer luck — and it often comes down to decisions made as much on instincts as on facts. Fortunately, there are ways to take some of the guesswork out of interviewing, and increase your chances of hiring an outstanding employee.

Get Your Act Together

A great job interview actually starts days ahead of time. It may appear spontaneous, when the moment arrives, but actually, it's the result of careful planning on your part.

How critical is that planning? Studies show that "off-the-cuff" interviews are no better than random selection, meaning that you may as well simply throw all of your resumes in the air and pick the candidate whose resume lands first. A planned interview, on the other hand, can provide you with insight and hard data you need to choose the best candidate from your resume pile. In the following sections, we discuss the interview details you should work out ahead of time.

Picking your team

Interviews generally include one person from the human resources department and at least one manager (usually more) from the department in which the candidate would work. The manager focuses primarily on the candidate's technical expertise, while the HR representative assesses the following:

- ✔ Whether or not an applicant meets the basic job specifications.
- ✔ The applicant's personality, attitude, and background.

However, if your company doesn't have an HR department, the hiring manager can assess the latter areas as well.

It's smart to have several interviewers, because this increases the chances that you'll ask all the right questions. Also, one interviewer may spot a strong point or weak area that another interviewer misses. But avoid interview overkill; we know of candidates who've been interviewed by six, seven, or even more team members, and they found the experience exhausting and annoying. Limit your interviews to five or fewer interviewers, unless you're filling a high-level executive position.

Deciding whether one interview is enough

We recommend having your candidate meet with all of your interview team members on a single day, rather than scheduling sessions on several days, whenever possible. Among the advantages of this approach are the following:

- ✔ You move the interview process along more quickly.
- ✔ You cause your candidate a minimum of stress and inconvenience. (Remember that your candidate is probably taking time off from her current job to interview with you.)

The disadvantage to conducting a single interview (which can be one session with several interviewers, or a series of sessions conducted one after the other on the same day) is that it's sometimes tough to schedule a single time when all of the parties can meet. If you must schedule a second interview day, do so — but schedule it quickly, to avoid losing your candidate to a competitor. And, unless you're hiring for a very high-level position, avoid scheduling three or more interviews. "Over-interviewing" makes your company appear unorganized and inefficient, and chases candidates away.

Prepping your players

Make sure each member of your interview team receives the candidate's resume at least 48 hours before an interview. Ask each interviewer to review the resume, and to jot down notes and questions. In addition, all members of your team should review information on any candidates previously interviewed for the position, so they can compare the new applicant's qualifications with those of other interviewees.

Be sure, too, that all members of your team know the exact time and location of the interview. Send this information to each interviewer in writing, and notify everyone promptly if you need to change the schedule.

Checking your baggage

Realize that each interviewer brings a collection of personal baggage to the interview. To prevent your interview team from responding to unstated (and often subconscious) biases, select a diverse team of interviewers when possible. That way, one person's biases can often be countered by another interviewer.

Also, if you're not absolutely certain that your interviewers are familiar with the laws governing hiring, provide them with written information on the discriminatory questions they're not allowed to ask. (See Chapter 21 for in-depth information on this topic.)

Don't assume that your managers will be sensitive interviewers, or instinctively know what they can and can't say. All too often, recruiters are stunned by managers who ask candidates blatantly illegal, rude, or inappropriate questions based on personal biases. (One recruiter, for example, recently shared a horror story about a hiring manager who ended an otherwise positive interview by suggesting that the candidate was overweight and needed to work out!) Train your managers beforehand, so you won't have to worry once you're in the interview room.

Is it "chemistry" — or bias?

We all know that it's both illegal and improper to judge applicants on the basis of age, sex, or ethnic background. But we don't always recognize our more subtle biases. Be sure, when interviewing, that you judge candidates fairly, without factoring in nonrelevant features such as the following:

✔ Weight

✔ Height

✔ Accent

✔ Attractiveness

✔ Taste in clothing

Also, learn to ask yourself, when making a first impression of your candidate, "On what am I basing this impression?" The more insight you gain into your own decision-making processes, the better you'll get at recognizing the difference between a gut instinct and a subconscious prejudice.

Planning your interview format

Decide whether you want to conduct a group interview, or a series of one-on-one interviews. Most companies prefer the one-on-one approach, and so do we. That's because group interviews, while they save time, can be intimidating.

If you do choose to conduct a series of interviews, work out the timing carefully so your candidate isn't kept waiting between meetings. And if your interviews run through the lunch hour, either take your candidate to lunch or make sure she gets a break so that she can get a bite to eat.

Meeting with your team members

Schedule at least one meeting before each interview, to make sure you're all on the same page. Begin by reviewing the job description, the required skills, and the salary and benefits you plan to offer.

Also, use this meeting to give your managers a pep talk, if necessary. Some managers view interviewing as a hassle or an interruption in a productive workday, and that attitude can translate into a negative attitude that turns off your candidates. Reinforce the message that good interviewing translates into filled job openings, leading in turn to more productivity, fewer problems, and a healthier bottom line.

Next, review the questions you plan to ask your candidate. If your firm doesn't have an interview form with required, standardized questions to ask each candidate, write down the essential questions your team will ask. Also, decide whether you want to conduct a structured interview, with set questions, or a flexible interview. (We recommend combining the two: Have a written list of your "must-ask" questions, but leave room for digressions that may unearth valuable information.)

Assign each interviewer to cover specific areas, so you won't duplicate efforts. Determine ahead of time which team member will assess the following:

- ✔ Technical skills
- ✔ Customer service and interpersonal skills
- ✔ Logical and critical thinking skills
- ✔ Personality
- ✔ Resourcefulness
- ✔ Ability to work with a team
- ✔ Ability to work under direction
- ✔ Ability to work individually
- ✔ Self-confidence
- ✔ Potential for growth

In addition, decide who will have the primary responsibility for selling the strong points of your company to your candidate. This assignment usually falls to the human resources representative, although every member of your interview team should help market the job and the company.

Decide on the order of the interview, and be sure to review the types of questions you CAN'T ask (see Chapter 21). In addition, select one team member to be responsible for following up with your candidate after the interview.

Selecting a comfortable location for your interview

You want your candidate to feel at ease, and you want to make a good impression — so if you conduct a group interview, pick an attractive and well-equipped area. Try to avoid boardroom interviews, where four or five of you stare across a huge table at your candidate; a casual setting is much less intimidating and will make your candidate feel more welcome.

Be sure that beverages will be available if your candidate desires them. Try to find a place that's private, too, so your interviewee can talk freely. Remind team members to have their assistants hold their calls, and keep other inter-ruptions to a minimum, during the interview time.

Increasing your managers' "interview IQ"

Your managers are talented at lots of things, but most of them probably aren't naturals when it comes to interviewing. Thus, you may want to consider offering training courses to teach your managers the basics of conducting an interview. To find information about good courses, visit the recruiting and human resources forums we discuss in Chapter 4.

Scheduling wisely

When you schedule an interview, allow plenty of time — and schedule some prep time and follow-up time as well. You'll need to budget adequate time for a quick review of your candidate's resume before the interview; for thorough questioning; for an office tour afterward; and, last but not least, for writing up your notes and impressions following the interview.

TIP

Impressing out-of-town candidates

If you're interviewing a candidate who's interested in relocating, it's vital to make a good impression during the interview process. Use this checklist to make sure your candidate's trip and interview go smoothly:

✔ Confirm travel arrangements, and be sure your candidate receives adequate information about these arrangements.

✔ Give your candidate the number of a contact person who can be reached day or night, in case difficulties arise.

✔ If possible, provide your candidate with a rental car. Also, be sure to reimburse your candidate for expenses.

✔ If you're serious about attracting a candidate, especially if you're at the final interview stage, pay to have the candidate's spouse or "significant other" visit your area. Also, ask a reputable real estate firm to provide information on your community.

✔ Make sure that no delays arise in the interview process. Your candidate most likely has other obligations and appointments, and may be inconvenienced or insulted if your interview doesn't happen according to plan. Delays will also reflect badly on your company's efficiency.

✔ Put your candidate up at a nice hotel, and have someone from your company treat him (and his family, if they've come along) to dinner at a nice restaurant at least once.

Also, pace yourself. Never schedule more than three interviews per day if your interview process is lengthy, and don't overdo it even if your interviews are short. We know we've stressed the need to move fast, especially when you're hiring for key positions. But if you hit "interview burn-out," your interview team's interest, enthusiasm, and attention are likely to dwindle — and your candidate is sure to notice.

Beginning the Interview: Break the Ice

Begin your interview by putting your candidate at ease. Meet her as soon as she arrives, rather than making her wait in your lobby. Also, coach your receptionist to be helpful, professional, and friendly when greeting your candidate. (Don't assume that this will happen without your input — see our horror story in the nearby sidebar, "How to lose a candidate before you say 'Hello'"!) If your candidate will be meeting different interviewers during the day, make sure each team member knows who's next in the chain, and who will escort your candidate directly to the next interview. Remember that candidates are very observant, and they'll judge your company climate by the friendliness, helpfulness, and efficiency of the employees they see.

Once you're in the interview room, break the ice by offering your candidate something to drink, introducing the members of your interviewing team, and starting with some friendly small talk to make everyone feel at ease. Then move on to the main purposes of your interview:

- ✔ Identifying your candidate's strengths and weaknesses.
- ✔ Allowing your candidate time to ask questions about you.
- ✔ Selling your company and the job.

How to lose a candidate before you say "hello"

One of our candidates arrived at a company for an interview, and gave the receptionist his name and the name of the manager he was to meet. The receptionist phoned the manager, who had stepped away from his desk.

Rather than tracking the manager down, the receptionist simply left a message — and then left our candidate cooling his heels while she chatted with a co-worker for nearly half an hour. To make a bad impression even worse, two employees entered the building arguing loudly, and continued their verbal battle in the lobby for several minutes.

By the time our candidate reached the interview, his mind was made up. Even though the interviewers treated him well, and did a great job of trying to sell him on the position, they couldn't erase the first impression created by the gossiping receptionist, the fighting employees, and the long wait in the lobby.

Interview Do's

Interviewing is a creative process, and interviews often take interesting twists and turns. Thus, there's no single list of right or wrong questions that will apply to every candidate and every situation. However, some general rules apply to almost all interviews. Among them are the following:

Listen more than you talk

The rule of thumb is to talk 25 percent of the time and listen 75 percent. The more your candidate talks, the more he'll reveal about himself. As an example of how effective silence can be, consider the difference between these two interviewers:

Interview #1:

Interviewer: "So, why did you switch from clinical work to research?"

Candidate: "It just suited me better."

Interviewer: "Okay. Now, tell me about your recent work . . ."

Interview #2:

Interviewer: "So, why did you switch from clinical work to research?"

Candidate: "It just suited me better."

Interviewer nods and looks encouragingly at candidate without saying anything.

Candidate (after several seconds go by): "I guess I realized I was getting too stressed out, trying to deal with my patients' problems and the pressures from the administration as well. Research is a calmer environment."

Note that in the second interview, the interviewer gains far more information from a single question. She discovers that her candidate may deal poorly with stressful environments, which could be a key factor in deciding whether or not to hire him — and she finds this out without saying a single word.

While silence is a powerful tool, however, don't allow pauses to grow uncomfortable. When your candidate runs out of things to say, help him out by picking up the conversational ball.

Ask smart questions

To make the most of your interview, ask open-ended questions that draw your candidate out. Of course, you'll need to ask a few easy-to-answer questions —

for example, "Do you have a security clearance?" "Can you work on weekends?" However, you'll get far more mileage out of open-ended questions and comments that make your candidates think.

Consider the difference between the open-ended questions in Approach 1, and the closed-ended questions in Approach 2:

Approach 1: "Are you a good problem-solver?"

Approach 2: "Can you describe a time in which you encountered a difficult work problem and solved it?"

Approach 1: "Do you know C++ well?"

Approach 2: "Can you describe a recent application you developed using C++, and explain why you feel C++ was the best choice in that situation?"

In each case, you'll notice that Approach 1 encourages a simple yes or no answer, while Approach 2 is likely to elicit a long, thoughtful response.

To get even more mileage from your questioning, combine open-ended questions with follow-ups. For example, ask your candidate, "Of all of the jobs you've held, which was the most rewarding?" When you get an answer, probe for more information: "Why was it rewarding?" "What specific areas of the job did you enjoy the most?"

Another good technique is the hypothetical question. If your applicant is applying for a management position at a store, for example, ask: "If a customer and a clerk are arguing over whether or not the customer can return a dress that's been stained, what would you do?"

Think before you speak

In a litigious age, it's critical to analyze every question before you ask it. Even the most innocuous off-the-cuff comment — "Wow, you must have worked at Motorola back in the days when they made transistors!" — can translate into a discrimination lawsuit, so don't ask a question unless you're sure it's legal. The most dangerous questions are the off-the-cuff queries that interviewers blurt out without thinking.

See Chapter 21 for an in-depth look at illegal interviewing questions. These include questions about the following:

- Age
- Marital status
- Children (or intent to have children)
- Race, color, ethnic background, or nationality

✔ Religion

✔ Military discharges (unless this relates to the job)

✔ Private life or sexual orientation

✔ Organizational affiliations (unless these pertain directly to the job)

✔ Disability (except for asking if a candidate is able to perform the essential functions of the job)

✔ Arrest record (except that you can ask about convictions)

Spot green lights

You can gain clues both from what your candidate says and from how she acts. Among the signs that your candidate is a winner are the following:

✔ She jumps at the chance to tell you about her favorite projects.

✔ Her "body language" suggests that she's open, eager, and forthcoming.

✔ She answers each question fully, rather than skirting some topics.

✔ She offers full explanations about job changes and other issues.

✔ Her skills are consistent with, or even exceed, those she's listed on her resume.

Spot red flags

If your candidate chats with you in a relaxed way, and then suddenly tenses up or stops making eye contact when you ask a question, probe further. It may be a coincidence — but it also may be evidence that she's hiding something. Also, watch out for candidates who do one or more of the following:

✔ Fail to explain gaps between jobs, or to offer credible reasons for leaving jobs.

✔ Change the subject quickly, instead of answering your question.

✔ Become defensive.

✔ Speak negatively about former employers or co-workers.

✔ Are abrupt or ill-mannered, or behave oddly.

✔ Make statements that don't match the information on their resumes.

✔ Are excessively long-winded.

✔ Seem interested only in salary, and not in other aspects of your job.

✔ Have unrealistic expectations about salary, refuse to offer information about their current or past salaries, or are vague about salary expectations (for example, saying, "I'm seeking a salary somewhere between $70,000 and $150,000").

If your warning buzzers go off at any point during an interview, keep questioning your applicant about the topic you're discussing. Use questions such as, "Can you tell me more about that?" or "Could you explain why you feel that way?"

Find your candidate's hot buttons

As you're interviewing, make notes about what's important to your candidate. Is he interested in learning new skills, or gaining more freedom over his work environment? Is he looking for a flexible schedule? Is he tired of his current long commute, and are you closer (or able to offer a telecommuting option)? Does he mention that he's looking for specific benefits or perks that you can provide? Write down the clues you obtain, and use these later to "sell" him on your job. Among the possible "hot buttons" you may spot are these:

✔ Benefits or perks

✔ Stock options

✔ Increased job prestige, authority, or autonomy

✔ Training opportunities

✔ Better office space/environment

✔ Less travel

✔ Telecommuting or flex time options

✔ Company size or location

✔ Ability to work on exciting projects

✔ Company culture

Remember: You're being interviewed, too!

Project a positive, friendly, enthusiastic image throughout the interview, and let your candidate know you're proud of your company. Provide plenty of information about your job opening, and encourage your candidate to ask questions. At the same time you're forming an opinion about him, he's forming an opinion about you — and you want it to be a good one. Among the questions you should be prepared to answer:

✔ What is your company's growth potential?

✔ Are you planning on expanding or improving your products or services?

✔ How strong are you financially? Have you had any recent layoffs? Are you expanding or cutting back?

✔ Why did the person who previously had this job leave?

✔ What is your company culture like? Are you casual? Flexible about work hours?

✔ When do you plan to make a decision on filling this position?

Take notes

When you're interviewing several candidates, it's easy to forget what each one said. Write down key points, so you can review them later. But be sure your notes, just like your conversations, pertain to issues relevant to the job, and remember that your scribbled notes are legally part of your hiring record — so be careful what you write.

Also, complete a written evaluation of your candidate soon after an interview, while your memory is still fresh. (See the sample evaluation form later in this chapter.)

Interview Don'ts

One of the biggest interview "no-no's," in our opinion, is to intentionally make your applicant uncomfortable — for example, by interrupting her, or asking rude or blunt questions. An uncomfortable interview translates, frequently, into a candidate who's no longer interested in your job.

We know that some experts recommend *stress interviews,* saying that putting a candidate on the spot reveals how well he or she deals with high-pressure situations. But in a world where employees are hard to find and almost all are being wooed by other companies, it's not a smart strategy to make your candidate dislike you! Prospects often make their choices based on how welcome they feel, so don't outsmart yourself by trying to gain an edge on your candidate. Instead, strive to make your applicants comfortable, and to ask fair questions.

In addition, avoid these common interviewing pitfalls that can leave you with false impressions, unanswered questions, unhappy candidates, or even legal problems:

✔ **Snap decisions:** Most interviewers give candidates a mental thumbs up or thumbs down within the first 5 minutes. That's a big mistake, and it's the major reason why interviewing is unscientific. It's fair to form a tentative opinion about your candidate's personality or professional appearance — "He dresses well," "She has a friendly smile" — but don't make a decision on the applicant's merits until your interview is well underway.

✔ **Getting too personal:** Avoid being overly friendly with your candidates, even if you like them and find that you have interests in common. If you get too chatty, you may accidentally ask questions about marital status, age, or other taboo topics.

✔ **Loaded questions:** There's only one right answer to a question such as, "Do you think it's important to work well with a team?" or, "Do you handle responsibility well?" — and your candidate knows it. Instead, ask questions such as, "If you're working with a team, and you have a disagreement, what's the best way to handle it?" or, "Discuss a time when you took responsibility for seeing a project through."

✔ **The "halo effect":** This occurs when you identify so strongly with one positive trait of your candidate that the resulting good feeling colors the rest of your interview. Watch for the halo effect, because it can blind you to your candidate's flaws.

✔ **Moral judgments:** If your candidate reveals that she has different religious or political views than you, or leads a lifestyle that isn't consistent with your moral beliefs, your gut instinct may be to think less of her. Spot that reaction instantly, and recognize that it's unfairly influencing your opinion about her job skills.

✔ **Bad-mouthing your competitors:** If you're trying to win your candidate away from her current job, it's tempting to disparage your rivals. But don't do it. It's unprofessional, and it makes you sound negative. It's fine to ask, "Is your current company offering you a matching 401(k)?" but it's not okay to say, "We're not surprised you want to leave your current firm — we hear they treat their employees badly."

✔ **Warp-speed interviewing:** No matter how late it is, and how rushed for time you are, give all of your applicants the time they need to "sell" themselves — or, conversely, to reveal their weak points. Often, the last ten minutes and the last few questions of an interview are the most revealing.

Good Question!

LINGO

There's no magic list of interview questions, and your choices will vary depending on the position for which you're hiring. However, here are some good basic queries that you can tailor to meet your needs.

✔ **To explore job skills:**

- "Here are the skills that are essential to the job. Do you have all of these skills? Can you describe how you used them in your previous job?"

- "Describe your experience, and how it can be applied to this job."

- "Describe a specific project where you used (skills) successfully."

- "Tell us specifically about the duties and responsibilities of your last job."

- "Is there any part of this job you feel you may not be qualified to perform?"

✔ **To explore the ability to work with a team, to work independently, and/or to display leadership:**

- "Describe a project in which you worked successfully as part of a group."

- "Describe a time when a co-worker disagreed with you, and how you handled the situation."

- "If you felt a team member was not carrying her weight, what would you do?"

- "Describe the advantages and disadvantages of working independently on a project."

- "When working independently, what techniques do you use to meet your deadlines?"

- "If you're assigned a project to handle independently, what would you do if problems arise?"

- "Describe a successful project you led."

- "Describe a problem you encountered as a project leader, and how you handled it."

- "Give some examples of how you motivate people to work hard."

- "What are your top three achievements in your current job?"

✔ **To explore attitude and personality:**

- "What types of people do you enjoy working with?"

- "Among the managers you've worked with, which do you admire the most and why?"

- "List three adjectives that best describe you."

- "What do you consider your greatest strengths? What do you consider your biggest weaknesses? How do you compensate for those weaknesses?"

- "What did you enjoy most about your previous job? What did you enjoy least?"

- "What would your ideal job be?"

- "Are there any environments in which you wouldn't be happy?" (This can be tailored to your company. For example, if you're a suit-and-tie firm, find out if your candidate is comfortable in a noncasual environment.)

✔ **To explore expectations:**

- "What benefits and perks are important to you?"

- "What is your career path? Where do you see yourself in 2 years? Five years?"

- "Why are you interested in leaving your current job? What are you seeking that your current job doesn't provide?"

You can find other good lists of interview questions at human resources sites on the Internet (see Chapter 4).

Money Matters

Eventually, your interview will come around to the important topic of salary. A single member of your interview team should be in charge of making an offer and negotiating with the candidate. This person should know exactly how flexible your company can be, in both the salary it can offer and the benefits it can provide.

If you're the person responsible for discussing salary issues, one good way to open the topic for discussion is simply to ask, "What are you currently earning?" Ask the candidate about her base pay, her bonus potential (if applicable), and her benefits, so you'll know if your offer is likely to be attractive. If your company doesn't have set salary grades, you may want to have several possible salary/benefit packages in mind, and use the candidate's answer to this question to judge which package is best. (For information on determining the right salary for your job, see Chapter 1.)

Now is also a good time to mention the topic of counteroffers. Ask your candidate how he will react if his current company responds to his plan to leave by offering him a better salary, more benefits, or other incentives to stay. (See Chapter 26 for more on the topic of counteroffers.)

Wrapping It Up

Give your applicant plenty of time to ask questions at the end of the interview, and do your best to answer them honestly and completely. Also, assign one interviewer as a wrap-up person. This person should be responsible for reviewing your company's offer, and making a final "sell" to your candidate.

If this is a final interview, and you're planning on making a job offer, give the candidate a tour of your office, and introduce any employees you run across on the tour. Be sure to include any highlights, such as an on-site gym or kitchen. If possible, steer your candidate toward some of your more outgoing employees, to help make a good first impression. However, don't give your potential employee any false impressions. (If he'll be working in a cubicle, for example, don't leave him with the idea that one of the nice offices you're touring will be his.)

At the end of the interview, thank your candidate and give him a heads-up about the next stage of the interview process. Tell him when he can expect you to contact him, and encourage him to call you if he has any questions. If you need to schedule another interview, explain when and with whom; if you're considering an offer, let the applicant know when to expect your decision.

To keep your strong points fresh in your candidate's mind, send him off with a packet of eye-catching, easy-to-read materials that "sell" your company's benefits and perks and emphasize your advantages. Also, give him a business card for each member of your interviewing team. And escort him personally to the lobby or elevator, to reinforce the positive impression you've created.

Above all, make sure your applicant leaves with a positive impression of your company. *This is true even if you don't intend to make a job offer to that applicant.* That's because your applicant will spread the word about you, and you want that word of mouth to be good. Thank your applicant sincerely for coming, and make him feel valued, whether he's a potential hire or not.

Also, be polite if your candidate tells you he's not interested. Over-selling your job can create hard feelings, so don't push too hard. Instead, thank him for coming, and part on friendly terms.

Keeping score

As soon as your candidate leaves, ask your team to rate him, using an official "scorecard" such as the one below. Remember that this form will be part of your applicant's official record, so spell out the reasoning behind your comments.

Rating your candidates

This is a very basic form that you can tailor to your own needs, depending on the type of position you're filling and the time you have to review each candidate. The more crucial the position you're filling is, the more detailed this form should be.

Applicant name _____

Date _____

Position _____

Circle the appropriate candidate rating (1=Excellent, 2=Above Average, 3=Average, 4=Below Average).

Does the candidate possess the skills essential for this position?	1 2 3 4
Does the candidate have the experience necessary for the job?	1 2 3 4
Does the candidate have the education/training necessary for the job?	1 2 3 4
Does the candidate exhibit the judgment skills, logic, decisiveness, confidence, verbal ability, and analytical skills needed for the job?	1 2 3 4

Overall impression:

_____

_____

_____

_____

Recommend employment for current opening? ___ yes ___ no

Recommended for future employment? ___ yes ___ no

Your team members should meet after the interview, rather than simply handing in evaluation forms, because discussion will help you clarify your candidate's strengths and weaknesses. If you disagree on some scores, discuss why, and try to come to a consensus.

Picking your finalist

As anyone who's ever judged a contest knows, it's often tough to pick the winner. And in this case, the stakes are high, because you're making a decision that can affect your company's productivity and profits for years to come.

Frequently, several people in a company participate in interviewing and selecting a candidate. Sometimes it's easy to agree on the candidate you want to hire. In other cases, your interview team may disagree — sometimes strongly — as to which candidate is the top choice. In the end, the hiring manager usually is responsible for saying yes or no. However, it's important to get input from every team member before that point, and it's always best if you can reach a consensus.

But what if you have three team members and three different opinions? Or what if you're the sole person responsible for making a hire, and you can't make up your mind? In either case, these tips can help you determine which candidate is your best pick:

- **Remember to focus primarily on job skills:** Personality is important. So is education. But when it's all said and done, you need someone who can do the job well, so make strong job skills and a proven track record your top priorities.

- **If your candidates match up evenly in skills and experience, consider each candidate's enthusiasm and willingness to learn new skills.** Also, consider whether each candidate is a good match for your work environment, and think about which candidate appears most likely to be able to establish good relationships with your current employees.

- **Compare candidates both *against each other* and *against the standards you set prior to interviewing.*** Sometimes it's easy to lose sight of your original goals, and revisiting your initial wish list for the position can clarify which candidate is right for the job. (See Chapter 17.)

  Also, you may discover that not one of your candidates meets the criteria you outlined before you started interviewing. If that's the case, decide whether you can safely rethink those criteria; if not, find additional candidates.

- **Be aware of the *order of interview* bias.** It's a fact that if three equally qualified candidates interview for your job, you're more likely to pick one of the latter two than you are to pick the first one. That's because you have high expectations at the beginning of the interview process, and you grow more realistic as you go along. To help avoid order of interview bias, refresh your memory by reviewing your written notes on each candidate.

Allow enough time for each member of your interview team to discuss the pros and cons of each candidate (while remembering, of course, that time is crucial). Where you disagree, compare notes, and see if you can come to an agreement. If so, your job is done! If not, then leave the decision to the person ultimately responsible. When you do, be totally supportive of the choice that person makes.

Not making an offer? Let 'em down gently

You want all of your applicants to have a good impression — even those you don't wind up hiring. A no-hire who tells people, "They were really nice — I hope they'll consider me for another position," is far better for your company than one who says, "I'm glad they turned me down — they were really unfriendly, and it took me weeks to get an answer from them."

So, in addition to treating every employee courteously during the interview, be sure to send a nice letter to the candidates who don't receive offers. Remember our rule: EVERY applicant could be your next hire, a future hire, a future customer, or a source for referrals — so treat each one well!

One note, however: Don't send your rejection letters out too soon. See Chapter 26 for advice on when to notify candidates that you've hired someone else.

Sample rejection letter

How you say no says a lot about your company. Here's an example of a polite note that can take some of the sting out of a turndown.

Dear [*applicant's name*],

Hiring decisions are always difficult, especially when several excellent candidates apply for a position. We are very impressed by your credentials and talents. We have offered the position of [*job opening*] to another applicant, but we would like to keep your application and paperwork on file for the next year in case we have another opening that may interest you.

Thank you for your time, and for your interest in our company. It was a pleasure to meet you, and we wish you the best of luck in your job search.

Sincerely,

[*Your name*]

Chapter 21

Avoiding Legal Land Mines

*W*atch your step! It's good advice in the modern business world, where seemingly minor slip-ups in job advertising, applications, interviewing, or hiring can leave you vulnerable to charges of discrimination.

To avoid legal headaches, you need to exercise caution in every step of the hiring process, from the day you place your ads to the day you sign on your new employees. And, the law aside, it's crucial to create a workplace atmosphere where no employee ever feels discriminated against, harassed, or threatened. Nothing hurts morale more than allowing prejudices to poison your work environment.

The first step in the process of ensuring that your workplace behaves fairly to all employees, and avoids legal hassles as well, is to understand the basics of the major U.S. laws against discrimination or unlawful hiring. This chapter provides a crash course.

The Civil Rights Act of 1964

Under this act, it's illegal for employers to discriminate on the basis of race, color, sex, religion, or national origin. One section of this law, Title VII, more familiarly known as the Equal Employment Opportunity law, specifically concerns hiring.

Know the facts before you hire

No basic book, including this one, can provide more than a quick overview of all the ins and outs of employment law. We recommend that you take an in-depth training course or college course on this topic, and that other managers and senior members of your recruiting team do the same. A few hours in class can save thousands of dollars in lawsuits — and possibly save your job as well.

While you're boning up on federal law, don't forget to research the laws of your state as well. Laws can vary widely; for example, some states forbid discrimination against smokers during the hiring process, while others do not. And laws change from year to year, so be sure to keep up with new rulings. (The Internet recruiting and human resources forums we discuss in Chapter 4 can be a big help.)

All companies with 15 or more employees are covered by Title VII. To avoid running afoul of this section, analyze every step of your hiring process to ensure that you aren't violating its provisions. This section provides some tips.

Advertising: Widening your net

To avoid the appearance (or, worse yet, the reality) of discriminatory hiring, be sure that your job postings are accessible to minority and female candidates. When you post job descriptions on Internet job boards, include several boards that focus on minority hiring (see Chapter 6). Participate in job fairs in ethnically diverse communities, and contact the Urban League and colleges in minority-rich areas for leads. Advertise in newspapers and on radio stations that target ethnic minorities, and consider placing ads in magazines or on Web sites that target female professionals.

When you advertise, never list requirements that can be construed as racist, sexist, or discriminatory to either religious or nonreligious individuals. For example, make note of the following:

- Don't say that you're looking for a male waiter, a female receptionist, or a "guy" to do landscaping. You can specify "attractive" only if it's an absolute necessity for the position — for example, if you're seeking models.

- Don't mention religion.

- Don't use words commonly associated with one gender or ethnic group; for example, don't ask for "burly" grocery baggers.

- Never ask applicants to send photos, unless you have a legitimate business reason. Photographs can be used to determine race or ethnicity.

- ✔ Be as specific as possible in listing the skills and training you require. This allows you to demonstrate that you rejected a candidate for being unqualified rather than because of discrimination, if a question arises.

- ✔ Be sure your ad focuses tightly on job skills, not personal characteristics.

- ✔ Specify in your ad that you are an equal opportunity employer.

Before placing an ad, read it over two or three times — and as you read, imagine that you're a job seeker of a different gender or ethnic background than your own. Would the ad attract you, or offend you? Be sure you've listed only what's called *BFOQs,* or *bona fide occupational qualifications.*

Also, be sure your recruiting brochures, as well as print or TV ads, feature people of both sexes and a mix of ethnic groups. The teams you send to job fairs and other public events should be as diverse as possible, too.

Applications and interviews: Keeping the process fair

Specify on your applications that you're an equal opportunity employer and that you do not discriminate on the basis of race, color, national origin, religion, disability status, veteran status, or gender. (See sample application in Chapter 19.) It should go without saying that you shouldn't ask questions about any of these characteristics. *In addition, avoid asking ANY of the questions in our "Busted!" charts in this chapter.* And balance your interviewing team, if it's at all possible. A woman candidate who's interviewed by five men and then rejected may wonder if sexism played a role. Conduct the same interviews with a three-man, two-woman team, and she'll have less reason for suspecting discrimination.

When you hire or reject candidates, document your decisions carefully in writing so that you'll have a paper trail if you're accused of discrimination. For example, if you choose a male candidate over a female because he has more experience, make sure your hiring record reflects your reasoning (for example, "Applicant A worked 6-plus years for a major national sales company." "Applicant B had only 3 months of prior sales experience."). If you reject an applicant because of limited English skills, or fail to hire a woman because she doesn't have the strength to lift a 50-pound box, be sure that you can demonstrate clearly that this directly impacts on the candidate's ability to do the job. And if you have any questions, consult with your company's legal staff before making a move.

Busted! The illegal questions interviewers ask most often

Interviews are dangerous territory, because even simple questions or casual conversation gambits can lead to legal woes. Here are some obvious, and not-so-obvious, illegal questions that interviewers all too often ask:

Questions that pinpoint an applicant's age

"When did you graduate?"

"Are your kids grown?"

"Do you think all of your years of experience might make you over-qualified for the job?"

Note: You can ask, "Are you over 18?" Also, you can require proof of age after you hire.

Questions about the applicant's children, either current or planned

"Hoping to have a little one soon?"

"Are you pregnant?"

"What childcare arrangements do you have?"

Note: You can ask about number and ages of dependents after hiring.

Questions about military discharges, unless you can show that the question directly relates to the job, questions about military service for other countries, requests for military records

"Were you honorably discharged?"

"You said you're from Germany. Did you serve in the Army there?"

Note: You can ask about service in the U.S. military, branch of service, rank attained, and job-related experience. You're also allowed to ask if the applicant is a member of the military reserves, and if this will affect work hours. After hiring, you can ask to see a military discharge certificate.

Questions about candidates' marital status, family, gender, or sexual orientation

"Where does your husband work?"

"Are you single?"

"If you have a spouse, would he/she be willing to relocate?"

"Do you go by Ms., Miss, or Mrs.?

"What was your maiden name?"

"Can you give us the names of some relatives as emergency contacts?"

Questions about the applicant's private social life or organization memberships

"You listed your GPA on your resume, but you didn't mention extracurricular activities. What social clubs did you belong to in college?"

Exception: You can ask about membership in trade or professional groups.

Questions about U.S. citizenship or national origin

"Are you a citizen?"

"What country are you from?"

"Are you a naturalized citizen?"

"My best friend's last name is Miras, and she's from Greece — are you from Greece too?"

"What is your native language?"

Note: You can ask, "Will you be able to provide proof of eligibility to work in the U.S. if hired?" *After* hiring, you can ask for proof of citizenship.

Questions about a candidate's disability

"Do you have a disability?"

"Do you have any medical problems?"

"Have you ever had a mental illness?"

"Have you ever had a disabling physical illness?"

Note: You can ask, "Can you perform the essential functions of the job for which you are applying?"

Questions about religion

"Do you have any religious beliefs that will affect your performance?"

"Are you active in any church groups?"

"Will you need to take Ramadan off?"

"You list St. Olaf's under education. Is that a Catholic school?"

Note: You are allowed to ask, "Can you work on Saturdays or Sundays?"

Questions about an applicant's arrest record

"Have you ever been arrested? What for?"

Note: You *can* ask about convictions, but to reject candidates with criminal records, you must show that the convictions have a direct bearing on job performance. For example, you can't reject a woman with a prostitution conviction for a job as a bookkeeper. However, you may be able to reject a convicted swindler for the same job.

The workplace: Protecting against prejudice

Unfortunately, the problems of the outside world almost always show up in our offices as well — and that goes for racial, sexual, and religious prejudice. You can't guarantee that all of your hires will arrive at the workplace free of such personal baggage, but you can — and, legally, you must — do all you can to prevent employees from acting on their biases. Among the steps you should take, both to insure fairness in hiring and to make sure current employees are treated fairly, are the following:

✔ **Watch your stats.** Is everyone in your accounting department male and white? (Or, conversely, is everyone in your advertising department female and Hispanic?) If you see questionable patterns, make sure your managers don't have hidden agendas. Also, keep an eye on promotions, to ensure that there's no *glass ceiling* for women or minorities — that is, no bias-based barrier to career advancement and promotion.

✔ **Offer training programs.** Hold seminars and workshops to teach your employees the rules against discrimination and sexual harassment. (Screen your training programs carefully, however. The sensitivity training field is booming, and while many programs are excellent, some are dreadful.) A company-wide effort to eliminate discrimination is good business — and it's excellent protection, if you're ever sued.

✔ **Investigate incidents immediately.** Be sure your employees know that violations will not be tolerated. Moreover, make it clear that this rule applies to everyone from the employees on the loading dock to the executives in the boardroom.

✔ **Establish clear policies in writing.** Because there are so many gray areas in discrimination and harassment laws, it's important to protect your company by spelling out as many rules as possible. Define unacceptable behaviors, and the consequences that will result. Have an attorney draft or at least review your list, to ensure that your requirements are legal and comprehensive. This is an area in which you don't want to take chances.

✔ **Comply with additional laws.** Federal contractors and subcontractors with 50 or more employees and contracts of more than $50,000 must also implement affirmative action programs. (For more information, check the Web site of the U.S. Department of Labor, at www.dol.gov.)

The Americans with Disabilities Act (ADA)

Just a few decades ago, many of America's most talented employees were shut out of the job market. Why? Because they were blind or deaf, relied on wheelchairs, or had other disabilities. In addition, employees who developed diabetes, cancer, and other diseases often lost their jobs, even if they were still capable of doing the work.

Fortunately, along with our old stereotypes about sex and race, our stereotypes about disabilities are falling away. Disabled employees are proving that they're more than able to compete in the work force, and employers in turn are finding a gold mine of qualified employees whom they may have overlooked just a few decades ago.

Busted, take two: The top illegal questions asked on applications

Applications are another area where you need to watch what you say. Illegal questions include the following:

✔ Birth date

✔ Marital status/questions about children

✔ Citizenship status

✔ Arrest record

✔ Relative to contact in case of emergency

✔ Maiden name

✔ Years of school attendance or graduation

The Americans with Disabilities Act is one driving force behind this change. By outlawing discrimination against individuals with qualified disabilities, the ADA allows large numbers of employees with a wide range of disabilities to enter the workforce as equals. However, the law is confusing, and even the most accommodating employers can find themselves in the docket defending against a discrimination claim.

On paper, the ADA seems fairly clear: It bans discrimination against qualified people with disabilities in all aspects of employment including recruiting, hiring, firing, promotions, pay, and training. Companies with at least 15 employees must comply with the law, which states that an employer must accommodate a disabled employee if he or she meets both of the following criteria:

- The employee is qualified for the job.
- The employee can perform "essential functions" of the job, with or without "reasonable accommodation." (Companies are exempt from making accommodations that would cause "undue hardship.")

In some cases, interpreting these requirements is easy. Suppose, for example, that a blind candidate applies for a position at your firm. Does she want a job as a programmer? Then if she can demonstrate that her blindness doesn't interfere with doing the job, it's illegal for you to deny her the job based on her blindness. Moreover, she can expect you to make reasonable accommodations for her blindness — for example, by purchasing software that translates computer text into spoken words. But does she want a job as a bus driver? Then, obviously, you can say no — and cite her disability as a reason — without fear of losing a discrimination suit.

Unfortunately, it isn't always that simple under ADA. The problem lies in defining the following:

- What is a disability?
- What is a "reasonable accommodation"?
- What is "undue hardship" on the part of the employer?

The following sections provide a little illumination. For more detailed assistance, you should consult with your company's legal staff.

Is the candidate disabled?

Under ADA, a job candidate or employee is considered as disabled if the individual

- Has a physical or mental impairment that substantially limits one or more major life activities;

> ✔ Has a record of such an impairment (for example, an employee who had successful cancer surgery years earlier may be considered as disabled); and/or
>
> ✔ Is regarded as having such an impairment. (For example, a candidate believed by other employees to have a mental disability may be qualified, even if the person does not claim to have a disability.)

Many of the disabilities that ADA covers are obvious: blindness, hearing loss, paralysis, epilepsy, heart disease. But many others aren't. For example, a recovered or currently recovering alcoholic or drug user is covered. Thus, if you're interviewing an administrative assistant who recently completed a rehabilitation program, you can't consider his past substance abuse as a reason for saying no. (You can, however, consider current abuse that impairs performance — but if you let an employee go for this reason, you must be able to prove that the dismissal is due to poor work habits, rather than to the substance abuse problem itself.)

Can the employee do the job — and how much will it cost me?

Under the ADA, you must make reasonable accommodations to enable a disabled employee to perform a job. This may mean adding ramps or bathrooms that accommodate wheelchairs, installing flashing lights for deaf employees who can't hear alarms, or scheduling flextime for an employee undergoing treatments for cancer.

If major accommodations are too difficult or expensive, you can legally reject the employee. But how expensive is "too expensive" — and how much hardship is "undue hardship"? That's one of the gray areas of the ADA. If you're a small business, you may be able to argue that adding a wheelchair ramp or an elevator could break you. If you aren't sure, consult with an attorney before turning down a disabled applicant.

However, it's smarter, if possible, to think of creative ways around the problem. For example, if you can't afford to install an elevator for a disabled candidate applying for a job as a manager, can you relocate her department to the first floor? If a candidate has epilepsy but the job requires some local travel, can you schedule his trips at regular times, and hire a college student at minimum wage to drive him? Before you say no to any candidate, make sure that the cost of coping with the disability is a severe burden, and that there's no simple solution that you're overlooking.

In general, the amount of money paid out by employers to accommodate disabled employees is small. According to the President's Committee on Employment of People with Disabilities, about two-thirds of employers pay $500 or less to make accommodations, another 12 percent pay $500 to $1,000, and only 22 percent pay more than $1,000.

What you can and can't do under ADA: Some pointers

Although it's sometimes difficult to determine how the ADA applies in various situations, you can use the following rules as a guideline:

✔ **You are allowed** to turn down a disabled applicant, if another applicant has superior skills.

✔ **You can't ask** an applicant to take a medical exam as a requirement for employment. However, you *can* make a job offer conditional on passing a post-offer medical exam, if the same exam is required of all entering employees in the same job category.

✔ **You are allowed to require** that a disabled candidate can perform *essential* job functions, as long as you provide reasonable accommodation as necessary. You can also hold disabled employees to the same standards as nondisabled employees in the case of *marginal* job duties — those that aren't absolutely necessary — unless their disability affects their ability to perform these tasks. If that's the case, then you must provide reasonable accommodation such as job restructuring.

And when you're considering the cost of making accommodations, factor in the benefits as well. Adding a wheelchair ramp, or training all of your employees in sign language, may make you a hit with disabled clients who aren't comfortable doing business with less accessible firms.

The Age Discrimination in Employment Act of 1967 (ADEA)

The ADEA makes it illegal to discriminate against job seekers or employees who are 40 years of age or older. Also, with a few exceptions, the ADEA prohibits you from establishing a mandatory retirement age. If your firm has 20 or more employees, this law applies to you.

Under the ADEA, you're not allowed to specify an age in your job descriptions, unless you can prove that it's necessary to the job. (For example, you can't specify "under 60" in an ad for waitresses, but you can specify "under 20" for models to promote children's sportswear at a department store.) You should not ask about age, either on applications or in interviews, except — as noted earlier — if you can demonstrate that the job requires candidates in a specific age group.

In addition, the ADEA requires you to offer older employees the same benefits you pay younger employees. However, you don't have to pay more for these benefits than you do for the rest of your workforce — meaning that you can reduce health or life or disability benefits for seniors, as long as you're paying the same amount out-of-pocket for younger and older employees.

While federal law covers only employees over the age of 40, many states have laws prohibiting age discrimination against anyone over 18; check to see if your state does.

One more word of caution: Telling an older job candidate that he or she is "overqualified" for a job can be interpreted as age discrimination, so avoid this phrase when you interview.

The Pregnancy Discrimination Act

Under this act, you can't refuse to hire a woman simply because she is pregnant, as long as she's able to perform the major functions of her job. The law requires you to treat pregnancy as a temporary disability, and to judge pregnant job applicants strictly on their ability to perform the jobs for which they are applying.

A separate Supreme Court ruling also makes it illegal for you to refuse to hire a pregnant woman for a job that could endanger her unborn child. To protect yourself from liability in such a situation, be sure your new hire receives information, in writing, about the risks entailed in the job.

The Equal Pay Act

The Equal Pay Act prohibits paying men and women different amounts for equal or "substantially equal" work — that is, jobs that are equal in skill, effort, and responsibility, and performed under similar working conditions. Here are some facts to know about this law:

- ✔ You must pay equivalent salaries to male and female employees, unless you can prove that the difference is due to seniority, a merit system, or another factor other than gender.
- ✔ You can't correct any wage disparity by lowering the salaries of either male or female employees.

Immigration Laws

With the skilled-worker crunch reaching crisis proportions, many firms are now looking outside the U.S. for talent. It's a smart way to expand your labor pool, but if you opt to recruit overseas or in Mexico or Canada, make sure you cover all the legal bases.

First, *all* employees, including noncitizen employees, must provide you with proof of identification. (Acceptable forms include driver's licenses and school ID cards.) In addition, all new employees — not just noncitizens — must fill out I-9 (Employment Eligibility Verification) forms. Employees who aren't U.S. citizens also need to provide you with documentation proving that they are able to work in the United States.

Because immigration laws change frequently, it's important to check with a labor attorney or immigration law specialist to make sure your hiring practices are in line with current regulations.

Busted, take three: The top illegal topics not to bring up in reference checking

It's smart to check your candidate's references (see Chapter 25), but be careful when you make those calls. Questions about any of the following topics are prohibited:

- Race or national origin

- Religion

- Medical history, or number of days missed due to illness (you may, however, simply ask if the candidate had a good attendance record)

- Marital status

- Age

- Number of workers' compensation injuries

- If the candidate is a smoker or nonsmoker (illegal in some states)

- Height or weight

- History of substance abuse

- Arrest records

- Disability

Chapter 22

Pre-Employment Testing

*B*ob says he's a whiz at Java — but how good is he really?

Susan wants a job as a copy editor, but she's fresh out of college. Can she do the job?

According to Arnie's resume, he can type 60 words per minute. But is that the truth?

Even when you have a good resume in hand and your candidate sounds like a dream come true, it's not always easy to know if your applicant is up to the job. Moreover, it's often difficult to be objective when you're picking a candidate based on interviews. That's why, in some cases, testing can help you make better-informed hiring decisions. Before you decide to evaluate your candidates, however, make sure your tests pass the grade.

Fair Versus Unfair Testing

To avoid legal problems when testing applicants, it's crucial to select your tools carefully and use them cautiously. You must meet the following criteria:

✔ Your tests must focus specifically on the skills needed for the job.

✔ Your tests must not screen out a disproportionate number of minority candidates. You must be able to show that your questions are not discriminatory. If the net effect is to exclude a large percentage of minority or female candidates, you're on shaky ground.

✔ Your tests can't be excessively difficult. Tests that require knowledge or skills beyond the needs of the job are discriminatory, because they often weed out candidates with strong job skills but without advanced education. (A Yale alumnus, for example, is much more likely than a community college grad to be able to answer questions about eighteenth-century British tax law — but that doesn't make him any more qualified to be a tax accountant.)

✔ Employees must get equal treatment. If you have six applicants for a programming position, and you test one, you need to test them all. It doesn't matter if the other five have proven track records.

✔ All candidates should be told up front that they'll be tested.

To Test or Not to Test

Testing increases the time it takes to hire an employee. In addition, it adds to the expense of the hiring process — and, as we noted, it can raise legal issues as well. Thus, it's important to decide whether or not your company will really benefit by testing job candidates.

How can you decide whether you should test or not? First, ask yourself if you can obtain accurate information about your candidates in other ways. If you're hiring for sales positions, for example, you may decide that your candidates' experience and track records provide sufficient information, and that you don't need to administer formal tests. On the other hand, you may find that personality tests provide useful insight about your candidates' customer interaction skills — a crucial factor in how successful they will be. But remember, if you decide to test a candidate, you will need to test all other candidates for that position.

Many employers test high-tech skills, because these can be hard to judge on the basis of a resume or an interview. If you need expertise in a range of programming languages, a candidate who knows only a few may be tempted to fib a bit, thinking, "I can always buy a few books and read up on HTML." Tests can reveal such a candidate's weakness, and help steer you toward a more qualified applicant.

In addition, tests can often rate a candidate's skills more objectively than the candidate can rate himself. Interestingly, studies tend to show that high performers underestimate their abilities, while low performers overestimate their talents. And testing is a useful tool for judging the expertise of college students with no job experience.

Testing is fairly standard in the high-tech industry, and you'll find a number of good tests on the market. Which brings us to another point: When possible, use well validated, standardized tests. When selecting a testing tool, access Internet recruiting or human resources forums (see Chapter 4) and ask which are the best.

If you decide to use tests, be careful not to base your hiring decisions too heavily on the results. In some cases, of course, tests in and of themselves can make the difference between saying yes or no to an applicant. Take our examples opening this chapter: If Bob flunks your Java test, Susan can't pass muster on a copy editing test, or Arnie types 12 words per minute on your typing test, then you're justified in turning them down. But other tests aren't as clear-cut, and tests don't always predict job ability. We've all known people who are natural-born test takers, and those who choke on exams even if they're smart and talented. Thus, in most cases, you'll need to consider testing as just one element of a hiring process that includes resume screening, reference checking, and interviewing.

Because the regulations governing testing can be complex, consult your company attorney before you implement a testing policy. You can also contact the U.S. Department of Labor and request a copy of their publication, "Testing and Assessment: An Employer's Guide to Good Practices."

Should You Outsource Your Testing?

Testing is more expensive if you use outside companies. However, outsourcing has powerful advantages. It ensures that your tests are standardized, helps to protect you in case of a lawsuit, and takes the burden of administering and scoring tests off your shoulders. But if you can test your candidate's skills fairly easily — for example, by administering a typing test, asking a copy editor to edit several pages of text, or asking a programmer to solve three or four programming problems — then outside tests may be a waste of money.

Don't Let Testing Get in the Way of Hiring!

While testing can weed out unqualified candidates, there's a chance that it can cost you good hires. Two factors to weigh, if you're deciding whether or not to test, are the following:

✔ **Speed of hiring:** Will you need to delay your hiring process significantly in order to get test results? If so, consider finding quicker or less formal means of evaluating your candidates' skills. Finding the best candidate won't do you any good, if that candidate is stolen away by a company that tests less and moves faster.

✔ **The comfort factor:** Candidates, especially experienced ones, don't like taking tedious tests. If you can determine your candidates' skills using job interviews, reference checking, and quick work samples, then avoid putting candidates through extensive testing.

Testing Is Just One Piece of the Puzzle

Above all, use tests only when you need them, and only as one part of a well-designed hiring process. In most cases, tests shouldn't be your only hiring tool. Used wisely in the right circumstances, however, tests can often save you from a disastrous hire, and steer you toward a winning candidate.

Best test strategies

To get the most from your recruiting and hiring dollars, use tests if the following apply in your situation:

✔ Your recruiting, training, and turnover costs are high.

✔ You typically have several good candidates for each position.

✔ It's easy to define the job skills you require, and tests can clearly differentiate between success and failure at these skills.

Know your testing terms

If you choose to purchase tests from a testing company, be sure to evaluate each test's *validity* and *reliability.* Here's what these terms mean:

✔ **Reliability** refers to how consistently a test measures a skill or characteristic. (If a person takes the test again, will she get a similar score or a very different score?)

✔ **Validity** refers to how well the test measures the skill it's intended to measure. (Do the people who receive high scores actually prove to be better performers than the people who receive low scores?) Validity is a particularly critical measure of a test, because high validity tells you that the test is a good predictor of job performance.

Test providers should provide you with information on the studies they've conducted to ensure that their tests are both reliable and valid.

Part V

Reeling in Your Catch: The Closing

In this part . . .

Y ou've interviewed your candidates, you've made your decision, and now it's time to close the deal. In this part, we discuss how to make your move. We start with tips on speeding up the interview-to-hire timing (Chapter 22), and then offer tips for keeping your prospect hooked during your negotiations (Chapter 23), checking references to make sure your choice is a winner (Chapter 24), and making an offer your candidate can't refuse (Chapter 25).

Chapter 23

After the Interview: Timing Is Everything!

As soon as a good candidate's resume hits your desk, the clock starts ticking — and in today's hiring market, that clock is ticking faster and faster. That doesn't mean that you should skip critical parts of the screening process. But it definitely means that you need to move quickly when it comes to contacting, interviewing, and hiring new employees. And it means that after the interview is over, and you select your winning candidate, you need to close the deal as fast as you can.

How Fast Do You Need to Move?

If you're hiring for technical positions, you already know the answer to this question: You need to move at light speed. In spite of recent layoffs, there are still far more openings for high-tech employees than there are candidates to fill the jobs, and almost every candidate can pick and choose from several offers.

Remember: By the time you've interviewed your high-tech whiz, the candidate has most likely interviewed with two or three other companies — and may plan to meet with several more shortly after leaving your office. Some of those companies will put offers on the table at the end of the interview. And odds are, several of them will make better offers than you.

The high-tech crunch

Think the recent rash of downsizings makes it easier to hire an information technology professional or other high-tech employee? Think again! Minor economic slowdowns, while they may temporarily ease the drought of computer experts, won't change the fact that the number of jobs for high-tech employees will continue to outstrip the number of qualified candidates for years to come. According to the U.S. Department of Commerce, by the year 2005, the United States will need more than 1 million more information technology employees (computer scientists and engineers, systems analysts, and computer programmers) than it needed in 1994 — and universities and colleges are turning out too few computer science majors to meet these needs.

Clearly, the way to play this game is to beat the other companies to the punch. Job seekers tire quickly of interviews, which are stressful and demanding. After the first few, they're looking for reasons to say yes to someone, so companies with efficient hiring processes are at a distinct advantage. Moreover, a quick, smooth hiring process creates a positive image, while moving slowly makes you look inefficient, unprofessional, and unorganized.

As a general rule, we suggest the following:

Resume review
↓
First contact: phone screen
↓
One face-to-face interview . . .
↓
Immediately followed by a roundtable discussion where the interviewers can provide their feedback. (As an alternative, provide an interview feedback database so you can receive input online.)
↓
Follow-up call to candidate, to assess the individual's interest level . . .
↓
Followed by an offer within two days. We recommend a verbal offer, followed by a written offer (see Chapter 26).
↓
Polite rejection letters to other candidates, as soon as your top candidate gives you a definite yes.

Time is also crucial if you're hiring top-level executives, especially if these people are active candidates. Qualified execs are always in demand, and they won't wait for you to make up your mind.

Hiring for contract positions should move even faster, in part because you're investing less in a contract employee and you don't need to offer vacation time, stock options, insurance, or other long-term benefits. Also, you're not looking for a long-term relationship but simply for someone capable enough to fill a temporary need or work on a particular project.

Getting Your Team into High Gear

No matter what position you're hiring for, however — from a top executive to a new receptionist — it's imperative to eliminate the down time from your hiring process. By using the tips in this section, you can shave a few hours, a day, or even a week or two off your hiring time.

Make your managers move

We know, we know: It's not _your_ fault that your best candidate is getting other offers while your technology director asks to interview more people "just to see who else is out there." And it's not your fault if your customer service manager says "sorry, no time" when you try to set up an interview. But no matter whose fault it is, managers who keep stalling create a bottleneck in your carefully designed hiring process.

How can you correct the problem? If you already created a clear-cut, efficient recruiting process (see Chapter 3), be assertive in making it work. If necessary, have the CEO explain to all of the managers that moving slowly is no longer an option.

Also, make the stakes clear to your managers. Explain that hiring delays result in the following:

- **Lost candidates:** The hotter the candidate, the less time she'll spend waiting for you to make an offer.

- **Lost money:** Hiring delays mean lost candidates, as we just noted — and lost candidates mean that recruiters will need to find, screen, and interview additional prospects. Pulling managers and recruiters away from their day-to-day duties to conduct interview after interview costs your firm money and takes a toll on productivity.

- **Bad choices:** After a while, hiring delays cause _interview fatigue_ to set in. As a result, managers who think they're holding out for the best candidate often wind up selecting someone second-rate instead.

- **Poor company image:** The candidates you chase off with a slow interview process will leave with a bad impression of your firm, and you can be sure they'll spread the word.

Flextime hiring

For recruiters, the 9-to-5 workday is a thing of the past. These days, plan on scheduling interviews before and after work, or even on weekends, so already-employed prospects can fit you into their schedules.

How far do some companies go to accommodate their candidates? A *Wall Street Journal* wire service article offers an example: "[The employee] was recruited for her job as communications manager for Blue Martini Software, Inc., of San Mateo, California, in an interview with a company manager at a bar around midnight on a Tuesday. The 'clincher' interview, at company headquarters, took place late on a Friday evening."

Establish one point of contact

Your hiring process will flow more smoothly and quickly, and fewer misunderstandings will arise, if you designate one person as the *point person* for the post-interview process. This person should do the following:

✔ Be the contact to whom all interviewers report their feedback.

✔ Be the contact for the candidate.

It's this person's responsibility to keep the hiring process moving quickly, and to keep the candidate in the loop at all times. This includes these activities:

✔ Contacting the candidate with feedback — either good or bad.

✔ Keeping the candidate informed by e-mail or phone if the selection process is still underway.

No candidate should go more than two or three days without hearing from you.

Avoid the quota trap

Many managers behave like Las Vegas gamblers: They keep hoping that the next spin — or, in their case, the next candidate — will be the winner. In the meantime, qualified candidates slip away one by one, and crucial positions go unfilled.

If this is a recurring problem in your organization, it's time to make your managers see the light. Explain that it's not necessary to interview ten candidates if the second or third one is a perfect match — and that your ideal candidate may be long gone by the time you've finished seven or eight other interviews.

Also, come up with figures to show how much your unfilled positions are costing the company in lost productivity, wasted recruiting costs, and the managers' own time.

"Parallel process" your candidates

Many companies interview one candidate at a time, calling the next prospect only if the current one isn't a perfect fit. You don't have time for this approach in today's hiring market; instead, see applicants as quickly as you can schedule them.

If you can, make an on-the-spot offer

Ask your bosses to consider giving one member of your interview team the authority to make an instant offer when a candidate shines in an interview. It's not an option you want to use frequently, but if it's truly a perfect match, an immediate offer can keep a dynamite employee from slipping away. Two of our client companies have even made offers to candidates during the phone screen stage, without ever meeting the prospects. While this is not the norm, it's sometimes the best way to go, so don't rule it out. You can always make a verbal offer contingent on reference checks, drug screening, and other criteria.

Fast Doesn't Mean Too Fast

While you want to remove all roadblocks to speedy hiring, moving too fast can cause problems as well — so don't pass on reference checking (see Chapter 25), don't rush your interviews, and do be sure that your interview team meets to review each candidate's qualifications thoroughly. Also, schedule all necessary drug tests and background checks.

Above all, don't hire the wrong person out of desperation. A too-hasty decision can result in a quick turnover, and that in turn can force you to begin the hiring process for that position all over again. (Ugh!) Avoid this unpleasant scenario by taking care to select the best candidate you can find for your job — but once you're sure that you're making the right decision, go "full speed ahead" to close the deal.

Chapter 24

Keeping Your Prospect Hooked

*N*o matter how fast your hiring process moves, there's almost always a little lag between the post-interview handshake and the offer letter. During this brief window of time you're vulnerable, and even the most enthusiastic candidates can slip off the hook if you're not careful. Thus, it's important to keep your candidate informed, interested, and in the loop.

Who Else Is after Your Candidate — and Can You Up Your Ante?

The biggest risk, at this stage of hiring, is that a competitor will extend a faster and possibly better offer. Remember that it's a given: If you love your candidate, your competitors will, too. So if you're considering making an offer to a candidate, be sure to ask the following questions:

✔ Are you interviewing with anyone else? If so, with whom?

✔ Have you received any other offers? If so, how much were you offered?

If the answer to either question is yes, always try to find out the names of the companies. Also, see if you can get a feel for how serious these companies are, how good their offers are, and how yours may fall short. Let your candidate know that there's some room for negotiation in your offer (if that's true), so he won't reject you immediately if another company's initial offer is better. And keep pointing out the advantages your company offers over the competition, without bad-mouthing the other firms. Do you have a shorter commute, more generous vacation hours, or an on-site gym? Remember your candidate's hot buttons, which you uncovered during your phone screen and interview (see Chapters 18 and 20), and keep pushing them.

Also, keep your hiring managers informed about competing offers to your candidate. They need to realize that a candidate with one or two great offers on the table won't wait, and they need to move quickly in response.

Staying in Touch: Why Constant Communication Is Crucial

Candidates hate waiting and wondering. They want feedback on their interviews, and they want to know if you're actively considering hiring them. Leave them hanging, and they'll imagine the worst. ("Did I answer that last question wrong?" "I knew that guy in the blue suit didn't like me." "They must be hiring someone else.") The more insecure they grow, the more eager they'll be to snap at an offer from another firm — especially one that's sending out friendly vibes.

Thus, it's critical, at each stage of the hiring process, to keep your candidates in the loop. E-mail or phone them regularly, and be sure to tell them, "Call me at any time if you want to know how the interview process is proceeding." Also, be frank with them if unavoidable delays occur. ("Our manager's wife just had triplets. We hope you can be patient and wait one more day until he can get back to the office.") Silence creates worry and discontent, and may drive candidates to accept other offers. Communication, conversely, lets your candidates know that they're still in the running, and often encourages them to hold off on taking other jobs.

Moreover, it's important to keep your candidates excited about your company and the position. Sound enthusiastic when you call or e-mail, and keep your company's assets fresh in your candidates' minds. Create the attitude that your candidates are already part of the team, and make them feel valued and respected.

Another advantage to staying in touch is that it gives you a chance to make sure that you and your candidate are truly a good match. As you get closer to the stage of making an offer, review the job duties with your prospect, and discuss any company policies and procedures she should know about (for example, drug screenings or background checks, required weekend work, or travel requirements). Also, go over your benefits, perks, and employee programs, so your candidate has a solid understanding of what you can offer.

The Spouse Factor: Selling the Whole Family on Your Company

Are you married? If so, would you buy a new house, or even a new car, without talking it over with your spouse? Probably not — and most likely you wouldn't accept a new job without getting your partner's input, either.

Keep this in mind when you're trying to win over candidates. While you can't legally ask your candidates if they're married, many will volunteer this information, and you can be responsive.

For example, when candidates mention that they're married, invite their husbands or wives to tour your office or join you for lunch. Also, encourage spouses to call with any questions, particularly about your benefits package — and make sure these questions get answered quickly. When you list your company's strong points, mention family-oriented perks, such as insurance coverage for dependents, or family picnics or parties.

Moreover, be aware that your candidate's spouse may play a crucial role in the family's financial decisions. Thus, the spouse may have as big a say as the candidate in deciding whether your benefits and salary are up to par. Always treat the candidate's spouse, and the entire family, as equal partners in the decision-making process.

If a candidate is considering relocating, it's especially crucial to sell the entire family on both your job and on your area. Send them information about your community, and make a point of asking if they have any special concerns. (For example, if your candidate has children, offer to provide information about local schools.) Local realtors and your Chamber of Commerce will be more than happy to provide you with materials to help you sell your community.

One issue that frequently arises is that of a spouse who's concerned about finding a new job if your candidate relocates. Again, you can assist, in this case by finding out the spouse's career interests, and sending information about companies in your area that may be a good match.

A "win-win" move

We once worked for a candidate on the West Coast who was considering taking a job in Austin, Texas. While he was interviewing with the Texas firm, Paula provided his wife with information about all aspects of life in Austin. The wife did additional research on her own, and decided that she really wanted to move to Austin for several reasons — better schools for her children, a lower cost of living, and more outdoor sporting activities for her son. By the time her husband received an offer, it was a done deal and the wife was already packing!

Chapter 25

The Pre-Employment Screening

*I*t's tempting to skip reference checking, and hope that your prospects are everything they say they are. In fact, most companies succumb to this temptation: Studies show that employers check the references of only about 20 percent of the people they hire.

However, a smart recruiter never forgoes the step of reference checking. Past employers can help you round out your portrait of your candidate, and decide whether his skills and personality are a good match for your job. In addition, reference checking can prevent you from hiring an unqualified, dishonest, or even dangerous employee.

This chapter takes you through the steps of screening your candidates' references, and evaluating the information you obtain.

What a Good Reference Tells You

Jane is applying for a job as a database administrator. So is Eric. Both of them interviewed well, and you're ready to flip a coin. Instead, you call their references, and talk to their former bosses.

Jane's boss says:

> *"Jane was amazing. She took over from day one, and immediately started implementing changes that made our system far more powerful. I wish she were staying, but we knew she'd find a better job soon because she's really management material and we don't have any management openings in her area."*

Eric's boss says:

> *"Eric? He's fine. Had to encourage him a little, to keep him working hard, but he did a pretty good job and everybody liked him. Not a real go-getter, but he's honest and dependable and gets along with everyone. Didn't like our suit-and-tie office, however — that's probably why he left."*

On the whole, these are both fairly good references. But your calls clue you in to important differences between your candidates:

- ✔ If you need a dynamic self-starter, Jane is your best bet.
- ✔ If you're hiring for a position with no chance of upward mobility, however, Jane may leave you in a few years to look for greener pastures.
- ✔ If your company culture isn't casual, Eric isn't a good match for you.
- ✔ Eric will need closer supervision than Jane.

Armed with this new information, you're in a better position to pick between your two front-runners. In cases like this, reference checking can make the difference between hiring Candidate A and Candidate B, even if both candidates pass their interviews with flying colors.

What a Bad Reference Tells You

Occasionally it happens: You call your candidate's former boss, and she says, "You're hiring WHO?" and laughs for 2 minutes non-stop. Or you receive a report that the prospect you're so hot to hire has a reputation for being lazy, rude, or even dishonest. Now what do you do?

First, call every reference on the applicant's list. If it's a skimpy list, call the prospect and ask for more contacts. In addition, ask if you can contact other people at the firm where the bad reference originated. Hold your judgment until you reach all of the references, because a single bad report could stem from personality conflicts or unfair grudges.

Also, look at the bad reference in context. If your candidate received the Employee of the Month award three times, got promoted regularly, and stayed with the same company for years, that's evidence that the ex-manager you talked to might have a chip on her shoulder rather than a fair gripe.

However, *two* bad references, particularly if they're from different companies, mean that your candidate could be trouble. Think about how serious the complaints are, and judge accordingly. And if you get three or more bad references, shop around for another hire.

In some cases, your reference checking will uncover the fact that your candidate's credentials, references, or academic degrees are fabrications. Most prospects don't tell flat-out lies on their resumes, but those who do are bad news. If they're lying about their skills, they're probably unqualified for your job. If they're lying about their experience or education, they may be the kind of people who lie about other things as well — such as who broke the copy machine, or why your petty cash box disappeared. And if they need to make up references, that tells you they probably lost their previous job under unpleasant circumstances.

How many applicants fib on their resumes? Unfortunately, lots. Experts say about one-third of resumes contain false information, and about 10 percent contain lies important enough to be grounds for rejection. That alone is a good reason to check the references of every applicant. But there's one more, equally important reason to check your applicants' references: According to the law, you can be sued for *negligent hiring* if you fail to check the background of an employee who later commits a criminal or irresponsible act.

Why References May Hesitate to Talk

Before you pick up that phone to start checking references, be aware of another fact: Checking references can occasionally cause legal trouble, rather than preventing it. In Chapter 21, we discuss the illegal questions you can't ask. (*Quick refresher: race or national origin, religion, medical history, number of days missed due to illness, marital status, number of worker's comp injuries, height, weight, history of substance abuse, arrest records, disability.*) It's also important to check state laws, which can vary. But even if you avoid those no-no's, you can still cause trouble for the ex-employer you're calling.

How? In one case, a court ruled that a construction company had to pay $250,000 in damages after a personnel manager, asked to give a reference on a former employee, offered a less-than-glowing reference based on second-hand information. The ruling and others like it have many ex-employers running scared, even though a number of states have laws protecting bad references based on concrete data such as poor performance reviews. Thus, when you call and say, "What can you tell me about this employee?" you'll sometimes obtain little information beyond the employee's job title and the dates of his employment.

Ironically, former employers who won't tell you about a bad employee are leaving themselves wide open for prosecution, too. In 1995, a Florida court found an insurance company liable for failing to reveal the violent history of an employee it terminated. Another insurance company hired him, and he later shot three employees at the second company.

Reference checking: Sample questions

If you're new to reference checking, it's a good idea to have a prepared list of questions. Here are some of the best standard queries:

(Applicant's name) has applied for a job at our firm. Would you be willing to serve as a reference? Your replies will be kept confidential.

In what capacity did you work with this individual?

When did (applicant) work for/with you? (Ask for exact dates.)

What were his/her job responsibilities?

We're considering (applicant) for the position of _____. Do you think he/she would perform this job well?

How would you describe (applicant's):

Attendance (*Remember: it's illegal to ask about medical reasons for absence!*)

Dependability

Judgment

Accuracy

Responsibility

Ability to get along with other employees

Skills

How would you characterize his/her work in general?

In which areas could this individual improve?

Why did he/she leave your firm?

If you had the opportunity to hire for a position, would you hire this individual? If no, why not?

What do you think this individual's strengths are?

Would you recommend this person for a leadership role? Why / why not?

Are there any environments or situations in which this individual would not per form well?

Remember to thank the person you speak with, and leave her with a good impression of your company. (Who knows — she may be the next employee to jump ship!)

So why try to check references? Because at the very least, you'll find out whether or not the employee actually worked for the firm. You'll also help protect yourself against negligent hiring suits. And even though employers are becoming more skittish about offering information, you'll often strike pay dirt and find a reference who's willing to answer most or all of your questions. When you do, the nearby sidebar, "Reference checking: Sample questions," offers a sample of what you should ask.

How to Avoid Stepping on Your Applicant's Toes

When you check references, be sure you don't upset your applicants unnecessarily by violating their privacy or giving away the secret that they're planning to leave their current jobs. Don't call your candidate's current boss without first checking to see if it's okay; if not, contact other references who aren't connected to your prospect's current company.

Also, check references only if you're really interested in a candidate. That way, you'll limit the chances of an unsuitable applicant deciding that she lost the job because she received an unfavorable reference from her former employer. You'll also save lots of time.

Include a statement on your application that gives you the right to check references. Here's an example:

> As a prerequisite for employment with XYZCorp, I understand that it will be necessary to verify my employment history and references. I have completed and reviewed the information contained in this application and, to the best of my knowledge, believe the information to be correct. I authorize the employers and references indicated on my application to release information requested by XYZCorp pertaining to my activities regarding unemployment, prior employment status, dates, titles of positions, duties, and salary information.

By signing this form (see our application in Chapter 19 for a shorter variant), your candidates acknowledge that you can and will contact the people they list.

What Background Checks Can Reveal

While you won't always uncover many clues about your candidate by calling references, you can find a wealth of information by running background checks. Among the facts you can find out are the following:

- Conviction record
- Driving record

✔ Social Security verification

✔ Credit history

✔ Education history

Before conducting background checks, have candidates sign agreements specifically allowing you to investigate them. Also, check with your company attorney for information about what information you can legally obtain under federal and state laws.

We recommend conducting at least a cursory background check for every employee, because even entry-level employees can be hiding secrets that can lead to lawsuits. (One fast-food company was sued, for example, when an employee committed a serious crime; the company had failed to uncover the fact that the employee had a prior record of such crimes.) At a minimum, check for a criminal record, and confirm the candidate's job history. For positions involving driving, also check your candidate's driving record. For higher-level positions, check your candidate's credit history if you think it's relevant, and investigate his education history to make sure he's telling the truth. And never, ever skip background checks if your employee will be interacting with children or handling large amounts of money.

What You Should Know About Drug Testing

Many companies require all applicants to take drug tests. If yours does, be sure to inform applicants, in writing, that passing a drug test is a prerequisite for employment. In addition, have a written substance abuse policy that lays out the consequences for drug use by employees.

What federal contractors need to know

If you are a federal contractor with contracts of $25,000 or more, you must comply with the Drug Free Workplace Act of 1988, which requires you to

✔ Certify that you will provide a drug-free workplace.

✔ Notify employees in writing that unlawful possession, distribution, manufacture, or use of a controlled substance on the job is prohibited, and state the consequences for violating company drug use policies.

✔ Establish an ongoing drug abuse awareness program.

✔ Require sanctions or remedial measures for any employee convicted of illegal drug use in the workplace.

State laws vary, and federal laws can change, so check with a labor attorney before embarking on a company-wide drug-testing program. Also, check with your attorney if your employees are involved in interstate transportation, because different laws may apply in this situation.

How to Decide if You Should Outsource Reference and Background Checks

In the Internet age, it's easy to find online firms that will run your reference and background checks for you. If you can afford them, they offer several big advantages over doing your own detective work. Advantages of outsourcing include the following:

✔ Using an agency puts one degree of separation between you and the reference. Often, that makes references more comfortable about telling all.

✔ You may be forced to give up after three or four unsuccessful attempts to reach a reference, because you're just too busy to pursue the issue. But an agency will keep calling until it gets results.

✔ Agencies know how to reach key people, and what questions to ask (and which not to ask).

✔ Agencies move fast, and they're inexpensive enough to be cost-effective for even most small companies.

If you decide to use an outside company to conduct background checks, reference checks, and/or drug screening, make sure the firm complies with federal and state laws — especially the Fair Credit Reporting Act. (This federal act governs how employers can obtain and use a wide range of personal information about employees.) To be safe, ask your company attorney to verify that the firm's methods are legal.

Whether or not you outsource reference and background checks, however, is less important than making sure they get done. A few phone calls can save you, your employer, and your company's clients a world of trouble, so be sure you find out if your applicants are hiding any big secrets — *before* you say, "You're hired."

Chapter 26

Making Your Move: When It's Time to Extend an Offer

According to experts, the top 10 percent of candidates are off the market and have new jobs within 10 days. The moral: You snooze, you lose! Once you're ready to make an offer, you need to move quickly to nail things down and ensure that your hard work pays off in a successful hire.

At this stage, you have three goals:

✔ Beating your competition to the candidate.

✔ Making the most tempting offer possible.

✔ Handling any indecision on the part of your candidate.

When You're Ready to Say "Yes"

When it's time to make an offer, remind your hiring managers that every delay lowers the chances that your candidate will accept. Your best strategy is to instill some healthy fear in your managers. Make it clear that they'll risk losing a good candidate if they drag their feet, and that they may be forced to begin the interview process all over again — something no one wants to do. Don't allow them to postpone making an offer unless they can give valid reasons.

> ### A bad case of "letter lag"
>
> One of our major clients wanted to extend an offer to a candidate, but couldn't find the offer letter file on the computer. The human resources person who normally sent the offer letters was out sick, and the letter ended up being sent out 5 days later — giving other companies an entire workweek to make offers to the candidate.

When you do get the go-ahead, make sure your offer letter goes out immediately — preferably the day you decide to extend an offer. Send the letter by overnight mail, or fax it and send a separate copy by overnight mail, so your candidate will know you're interested. Ask the candidate to sign the letter and return it, either by fax or by mail, and be sure to enclose a return envelope.

Also, make sure the person extending the offer has the authority to do so! We've heard of cases in which firms had to rescind offer letters sent by unauthorized employees, or letters that contained promises the sender wasn't authorized to make. This is a nightmare scenario, and creates the impression that your company is unprofessional — or, worse yet, that you renege on agreements.

The question of who is authorized to make an offer should be resolved long before the offer-letter stage (see Chapter 3). Make sure this person, or someone directly authorized by the person, is in charge of sending your offer, and knows exactly what you can offer. While only this person should have the authority to initiate the letter, at least two people in the human resources department should know how to perform the nuts-and-bolts task of typing it, printing it out, and mailing it. This way, if the person in charge of sending the letter isn't in the office, she can delegate this task — making sure, of course, that the letter says what it should.

Feeling Out the Market: Is Your Offer Competitive?

Before sending your letter, review the package you're offering your candidate. Did you research the market, to make sure you're competitive (see Chapters 1 and 3)? Do you know how your offer compares to the salary, benefits, and perks that other firms are likely to offer? Are you up-to-date about the market value of the skills your candidate possesses? This last is particularly crucial in high-tech fields, where people with hot skill sets can demand top-of-the-line salaries.

Other points to consider:

✔ If you came to a tentative agreement about salary during the interview stage, do not undercut the amount you agreed on. Doing so tells your candidate a) that you were less than up-front during the interview stage, and b) that you don't value him.

✔ Your offer should be at least comparable to the salary your candidate made at his past job, and preferably higher. A 5 to 10 percent increase is typical.

Writing the Offer Letter

If you're hiring a retail clerk or short-order cook, a verbal offer is usually sufficient. Candidates for critical positions, however, should receive both a verbal and a written offer. (Make both on the same day, if possible.) A written offer spells out the details of your agreement, and prevents misunderstandings. In addition, it can help protect you legally.

It's smart to have a standard offer letter already drafted and reviewed by your company attorney, so you don't need to write a new letter each time. Customize this letter for your candidate, be sure it's error-free, and check to see that you've included all of the following:

✔ A warm welcome to your candidate.

✔ The job title.

✔ The starting date.

✔ The salary rate and classification.

✔ An outline of any bonuses, stock options, commission structures, vacations, insurance, and other benefits negotiated during the hiring process.

✔ The name and title of the person to whom the candidate will report.

✔ Any requirements on which your offer is contingent (for example, medical evaluations or background checks).

✔ Additional specifics (for example, whether the candidate needs to purchase a uniform or equipment, or join a union).

✔ Information about your orientation program.

Sample offer letter

You'll save time if you create a standard offer letter that's ready to modify and send at a moment's notice. Here's a helpful template you can use as a starting point:

[*Date*]

[*Name and address*]

Dear [*Candidate's Name*]:

It is with great pleasure that we extend to you an offer of employment for the position of [job title]. This letter sets forth the terms of our offer.

You will be employed at a starting salary of $_____. In addition, you will receive _____ weeks of paid vacation for each full year of employment. Your benefits will include free medical insurance for yourself and your dependents; a dental plan; a vision plan; and a matching 401(k) plan. In addition, as discussed during your interview, we will include a $1,000 signing bonus.

Your immediate supervisor will be [*name, position*], and your first day of employment will be [*date*].

[*If you are an employment at will state, add:*] You are being hired on an "at will" basis, which means that either you or the company may terminate your employment at any time and for any reason or no reason. Please note that your employment is contingent upon our receipt of satisfactory results from the pre-employment drug screening; instructions for completing this test are enclosed.

If these terms are agreeable to you, please sign and date this letter below, and return it to [*company contact*] prior to [*date*]. This letter will supercede any prior agreements or offers, oral or written, on behalf of the company, and can be amended only by a written agreement signed by both you and an authorized representative of the company.

We are delighted that you are interested in joining our company, and we are looking forward to having you join our team. We will contact you regarding our orientation program, which will provide you with an introduction to our firm, our people, our company policies, and the benefits to which you are entitled. Welcome to [*company name*]!

Sincerely,

[*Company Name*]

By: [*your name and title*]

Agreed and Accepted:

Employee signature:_____

Date:_____

Creative writing: Playing to your candidate's hot buttons

An offer letter can be enthusiastic and professional at the same time. Use yours to convey your excitement at making an offer, and to play up the advantages your company offers. Remember the "hot buttons" you spotted when interviewing your candidate (see Chapters 18 and 20), and include them in your letter. If your candidate negotiated more vacation time or a sign-on bonus, be sure your letter covers these points, so your candidate won't call and say, "You didn't mention my bonus — did you forget?" Remember, at this point you're still selling your job and your company, and every feature you point out — even the smallest — can help win your candidate over.

Watch your words!

When is an offer letter more than just a letter? When it's construed as a contract between you and your prospect. If you renege on the statements in your offer letter, a job candidate may be able to argue successfully that you violated a contractual agreement. To protect yourself, follow these rules when you write your letter:

- Don't write the letter until you're sure you're hiring the employee! If you send your candidate an offer letter, and two days later your hiring manager says, "Never mind — we're scaling back that project, and we don't need him," your prospect can make a good case that he was damaged — especially if he just quit his former job when he received your offer.

- Make your wording as specific as possible.

- Be sure you can back every promise you make. Can you really offer your candidate a waiver on the waiting period for health insurance? Is your offer of 2,000 stock options acceptable to management? Don't put it in writing, until you know you're on solid ground. If necessary, run your offer letter by your superiors and have them sign off on it.

- Be sure you note that you're hiring the employee under an *employment at will* condition, if this is allowed in your state. (Employment at will means that the employer can terminate the employee, with or without cause, at any time.)

Selling the Offer to Your Candidate

Some candidates will be thrilled when your offer arrives. Others will say, "I'm just not sure...." If your candidate expresses doubts about your offer, be prepared to discuss his concerns in a positive and persuasive way.

The most common sticking point, of course, is money. What should you do if your candidate calls and says, "I thought it over, and the salary is a little low"? Prepare for this possibility by deciding in advance how flexible you can be. If there's no room for compromise, or if you feel that the salary you've offered is more than fair, try to stress the other advantages of your offer: benefits, perks, commute time, vacation days, 6-month salary review, opportunities for growth, employer-paid training, and so on.

The same is true for other aspects of your offer. Negotiate where you can, while being cautious not to offer such a generous package that you strain your budget or make your current employees feel cheated by comparison. Where you can't negotiate, emphasize any benefits or perks that can compensate for the problem spots in your offer.

Often, doubts arise simply because your candidates don't have enough facts. If a candidate says, "I'm not sure I like your medical plan," for example, immediately arrange for a human resources person to call and answer any questions about the plan. Keep your candidate talking, so you can pinpoint questions (Does 25 percent travel really mean only 25 percent? Will the company help pay for me to earn an advanced degree? How flexible are the flex hours?) and quickly provide accurate information.

Also, spot what's most important to your candidate. If gaining exposure to interesting technology excites him, ask a technical manager to contact him and talk up the exciting projects the company has underway. If benefits are a priority, ask an HR person to call and review your package in-depth.

And always sell, sell, sell. Each time you talk with your candidate, keep pointing out the qualities that make your company an outstanding choice. Take any steps you can to make your offer attractive, and add to it if possible.

On the other hand, you may need to be firm if a candidate unceasingly attempts to up the ante. At some point, simply say, "That's the best we can do — we hope it's an attractive package." After all, a candidate who crosses the line between assertive and aggressive may not be the best person to hire.

"My Current Boss Wants Me to Stay"

Often, if your candidate is already employed, his current company will scramble to make a counteroffer when they discover that he's planning to leave. This is a tricky moment, because taking a new job is stressful and your prospect may be tempted to stay on familiar turf.

In many cases, you can discuss counteroffers with your candidate even before the other company has time to make such an offer. Sound out the candidate, and get a feel for how he plans to handle a counteroffer if one is made. Either at this stage or later, if a counteroffer situation actually arises, point out to your candidate that staying with his current company has its pitfalls — and they can be major. Among the risks of accepting a counteroffer that you can discuss with your candidate are the following:

✔ Counteroffers are generally just stalling maneuvers, to give a company time to replace an employee.

✔ Companies may consider employees who've been bought back with a counteroffer as disloyal, and promotions and advancement are highly unlikely.

✔ Employees who accept counteroffers are often the first ones laid off during cutbacks.

✔ Statistics show that employees who accept counteroffers are very likely to leave their jobs soon afterward. A recent *Wall Street Journal* survey found that more than half of individuals receiving counteroffers after turning in their resignations accepted them — but within 18 months, 93 percent of those accepting counteroffers either resigned or were fired.

Also, ask your prospect, "How many of the problems that made you want to leave your job still exist?" Usually money isn't the only reason that top producers leave a company. Point out the advantages your firm has over his current employer — for example, better benefits, training programs, or opportunities for advancement.

If that isn't enough to sway him, talk with management about upping your offer. If he's worth enough for his old company to shell out extra money, he may be worth fighting for. However, don't get into an extended bidding war over a candidate. If you get involved in an escalating salary battle, you're likely to wind up with an overpaid employee who's making more than your company can really afford — and you're likely to alienate other employees who didn't play the counteroffer game. Moreover, a candidate who's primarily driven by money is one who's likely to leave you in a heartbeat if a more lucrative offer comes along.

Setting a Date

Pin down a date for getting a yes or a no from your candidate, either by including a deadline for acceptance in the offer letter, or by asking your candidate how long it will take to make a decision. Don't threaten the candidate with a hard-and-fast deadline — "You need to respond in 24 hours, or we'll offer the job to someone else" — but do be assertive. Remind the candidate that you're eager to fill the position quickly, because the job is important.

Also, set a starting date in your offer letter. When you do so, bear in mind that you may need to adjust this date slightly. Many candidates need to give two weeks notice to current employers, while some need to start right away. Be as accommodating as possible, while allowing enough time to arrange for a desk, computer, security badge, and so on for your new employee.

The Right Way to Handle a "No"

In some cases, you'll find that you simply can't make an offer good enough to sell your candidate on your job. When this happens, be sure to handle the situation with tact and class. Make it clear that you're unable to raise your offer, but be careful not to appear angry or upset. Instead, say, "I'm really sorry we can't match what you're looking for, because we're very impressed by you. If your needs change, we'd be very happy if you'd consider working for us in the future."

One company scored major points with a candidate who rejected their offer by saying, "We hope you'll consider us down the road. And the offer we made last week to take you and your wife out to lunch still stands, even after you take the other job!" It was a professional way to say, "No hard feelings," and the company is tops on the list of the candidate's favorites — meaning that if his requirements change, they may net themselves an easy hire.

Also, try turning a negative into a positive by saying, "We're so sorry you won't be joining our team. We think you have a lot of talent, and we need someone just like you. Do you know of anyone with skills similar to yours who would be interested in our company?" Your candidate may very well respond by offering the names of other people who'll turn out to be good prospects.

If you lose your top candidate to another company, follow up in a month or so, and ask if it's going well. If the new job isn't working out, he may be too embarrassed to call and ask if your position is still open — so give him an opportunity by making the call yourself.

The Right Way to Handle a "Yes"

If your candidate accepts the job you're offering, let her know that you're excited. Get her signature on the offer letter, and discuss the possibility of counteroffers (see our advice earlier in this chapter in the section, "'My Current Boss Wants Me to Stay'"), because even a candidate who has signed an offer can sometimes surprise you by accepting a last-minute counteroffer. Also, stay in touch during the time between her acceptance and her first day at work. Too often we woo candidates enthusiastically, and then ignore them once they've signed.

Because starting a new job is nerve-wracking, help ease the way by providing as much information as possible. Tell your new employee where she'll park, make sure she knows if she needs to take a drug test or get a security badge, and have her new supervisor give her a call to welcome her enthusiastically. Also, mail her a few copies of recent company newsletters, and consider sending her a "welcome to the company" card, or a basket with a company T-shirt, mug, or other goodies. The more at home she feels, the better off both she and your company will be.

What Should You Tell Your Runners-Up?

It's a pleasure to call your top choice for a job and say, "We want to make you an offer." It's less fun to call your other interviewees and tell them you're *not* selecting them. But don't let this chore slide, assuming that the candidates you don't hire will figure out the bad news eventually. This is rude, and it gives your company a bad reputation that can cause you to lose candidates in the future. (Besides, you may wind up needing your second-place candidate in the future!)

Also, put yourself in your candidates' shoes. They're probably juggling several job offers, or deciding whether to schedule additional interviews, and a delay in giving them your news could keep them from accepting another good offer. So break the news gently, thank your candidates, and tell them you'll keep them in mind for future opportunities. (See sample rejection letter in Chapter 20.)

However, don't jump the gun on calling your back-up candidates and turning them away. There's always a chance that the candidate you select will surprise you by calling the next week and saying, "I'm sorry, but I can't take your job after all." So treat all good candidates as first-choice candidates until your job offer is a done deal.

When you do break the news to the candidates you didn't select, plan what to say when they ask (and they probably will) — "What made you choose someone else?" In almost all cases, the best response is simply, "We found another candidate whose skill set/experience matched our needs more closely."

Do *not* tell a candidate if she received bad references; if you do, you'll violate the confidence of the people who gave you those references.

Part VI

Once You Catch Them, How Do You Keep Them?

The 5th Wave

By Rich Tennant

In this part . . .

It's a happy day when you finally fill your most critical job openings, but your work isn't over yet. Now you need to plan a strategy for keeping those employees on board — not an easy task, when other companies are working day and night to lure them away. In Chapter 27, we show just how expensive employee turnover is, in terms of money, morale, and productivity. The good news is that you can avoid that expense by keeping your employees happy, and in Chapters 28 and 29, we offer a host of retention techniques to help you achieve that goal. Also, in Chapter 30, we provide advice on how to thwart other companies who try to steal your best employees away.

Chapter 27

The High Cost of Turnover

In This Chapter
- Wasted time and money
- The damage to productivity
- The damage to morale
- Those lost agency fees — ouch!

It's like a bad country-and-western song: You woo 'em, you win 'em, and then they break your heart. Statistics show that around 60 percent of employees leave a company within 5 years; and in the high-tech field, the turnover rate is mind-boggling. It's also costly, in terms of money, morale, and productivity.

But don't despair, because with a combination of old-fashioned common sense and innovative new ideas, you can cut your employee turnover to a level that will make your competitors green with envy. This chapter looks at why developing powerful retention strategies is critical.

FACTS & FIGURES

The revolving door

Employee turnover can take a tremendous toll on your company. New numbers from Sibson & Co. paint a particularly grim picture for the high-tech industry, where turnover is averaging 25 percent. Other fields in which employees are hard to retain include sales, marketing, and customer sales and support. But employees in all categories are less loyal to their companies than they were 10 years ago — and with good reason. The days of working for one company for a lifetime are gone, and with layoffs and downsizings a common occurrence, today's employees realize that they need to be as loyal to themselves and their own career goals as to their employers.

Employee Turnover Wastes Time and Money

When employees leave within a few months, you lose almost all the money you put into hiring them. Even if they stay for a year or two, you just begin to break even on the cost of hiring them in the first place. Just how big is that cost? To find out, factor in all of these expenses:

- ✔ Time spent writing job descriptions
- ✔ Advertising costs (print and online)
- ✔ Time spent collecting, sorting, and reviewing resumes
- ✔ Interview time
- ✔ Agency fees
- ✔ Referral bonuses
- ✔ Time spent at job fairs
- ✔ Travel expenses — yours
- ✔ Travel expenses — your candidate's, if you paid for them
- ✔ Relocation expenses
- ✔ Drug screens, background checks, and other screening
- ✔ The cost of your recruiting Web site
- ✔ Training expenses
- ✔ The cost of employee orientation

In addition, of course, you need to factor in lost profits, and the overtime your other employees work when your firm is short-handed.

The following sections provide a little more detail on just some of the costs you can anticipate when your staff turns over.

Declining morale

The loss of a key employee often takes the wind out of an entire department, or even an entire company. Staff members who worked closely with the departing employee may worry about how their projects will fare. In addition, there's the stress of integrating a new person into the team, and of being understaffed during the time it takes to fill your vacant position.

Calculating the cost of those lost employees

How much did it cost to hire that employee who left 3 months later for another job? Figure your cost-of-hire using this formula:

COST PER HIRE =

All annual recruiting expenses, including salaries*

The total number of employees hired over a year

*Calculate the number of hours spent solely on recruiting functions — for example, if an

HR person spends 20 hours each week on recruiting efforts, include 20 hours per week of her salary as a recruiting expense

The average cost-per-hire for a professional employee ranges from $12,000 to $20,000 per year, but the number can range from $1,000 to $40,000. The more skilled or harder-to-find your employee is, the bigger the hit to your budget will be.

Worse yet, the loss of a key employee raises questions in other employees' minds. Employees start wondering, "Why are our best people leaving?" "Should I think about moving on myself?" "Is this company heading in the wrong direction?" This can lead to a *domino effect,* in which one employee's resignation sets off a mass departure. (It doesn't help, of course, when the departing employee encourages others to follow his lead — often to obtain a referral bonus from the new firm.)

Plummeting productivity

Turnover can lead to reduced productivity, as other employees are forced to fill in for an employee who left. Often, the employees who take up the slack aren't as skilled in the ex-employee's area. Other times, they're already stretched to the max, and must work overtime. This can lead to mistakes that can cost you customers.

Swallowing those agency fees — gulp!

If you use an outside agency, the fees you pay per-hire can be substantial. You'll get your money's worth for that fee — and much more, if your employee stays for several years. If not, you can be out thousands of dollars in agency fees — or, if your defector is a top-level executive, even tens of thousands of dollars.

An Ounce of Prevention . . .

Clearly, it hurts to say goodbye, especially when the employee who's leaving is experienced, or in a field where qualified employees are next-to-impossible to find. So keep your turnover rates low with a strong dose of preventive medicine in the form of an aggressive retention program (see Chapter 28). It'll cost you some effort and money to create an employee-friendly company, but in the long run both your employees and your company will be better off.

How far can turnover ripples spread?

In addition to causing problems within your company, high turnover rates can affect how investors and competitors view you. For example:

✔ Vacancies may signal to competing firms that your company is weak, thus encouraging them to lure away your remaining employees, or tempting them to aim for a greater share of your market.

✔ Analysts may see your high vacancy rate as a sign that your company is becoming less desirable as an investment.

✔ Excessive turnover can negatively affect merger/partnership plans.

Chapter 28

Make Your Employees Love You

*T*he solution to turnover problems is simple: Keep your employees happy! "Easy for you to say," you may reply. "But how do I do it?" The answer is: Offer good salaries and benefits, but, even more importantly, make your work environment so attractive that your star employees stick with you instead of straying.

Good pay and good benefits are virtual necessities, but money alone won't do the trick. Companies are like families, and a dysfunctional firm can pay employees top dollar and still have a revolving-door problem. Conversely, many cash-poor companies are able to create remarkable company loyalty, keeping employees on board for years.

That doesn't mean you should skimp on money, benefits, and perks. Obviously, most employees go where the money is — and they want good healthcare, investment plans, and other benefits as well (see Chapter 1). In addition, a well-designed benefits package weighs heavily in your favor when your current employees receive tempting offers from other firms.

Thus, your first step should be to ensure that your salaries are competitive, and that your benefits not only attract new employees but also satisfy current employees. (The perks that entice new employees to sign on with you aren't always the same perks that keep current employees loyal.) According to a survey in June 2000 by the magazine, *Hrfocus,* the benefits, perks, and policies that companies find most useful in promoting retention include those found in Table 28-1.

Table 28-1	Most Popular Benefits
Benefit/perk	*Percentage of companies offering*
More office social events	46%
More flextime options	44%
More input encouraged from employees on policies and procedures	41%
Performance bonuses	39%
Casual dress days	34%
Higher raises	28%
Increased vacation/leave-time	23%
Telecommuting options	21%
Employee entertainment and service discounts	20%
Job-sharing options	14%
In-office services (for example, free dry cleaning)	13%
Comp time	12%
Diversity initiatives	12%
Sabbaticals	3%
Employees allowed to bring pets to the office	2%

Notice that lifestyle factors — for example, having a voice in company policy and having opportunities to socialize with colleagues — often rank as high as the perks that cost you money. Similarly, the 2000 Information Technology Attraction & Retention Survey, conducted by the high-tech trade association, AeA, found that perks and benefits are important to high-tech employees, but lifestyle issues are even more important. Following are the factors that keep IT employees loyal, according to the AeA survey:

✔ Challenging work assignments

✔ Favorable work environment

✔ Flextime

✔ Stock options

✔ Additional vacation

✔ Support for career/family values

- Everyday casual dress
- High-quality supervision and leadership
- Visionary technical leadership
- Cross-functional assignments
- Tuition training/reimbursement
- 401(k) matching

As you develop your retention strategy, it's critical to realize that perks, benefits, and good salaries are just the starting point. In addition, you want to create a culture that treats employees as valued family members and talented assets, and keeps them involved and challenged. And the best time to begin is on Day One.

Orientation: Starting Off on the Right Foot

New hires often feel as though they've landed on an alien planet. They lack even the most basic information — Where's the restroom? How does this phone system work? Who do I talk to about getting a stapler? It's nerve-wracking, and so is being in a building full of strangers. Factor in the fears all new employees have about proving themselves to new supervisors and co-workers, and you have a recipe for sky-high stress levels.

You can reduce those stress levels, however, by taking a few simple steps to welcome each new employee to your firm:

- **Ask supervisors to phone new employees a few days before they start.** Extend a friendly "hello — we're looking forward to you joining us!" This gives your new hires a chance to ask questions and finalize any last-minute details.

- **If you have enough new recruits, hold orientation meetings.** These meetings give newbies a chance to learn about the company while they bond with other employees in the same boat. Be sure the person conducting your orientation is warm and welcoming, and make the sessions informal and fun. The orientation session should cover all of the basic employee questions — for example: Where do I park? What time do I show up for work? Where does everyone go for lunch?

✔ **Equip your new employees with all of the essentials.** Have your new arrivals' desks, chairs, and computers set up and ready to go, have their parking cards and building access cards ready, and set up their e-mail addresses. Be sure they're supplied with everything from pens and paper clips to a calendar and a company coffee mug. Also, if you can afford it, make new employees feel even more welcome by arranging to have a bouquet of fresh flowers or a basket of goodies delivered during their first day, with a friendly note — "Welcome to XYZ Corp — We're Glad You've Joined the Team!" If that's not in the budget, have department members sign a welcome card and leave it on the employee's desk, or send an electronic card via e-mail.

✔ **Assign supervisors or mentor employees to meet new employees in the lobby.** On their first day, the mentors should take them to lunch, show them around the office, introduce them to their co-workers, and answer any questions. Tell your new hires that they can reach their mentors by phone or e-mail any time during the first week or two, if they have questions.

✔ **Be sure your new employees are a part of the team.** Send them invites to any upcoming company events (parties, picnics, company softball games, and so on). Also, make sure they receive plenty of lunch invitations.

✔ **Consider starting your employee in the middle of the week.** MWW/Savitt, a Seattle PR firm, has new employees start on Friday, and introduces them to their co-workers during a Friday-afternoon happy hour over a red-wagon-full of drinks. It's a great icebreaker that makes newcomers feel like part of the family by the time they show up the next Monday.

Also, make sure new employees know the ground rules. Don't scare them with too many lectures, but do give them written information about your company's policies on dress and behavior, so they won't make any embarrassing mistakes.

Don't Let the Honeymoon End!

Your new employees' first few days at your company are important, but no more important than the 1,000 days that follow. With other companies working hard to lure your employees away, you need to work hard every day, all year long, to keep them loyal.

Retention efforts need to start at the top, so your first job is to convince upper management of the need to keep employees happy. Show them the stats we outline in the Chapter 27, and convince them that the dollars and energy they spend on retention are a good investment. Hammer home the message, "Retention equals higher productivity, more efficiency, and a healthier bottom line."

Once management is on board, work with them to create a company-wide plan for cultivating your employees. Your goals should include the following:

- Recognizing employees' contributions
- Encouraging career growth and training
- Acknowledging individuality
- Developing a strong company culture
- Communicating during good times and bad
- Preventing burnout
- Identifying problem managers who may drive good employees away

The importance of recognition

There's an old story about a little boy who didn't speak a word for his first 5 years. Finally, one day he turned to his mother and said, "I don't like these carrots."

His mother, crying with joy over her son's first words, said, "Why didn't you ever say anything before?"

"Because," he said, "Up till now, everything's been fine."

Unfortunately, that's how many managers behave. Too often, they give employees less attention than potted plants, as long as the employees are producing. But even the most self-motivated employee likes to hear, "Hey — you're doing a great job." If your managers aren't doing their part to acknowledge employees' contributions, encourage them to make a greater effort.

Recognition comes in different forms, from a "thanks for staying late" to a framed Employee of the Month certificate. It's not necessary for managers to pat employees on the backs every few minutes — in fact, over-praising sounds insincere and becomes meaningless — but it *is* important to let employees know when they're doing good work.

It's also important to make sure this recognition reflects the importance of your employees' achievements. In an article in Knowledge@Wharton, management professor Anne Cummings tells the story of an MBA student she met recently. The student, while working earlier at an aircraft manufacturing firm, had come up with an idea that's likely to save the company millions of dollars, and save aircraft passengers' lives. The company recognized this achievement by presenting the young man with a pen set. He presented them, shortly afterward, with his resignation.

Why? Cummings says, "He told me that he would rather have gotten nothing. But what he would really have preferred was an offer of more autonomy, or another project to work on, or to be given two incoming engineers to help him develop a new idea."

The message: Recognition often means more than a plaque or a pen set. An employee who contributes in a major way to making your operation more efficient and more profitable should be rewarded with something more substantial, such as the following:

- More freedom to pursue projects and try new ideas
- More authority
- More resources — for example, an increased budget for software, books, or other resources
- More training

"Grow" your employees

Whether your employees are fresh out of college or ready for their 40-year pins, they're still learning and growing. The more you help them, the more loyal they'll be — and the more valuable they'll be as well. To keep your employees' skills sharp and their interest level high, offer them the following:

- Challenging work
- Training
- Career advancement opportunities

All three of these factors will influence how contented your employees are, how productive they are, and how likely they are to stay put.

Challenging work

Ever play Monopoly with a 5-year-old? It ought to be fun. After all, you win every time, because all your opponent cares about is whether he gets to move the car or the dog. But almost any grown-up prefers to play Monopoly with another experienced player. That's because when we play games, we want a challenge.

It's the same with work: While a few employees want easy jobs, the majority yearn to stretch their minds and test their skills. To prevent employees from heading to more exciting companies, encourage your management team to give top performers challenging assignments. Managers should routinely ask their top employees these questions:

✔ Is this work interesting?

✔ Are there other projects you'd like to participate in?

✔ Can this job be improved? How?

✔ Is there too much "grunt work" involved in this job? (If so, you may want to hire an assistant to take over some of the employee's functions.)

If key employees express dissatisfaction with their work, managers should do what it takes to make their jobs more challenging and more rewarding. If necessary, consider lateral transfers to other projects or departments. It's easier to move good producers than to replace them.

Training

Continuing education is a necessity, not a luxury, for employees in high-tech or medical fields, where yesterday's progressive technology is today's old news. In fact, IT employees regularly list training as one of the top selling points when they look for new jobs. So pay for your HTML programmers to learn XML, or send your radiology techs to courses on new imaging techniques. Training costs money, but it benefits you in two major ways:

✔ It keeps your employees knowledgeable about developments in their fields, and thus makes your company more efficient.

✔ It encourages employees to be loyal to your firm, because they see their job as a path to a better future — not a dead end.

Moreover, training your employees is easy, no matter where your company is and no matter how big a budget it has. If you're near a junior college, college, or university, you can send employees to classes. Too difficult to work schooling around your employees' schedules? Then pay for online training programs. Advantages of online training include the following:

✔ **Flexibility:** Employees can take classes at work or at home. Some online training programs offer lectures at specific times, while others let participants access course materials at any time.

✔ **Self-paced formats:** Online classes usually allow participants to proceed as quickly or slowly as they wish.

✔ **Options:** Online training portals offer courses in hundreds of skills, and they're tailored for employees at different skill levels.

✔ **Different pricing levels:** Costs depend on the type and length of training.

Be sure your company chooses online programs carefully, because some are better than others. For information on which programs to check out and which to avoid, access the human resources forums on the Internet (see Chapter 4) and ask for recommendations. Also, consider offering a bonus to employees who complete a class or earn a certification. It's an added incentive for your employees to invest time and effort in improving their skills.

Who should you train? Obviously you want your skilled employees to upgrade their abilities, but don't limit your focus to these employees. Offer your receptionists a quick course on communication skills, bring in a customer service consultant to train your retail staff, or send your factory workers to a safety skills training course. Your employees will approach their jobs with new interest and confidence, and both they and your company will benefit.

Opportunities for advancement

Employees who see that hard work pays off, in the form of promotions and bigger paychecks, will be motivated to stick with your company and to work hard at their jobs. Thus, your company should make it clear that good candidates for promotions won't be passed over in favor of outsiders.

A *promote-from-within* policy, in addition to increasing morale and helping you retain high-quality employees, can make your firm more efficient. After all, your current employees already know your company, your products and services, and how to get things done. And you know them, too — their strengths, weaknesses, and job history — because they've had a chance to prove themselves.

We don't recommend limiting yourself to internal promotions, because "new blood" makes a company stronger by bringing in innovative thinkers and making your workforce more diverse. But we do recommend giving qualified employees a fair shot when a position opens up. If you don't offer a top-notch employee a crack at a management position, she'll find one anyway — at someone else's company.

In addition, let employees with the proper skills move around horizontally, if they're tired of their old jobs. Often, an employee who's not a perfect fit in one job or department will blossom in another.

Let your employees be people

Your administrative assistant has a Venus' flytrap on his desk, your lead programmer listens to heavy metal music all day on his Walkman, and your systems administrator has a full-color poster of Brad Pitt hanging on her wall. What should you do?

Nothing. More and more, companies are treating employees like human beings — and that means allowing them to be creative or even a little eccentric. Also, with employees working longer and longer hours, companies are recognizing the value of letting employees transform their offices into a home away from home. So let your employees be themselves, as long as:

Net surfing at work: A balancing act

These days, surfing the Net is a favorite break-time activity among high-tech employees. It's smart to allow your employees access to the Internet at work, but it's also smart to institute policies to protect yourself against legal problems or lost productivity. Experts suggest that you have employees sign a policy specifying that they will not visit pornographic sites or use e-mail to send harassing messages.

✔ They don't make public office areas look unprofessional.

✔ They don't distract or offend other employees.

✔ They don't violate sexual harassment rules or other company policies.

Allow your employees to express themselves by relaxing your dress code if possible, and by ignoring oddball office decor. This rule is particularly important if you employ programmers and other "techies," who tend to be highly individualistic.

Also, be flexible about allowing employees to do some personal tasks during work hours. Offer your employees the freedom, within reasonable limits, to do the following:

✔ Make a few personal phone calls

✔ Send and receive personal e-mails

✔ Do online shopping during breaks

Have a heart

Employees will be loyal to you if you're loyal to them, particularly when they're going through tough times. Make it part of your job to find out if an employee suffers a serious personal crisis — for example, if a billing clerk's house burns down, or a secretary's child needs heart surgery in another city — and to plan a response. In such cases, your company should pull together and offer both moral support (in the form of cards, e-mails, and so on) and practical support. For example, your company could create a fund to help the employee whose home burned down, or chip in on the hotel bill for the employee with the sick child.

Gestures such as these forge strong bonds between companies and their employees — and if you stick with them when they're down, your employees are likely to return the favor some day if you hit a rough patch.

On a more routine basis, be aware that today's employees are torn between family needs and job needs. Look for ways to help them resolve this conflict — for example, by expanding your flextime or telecommuting options. And be flexible if top performers ask for a little extra time off to handle family problems, attend their kids' holiday recitals, get an annual checkup, or coach a few Little League games.

Build a winning company culture

We choose our friends because they're generous, fun, and smart. Companies, too, have personalities — and some create loyal employees, while others drive employees away. To create a successful company culture, follow these rules:

Be generous

Make your employees proud to be associated with you, by participating in projects that improve your community, such as Habitat for Humanity, Toys for Tots, the Make-A-Wish Foundation, races to raise funding for medical research, or tutoring in elementary schools.

Also, make donations to charities, and consider matching employee donations. And, if possible, offer employees time off to participate in charitable activities.

One caution: If you offer to match employees' donations to charities, or to provide grants to employees' favorite charities as some companies do, be sure to lay down clear rules about what types of charities you will and won't support. (Most businesses rule out donations to political groups or other controversial organizations.) Also, be sure the IRS recognizes the charities as non-profit.

For more ideas on becoming involved in charitable activities, see Chapters 11 and 14.

Be fun

Make your employees *want* to come to work — yes, it's possible! — by encouraging them to have fun on the job. Excite@Home offers an alternative to stairs and elevators: Their employees can slide between floors in red tube slides. Employees at Gymboree break every Thursday afternoon for a cut-throat game of four-square, while Advertising City has a full basketball court, Tilt-a-Whirl cars, and punching bags with pictures of the bosses' faces.

Obviously, not everyone can afford bumper cars and basketball courts. But you can encourage employees to let their hair down, with everything from silly contests to movie breaks in the cafeteria. Granted, you can't go as far with this idea if you run a funeral home as you can if you're a high-tech Silicon Valley firm; but there's always a way to inject humor into the workplace, without being unprofessional.

Also, perform "random acts of kindness" for your employees. Surprise them one morning with an array of fancy pastries, or put $25 gift certificates in their paychecks two or three times a year. Keep them guessing — and keep them happy.

Communicate

A friend of ours used to work in a community hospital. One day the hospital's CEO issued a new protocol, suggested by a consulting firm, for admitting and handling ER patients. The boss didn't see any reason to run this new protocol by the ER staff — after all, the plan was devised by experts!

When our friend asked the lead ER nurse how she felt about the new protocol, the nurse replied sarcastically, "It's fabulous. It's such a dumb plan that it'll kill at least a tenth of our patients right off the bat, so we'll have plenty of time for the rest of them." (Luckily, the protocol died a quick death, before any patients came to harm.)

What's the moral? Communication is critical. Your employees are experts at what they do, and they have good ideas to share — ideas that can make their jobs, and your company, better. Too often, managers feel that only they (or the expensive consultants they hire) are experts at how a job should be done. But frequently, the plumber in plant maintenance or the buyer in your supply department can spot problems, and identify solutions for them, long before management can. And by asking your employees for their input, you'll show them that they're valued and respected.

To find out what your employees think about their jobs and your company, invite them to regular meetings. One firm, for example, holds informal brown-bag lunches once a month, where any employee can dine with top management officials to voice concerns or suggest improvements. Also, survey your employees regularly (see Chapter 29) to find out what they like and dislike about working for you.

It's even more important to keep the lines of communication open when crises hit your company. If you're hit by a major product recall, or your stock takes a nosedive, your employees will hear about it instantly. And bad news, in addition to traveling fast, quickly mutates into rumors that are generally far worse than the truth. So don't stonewall or hide from your employees during bad times. Instead, tell them the truth, as much as possible. Set up a hot line to answer their questions, or send out daily bulletins explaining what's being done to resolve the situation. Also, encourage two-way communication by asking managers to hold meetings and let employees discuss their fears and concerns.

Watch out for burnout!

In a world with too few employees to go around, companies tend to compensate with the "Golden Goose" strategy: They hire a few good employees and then work them to death. It's a counter-productive strategy, which can cause you to lose your best employees and make it difficult to find new ones.

Two groups of employees prone to job burnout — high tech employees, and medical employees — are also two of the most difficult groups to recruit. If you recruit employees in these two fields in particular, be sure you have a good "anti-burnout" policy in place. Also watch for burnout if many of your employees are parents of young children, because juggling family, childcare, and work demands can drive a stressed-out employee to seek a job with shorter hours.

How can you tell if the workload is too much for your employees? Suspect burnout if previously efficient, cheerful employees start showing these warning signs on a regular basis:

- ✔ "Blow-ups" over minor problems
- ✔ Fatigue
- ✔ Reduced productivity
- ✔ Forgetfulness and failure to finish projects on time
- ✔ Frequent complaining or sullen attitude

If you suspect that burnout is an issue, talk to management about hiring more employees, bringing in contract employees at least temporarily, and providing employees with company gyms, nap rooms, or other stress-reducing perks. Also, consider adding perks that reduce stress in other areas of your employees' lives. Onsite dry cleaning, errand-running, or car washes can reduce overworked employees' stress, by giving them more free time when they're not at the office.

Occasionally, you'll need to ask employees to burn the candle at both ends. If your new software develops a glitch 3 days before its release date, or your hospital has to react to a massive flu epidemic, then employees will need to respond — and most will, without too much complaining. The problem arises when the exceptional becomes the norm — that is, when employees routinely need to work 10, 12, even 14 hours a day. If that's the case at your firm, either hire more employees to do the same job, or hire more support personnel to take off some of the load. It's smarter to hire one new person than to risk losing an entire team, or even one experienced team member.

When your employees *do* need to work long hours, try to make the experience as painless as possible. Staging an all-nighter to get a new release out on time? Then bring in dinner — and not just pizza every time (unless that's what your employees want). Or take everyone out to a nice restaurant for a break, before you head back to the grind.

Also, compensate for long hours by cutting employees a little slack during quiet times. Even if your employees are salaried, let them sneak out early a few days in a row if they stayed till midnight every night the week before. And, of course, remember to say, "Thanks — you did a great job." A small reward, such as a bouquet of fresh flowers or even a thank-you card, won't hurt either.

Identify the problem managers

Almost every manager rubs a few employees the wrong way. However, some managers actively drive employees away, by being hypercritical or unsupportive, taking credit for their employees' work, assigning impossible tasks, playing favorites, structuring assignments poorly, or otherwise making life miserable for everyone.

How can you spot these problem bosses? Often, it's simple. You'll place five new employees in a manager's department, only to have four of them leave within the first six months. And their replacements will quit just as fast, leaving the department chronically understaffed. Other times, you'll hear complaints through the grapevine. If you sense widespread dissatisfaction within a department, meet with the manager and tactfully discuss employee retention tactics. If that doesn't work, you may have to go higher up. Remind your supervisors that replacing dozens of employees, time after time, is far more costly than correcting the mistakes of one manager.

Relax — it's company policy!

Interwoven, a high-tech firm in Sunnyvale, California, has a "Stop and Smell the Roses" program that encourages employees to leave the office for fun group activities such as white-water rafting. In addition, the company employs a professional triathlete who works one-on-one as a personal lifestyle coach for employees, designing customized diet, exercise, and fitness programs. The company also offers a weekly e-mailed wellness newsletter, yoga classes, and other health-oriented activities. "People tend to forget about stock options," vice president Gary Wimp told *InfoWorld*. "They are more concerned with the day-to-day work environment and the way they're treated."

Identify problems and fix them

Keep an eye out for minor or major problems that detract from your company's attractiveness. Do your night nurses have trouble finding childcare? Do employees hate your parking arrangements, your cafeteria food, or your grungy employee lounge? Most likely, none of these problems is important enough, in and of itself, to make employees leave — but even small irritants can contribute to defections when employees are already dissatisfied.

If you discover problems that inconvenience or irritate employees, talk to management about correcting them. Also, post a suggestion box in the cafeteria so that employees can share complaints and ideas for improvements.

The Bottom Line: Employees Count!

In today's labor market, your employees are as valuable as the people who buy your products or services. So listen to your employees. Recognize their accomplishments, and help them with their problems. Train them, promote them, challenge them, and encourage them. Make them proud of what they do, and what your company stands for. If you do, you'll convert them from a group of strangers to a loyal team that will repay your efforts a hundredfold — and you'll make it nearly impossible for another company to steal them away.

Chapter 29

How You Know They're Happy — Measuring Employee Satisfaction

. . . .

In This Chapter

▶ Surveys: Giving your employees a voice

▶ Focus groups: Zeroing in on specific issues

▶ Annual reviews: Finding out what your employees think of *you*

▶ Exit interviews: Learning from your mistakes

. . . .

*E*d Koch, the former mayor of New York City, loved to stop folks on the street and ask, "How am I doing?" He knew that when you ask people for their opinions, you gain valuable information and create goodwill in the process.

What's true for politicians is equally true in the business world. That's why smart companies survey their customers — and why really smart companies survey their employees as well. The tools that savvy firms use to gauge employee satisfaction include the following:

✔ Periodic surveys, both formal and informal

✔ Focus groups, to explore important single issues

✔ Annual reviews

✔ Exit interviews

Accurate opinion gathering, however, involves more than simply asking, "How am I doing?" To get the most from your surveys and interviews, you need to design your questions well, interpret the answers correctly, and use the results wisely.

Taking the Pulse of Your Workforce: The Employee Satisfaction Survey

The best way to find out if you're meeting your employees' needs is to ask them, and the easiest way to do that is by conducting surveys. We recommend conducting surveys regularly (how often depends on the size of your staff, the available time, and your resources), to find out how your employees feel about issues including the following:

- Their benefits and compensation
- Their opportunities for training, growth, and advancement
- Their work environment and the company culture
- Your company's products, services, and future directions

Choosing your strategy: in-house surveys versus consultants

If you decide to survey your employees, your first decision will be whether to do it yourself or outsource the job. Conducting your own surveys is far cheaper, and it's often easier than getting an outside consultant up to speed. If you're a small organization, and you have a good feel for the questions you want to ask your employees, the do-it-yourself survey is a good approach.

However, many large companies hire outside firms, because designing and tabulating surveys is a big job. Outside companies have other advantages, too:

- Because these firms are experienced in doing surveys, they have a good idea of which questions yield results and which don't.
- They can provide statistical analyses to help you make sense of the data you collect.
- They can help you benchmark your survey results, by explaining how they compare to industry-wide results.
- Employees are more likely to open up to a neutral party.

If you use an outside company to conduct your surveys, be sure to choose one carefully. Check with human resources forums on the Internet (for example, the HRNet forum at www.the-hrnet.com), and ask participants what companies they recommend. Also, ask for references when you interview survey consultants. Call the companies for whom they've conducted surveys, and ask if they were satisfied.

Choosing your questions

If you choose to keep your surveying in-house, your first step is to create your survey tool. You can build one from scratch, or select an off-the-shelf form. If you design your own questions, you can tailor them to your company's specific needs; on the other hand, a canned survey may include good questions you hadn't considered. The best solution: Purchase one or two ready-made forms, and then customize the questions to suit your company.

In planning your survey questions, follow these rules:

- ✔ **Invite a range of managers and employees to the meetings at which you develop your survey:** The more input you have, the more meaningful your survey results will be.

- ✔ **Ask yourself, "What will we do with the results of this question?"** The Number One rule of surveying is: *Never survey unless you plan to act on the survey results.* Don't survey your employees about your training programs for example, if you know you can't afford to offer better ones. Instead, pick areas in which you're willing and able to remedy any weaknesses that your employees point out.

- ✔ **Respect your employees' time:** Employees love to tell you their opinions, but they don't want to spend all day doing it. Ask enough questions to make your survey useful, but avoid overkill. You may want to do one large survey, and follow it with several smaller surveys that focus on specific topics.

- ✔ **Use a combination of ratings, multiple choice questions, and essay questions:** For example, ask your employees to rate your healthcare plan's selection of doctors on a scale from one to five, and then ask, "What in particular do you like/dislike about your choice of doctors?" Or ask your employees if they agree or disagree with the statement, "My manager pressures me to work faster, even if quality suffers," and then ask for examples. This will give you easy-to-tabulate data *and* in-depth insight into the opinions behind that data.

- ✔ **Keep your questions unbiased — and don't shy away from the tough ones:** We've all seen this kind of survey: "Given Candidate Z's strong commitment to America's children, do you think his election will benefit your family?" Avoid using this type of loaded question to influence your employees' answers. Also, resist the urge to fill your survey with questions that you think will get positive responses. Instead, give your employees an opportunity to voice their opinions on topics where you know problems exist. (Again, however, don't ask about problems if your company isn't willing to solve them!)

✔ **Provoke thought:** Throw in interesting questions such as the following: "What are the three biggest challenges our company faces?" "What are the biggest obstacles to productivity in your job?" "What would you change, if you were the CEO?" Also, ask your employees to go beyond merely identifying problems, and encourage them to offer solutions as well.

Doing a trial run

When you think your survey is on target, do a dry run. Ask a small group of employees to complete the survey and tell you if your questions are clear and easy to answer. Be sure to select a range of employees, from different departments and with different skill levels.

Ask your test group: Were the questions clear and concise? Were you able to express your opinions adequately using this format? Were the questions relevant? Can you think of any additional questions we should have included? Also, tabulate your test surveys to make sure your scoring system provides you with valid and useful data.

Make any necessary adjustments based on this initial test, and ask your test group to review the changes you make.

Getting your survey to your employees

The two issues to consider, when your survey is ready to go, are the following:

✔ When to survey

✔ How to conduct your survey

Time your surveys right, so they don't hit during "crunch" periods. If your company plans a new software release in March, for example, survey your employees in April, when the release is out and everyone's had time to catch their breath. If possible, avoid surveying employees during layoffs, major reorganizations, or other periods of significant change.

Publicize your survey in advance, emphasizing to employees that their input is important. Also, if you're surveying only some of your employees, explain why. Otherwise, the employees who aren't surveyed may get the impression that you don't value their opinions.

When you conduct a major survey, it's a good idea to post it online. (If only some of your employees have e-mail or Web access, have paper copies available too.) Tell supervisors to give employees sufficient time to complete the survey during work hours. Allow employees several days to return the survey, and encourage them to make candid responses.

Also assure your employees that you will respect their confidentiality, so they'll be willing to tell you what they really think. If you use an outside firm to conduct your survey, they will devise a coding scheme to protect your employees' confidentiality. If you use an in-house survey, consult the human resources forums we list in Chapter 4 for advice on devising your own system.

Dealing with your data

Often employees become cynical because surveys disappear into a corporate black hole. Don't let this happen at your firm! Instead, move fast to tabulate your survey data, present the results to management, and create a plan for dealing with your employees' concerns. As soon as you're ready, provide feedback to your employees about the following:

- ✔ The strong points your survey revealed (for example, did 90 percent of your employees say your employee referral program is excellent?)
- ✔ The weaknesses the survey uncovered
- ✔ How management plans to address these weaknesses
- ✔ The timetable for making the needed changes

Afterward, keep your employees posted about your progress in solving the identified problems, by sending e-mails or publishing articles in your company newsletter. (If a problem requires long-term solutions, issue regular progress reports.) Also, measure the success of these solutions. If a survey reveals major problems, and your company takes steps to correct these problems, re-survey your employees within a reasonable amount of time to see if management's fix really worked. By being responsive to surveys, you'll give employees a sense of ownership in your company, showing them that their opinions matter.

The power of the ballot box

Should you give your employees the vote? It works for Colorbrite, a printing business in Minneapolis that routinely lets its 115 employees vote on company issues that concern them. The company's owner has veto power, but rarely uses it. Among recent votes: Employees opted to sell their game room equipment; to give themselves restaurant gift certificates on their anniversaries; and to pay larger signing bonuses to lure more sales reps. Two-thirds voted against getting a company car, and a plan to "hire" a company cat after the firm's first mouse-sighting was also vetoed! The "one worker, one vote" plan is a big hit with current employees, and helps to attract new ones as well.

Focus Groups

If you don't have the time or money to conduct a survey, or you're looking for extensive feedback on a particular issue, consider conducting a focus group. Focus groups, which consist of a small group of employees sharing ideas in an informal discussion, are inexpensive, quick, and often highly effective.

The first step in conducting a focus group is to define your topic and the questions you wish to ask. Since focus groups usually last only one to two hours, and you can realistically cover only five or ten questions per hour, make every question count.

Next, take care to select participants who reflect a good cross-section of your staff. Make sure you include men and women, junior and long-time employees, management and non-management personnel, and others in different departments.

To obtain the best results, be an assertive moderator and keep your participants on track. Occasional digressions are fun, and can help participants open up, but it's important to keep returning to your key questions. Also, avoid letting one or two assertive people "hijack" your group. Instead, make a point of calling on your quieter members for opinions. Be sure, too, that you don't become defensive. You're looking for honest input, not flattery, so thank participants sincerely if they give you their candid opinions — even if they aren't the opinions you want to hear.

One good trick for getting true opinions, rather than just "me-tooism," is to ask a question, and ask your focus group members to write down their answers without discussing their opinions with the other participants. Then ask the participants to read their answers. This ensures that you'll get their original thoughts, even if they've disagreed with the others.

At the end of your meeting, summarize the results as you see them, and make sure the participants agree with your assessment. Also, be sure they get feedback about any actions the company takes in response to their input. When writing up sensitive feedback in notes or minutes, leave out the names of employees making the comments, if this is possible.

The Annual Review: Do Your Employees Still Love You?

In the past, annual reviews focused only on employees — were they producing, did they deserve raises, or did they need to improve their efforts? Now, however, it's a two-way street, and employees are just as likely to tell their bosses, "You need to work on a few areas."

This is a trend that makes some managers nervous, but it's one that you should encourage. After all, it's far easier to discover what's making key employees unhappy and fix it, than it is to replace them a few months down the line.

To find out how satisfied your employees are, suggest that managers ask questions such as these during annual reviews:

✔ Are you happy here?

✔ Do you feel that management is supportive?

✔ Do you feel that your efforts are recognized?

✔ Do you see any serious deficiencies in our salary or benefit package?

✔ Do you have any problems with your work environment?

✔ Are you receiving enough training?

✔ Do you have the materials you need to do your job well?

✔ Are project assignments fair?

✔ Do you find your job challenging?

✔ Are you experiencing any problems with burnout?

✔ What do you like most — and least — about this job?

✔ What can we do to make your job more rewarding?

✔ If you were in charge of this department, what would you change?

Obviously, you'll want to tailor this list to the employee you're reviewing. Make a particular effort to identify any problems that your highly skilled, hard-to-replace employees may be experiencing, and address these problems quickly, because replacing key employees takes a great deal of time and money. But every one of your employees is important, so ask all of them whether they're happy, and whether their work environment could be improved.

Exit Interviews: Finding Out What Went Wrong — and Fixing the Problem

Strangely, one of your best retention tools is the exit interview. That's because an employee who's leaving may be more honest with you about your company's flaws than one who's still working for you. We suggest combining a face-to-face exit interview with a written questionnaire, because some dissatisfied employees will open up to a friendly interviewer, while others are more comfortable discussing their complaints on paper.

When you conduct an exit interview, try to get specifics. For example, if an employee says, "I didn't like the atmosphere," find out why. Did the employee feel left out, under-appreciated, mistreated, over-stressed, or out-of-place? The more you learn, the better your odds of avoiding the same problem in the future. (One way to get specific input: Leave lots of room for comments on any written exit interview forms.) Among good questions to ask are the following:

- Why are you leaving?

- What's the most important thing we could have done differently, to make you stay?

- Was your salary satisfactory? Were your benefits satisfactory?

- Did you feel that you had an opportunity to learn new skills here?

- Did you feel that there was opportunity for advancement?

- Did your manager support you? Recognize your efforts? Assign you a fair workload?

- Did you feel that your job was meaningful? Challenging? Well structured?

- Did you feel comfortable communicating suggestions, criticisms, or questions to your co-workers or management?

- Did you have any problems dealing with your co-workers?

- What did you like best about working for us? What did you like least?

- How would you improve your department, or this company as a whole, if you were in charge? How would you improve productivity? Morale?

- What is your new company offering you that we didn't offer?

- If the problems you've cited were resolved, would you consider returning? If not, why not?

Above all, part ways on a friendly note. Tell your departing employees how much you've enjoyed knowing them, thank them for their contributions to your company, and sincerely wish them good luck. You never know when they might want to come back, so don't slam the door on a future opportunity.

Also, if your departing employees seem a little ambivalent ("I know I'm going to miss this place, but I think the new company is more interesting"), give them a call a month or so after they leave and ask, "How's it going?" The grass frequently looks greener than it really is on the other side, and a few of your former co-workers may be wishing they hadn't switched jobs. If so, you may be able to get them back.

Of course, the trickiest part of the exit interview is passing on what you've learned to the people in charge. Try to do this in a positive way, but don't beat around the bush. If you're losing critical employees because the nursing director plays favorites or the marketing manager demands too much overtime, bring these problems to the attention of the individuals in question. If that doesn't work, go higher up. By being assertive at this stage, you'll prevent employee defections in the future — even if you step on a few toes in the process.

Chapter 30

Keep the Competition from Stealing Your Employees

*Y*ou don't leave the keys to your car in the ignition, and tape a note to the windshield saying, "Help yourself — the door's unlocked!" Yet many companies are nearly as lax in protecting a much more valuable investment: their employees.

It's a major mistake, because a primary way to find excellent employees is to hire those employees away from other companies. Even the most ethical competitors work hard to lure your employees away, because that's how the game is played today. So think of your employees as the equivalent of expensive BMWs, and think of your competitors as people just waiting to steal those BMWs. Don't let it happen!

The first step in guarding your employees, of course, is to make them happy (see Chapter 28). Pay market value for your employees, offer them opportunities for advancement, create a strong company culture, provide training programs, and offer competitive benefits and perks. But that's not enough. Even a happy employee may be tempted by a higher salary, longer vacations, or other incentives you can't offer. Moreover, many of your competitors now believe that all's fair in love, war, and recruiting — so keep the competition from finding your employees in the first place, by implementing the "anti-raid" tactics we outline in this chapter.

How devastating can a raid be?

If you're having trouble convincing management to adopt anti-raiding strategies, remind them that you could lose more than just one employee — you could lose an entire department. Often, competing companies succeed in hiring away a half-dozen or more key employees at a single time. A mass exodus like this can bring a major project to its knees, and cost your firm thousands (possibly even millions) of dollars.

To raise the level of concern about this issue, ask your management team to consider these points:

✔ Could we afford to lose every key person in our most critical department?

✔ Could we afford to lose all of them in the same month?

✔ If we lost several key people in a department, would the remaining staff be able to train new employees quickly enough to avoid damage to our company?

✔ Would the loss of several key employees at once, due to raids by other companies, seriously affect our product design/development/sales?

Get your managers to contemplate such worst-case scenarios, because all too often, these scenarios come true for companies that fail to take steps to protect their employees from their competitors.

Watch What You Say on the Web!

In Chapter 6, we tell you how to search public and private pages of Web sites to find lists of employees. It's legal and ethical, but you don't want other people to use the same tricks on you! So don't list your employees' names and e-mail addresses on your Web site, even on pages you think are safe from the public eye. And if you're tempted to include a Web page feature on your sales team and the major deal they just closed, that's fine — but don't list their names, or you'll provide easy information for competing companies or outside recruiters seeking good prospects for their open sales positions.

You'll probably want to include the names and bios of your management team on your site, but limit employee info in general. Also, ask your technical staff to create a good firewall to keep people from snooping through Web pages that are supposed to be off-limits. If you list your organizational charts and other sensitive information online, make sure they're safely behind that firewall.

Beware the Directory

It seems so innocuous: That little booklet listing all of your employees' names, phone numbers, and e-mails. But, to return to our BMW analogy, think of your employee directory as the keys to an expensive car. Would you leave those keys lying around where any stranger could pick them up? No — and don't be relaxed about guarding your directory, either.

Competitors may try to get to your directory by manipulating your employees. How? A recruiter will stop by your new administrative assistant's desk and say innocently, "I need to look up a phone number of an employee. Do you have a spare copy of your employee directory?" (Some recruiters go even further, offering employees cash in exchange for directories. And not just a little cash, either; directories for hot high-tech companies now go for thousands of dollars.) Competitors may also contact your mailroom employees, asking for mailing lists.

To prevent naïve employees from leaking your employee information, establish and enforce these rules:

- ✔ Employees may not give directories or mailing lists to non-employees under any circumstances.
- ✔ Copies of directories must be kept on the premises at all times.

With these formal rules in place, you'll limit competitors' access to your employees. In addition, you'll be in a good position to discipline any employee who's caught selling your company directory to a competitor. Make it clear that this is unacceptable and is grounds for dismissal.

Also, consider eliminating hard copies of your directory, and putting this information online — but only where it's safe (see previous section). You may also want to limit employees' access to information about people outside their own departments.

Educate Your Gatekeepers

The most important weapon in the arsenal of a competitor trying to lure away your employees is the telephone, so educate your receptionists to screen out calls from recruiters. Here are some examples of calls that should raise your receptionists' suspicions:

- ✔ "Hi, I'm a student doing my Master's thesis on pharmaceutical research, and I'm wondering if I could get the numbers of some of your researchers so I can interview them."

✔ "We're planning a seminar on geriatric nursing, and I'd like to get a copy of your company directory so we can contact nurses who may be interested in participating."

✔ "I'm Bob's brother. You know Bob, the tech department manager? My wife and I want to invite his employees to a surprise party for him — can you give me their names and extensions?"

✔ "Hello, my name is John and I represent a new software product. We'd like to talk with your Chief Technology Officer to see if your company might be interested in beta-testing our product. Is he or she in?"

✔ "Linda Smith just called me, and I'm returning her call. Please transfer me to her."

The rule of thumb for receptionists should be if the caller doesn't know the name or extension of an employee, don't give it out. Instead, the receptionist should get the name of the caller, and verify the legitimacy of any suspicious calls (for example, by calling Linda Smith in the example above, and asking, "Were you expecting a return call from Bob Johnson?"). When in doubt, receptionists can also refer callers to department managers who can decide whether the calls are legitimate requests or merely ploys to get your employees' names and phone numbers.

But don't just train your receptionists; instead, teach all employees not to give away too much information. If you've created a sense of loyalty and team commitment, your employees will understand the importance of protecting your "people assets."

Counter these tricks

If the same individual continues to call your company time after time, asking for a different person each time, it's quite likely to be a recruiter going down a list of your employees and trying to reach them. If you have caller ID technology, you can spot this, because the same number will come up again and again.

Here's another trick some recruiters use: They call into a company after the end of the workday, and use the automated phone directory to reach employees' voice mail. While you can't do away with your after-hours automated phone system, consider limiting the information you provide to employees' names and/or extension numbers, and leaving out their job titles or departments.

Offer Retention Bonuses

If the competition for your employees is really ruthless, consider upping the ante by instituting a team retention bonus. Under this plan, departments or key teams receive a cash bonus if every person in the group is still with the company after a 3-month, 6-month, or 12-month period. A team retention bonus costs some money, but it's a powerful tool because employees who depart feel as though they've let down their co-workers.

A team bonus should be large enough to cause some excitement. Also, consider offering a graduated bonus; for example, you might pay $100 per employee for 80 percent retention, and $200 for full retention. Employees terminated by the company should not count against the rest of the team.

Use Ethical Recruiting Agencies

One unbreakable rule of recruiting agencies is "Don't recruit your client's employees." It's unthinkable to place an employee with XYZ Corp on Tuesday, while trying to steal a different XYZ employee away for a competitor on Thursday. Unfortunately, a handful of unethical recruiters will do the unthinkable.

That's why it's important, if you outsource some of your jobs, to make sure the agencies you hire are ethical and don't have a history of recruiting from their clients. We talk about checking recruiting agencies' references in Chapter 13, but it bears repeating here: Check with other clients, to make sure the agencies you're thinking of hiring have sterling reputations. An agency that finds three employees for you, and then steals four away, isn't doing you any favors!

Consider Non-Compete Agreements

You can put some muscle behind your efforts to keep your employees where they belong by having them sign non-compete agreements. These agreements require employees to agree not to compete with the company for a specified time within a specific geographic region. Their effect: To discourage employees from departing and sharing your company secrets with competitors, or from leaving and starting their own companies using your technologies.

In general, such agreements must be signed at the time of hiring. State laws differ, so check with your company attorney if you're thinking of making non-compete agreements a requirement for employment.

Part VII
The Part of Tens

The 5th Wave   By Rich Tennant

"Ooh – I think we've found our man."

In this part . . .

Every For Dummies book includes a Part of Tens, where you can always find a little of this (usually ten) and a little of that (also usually ten). We offer some tips for recruiting successfully, some things to avoid when interviewing, and a few ideas about where to get some great referral program rewards.

Chapter 31

Ten Keys to Being a Successful Recruiter

. . . .

In This Chapter

▶ Build relationships and networks

▶ Maximize your time

▶ Learn, grow, prosper

▶ More traits and actions that translate into success

. . . .

You spend hours defining the qualities that you're seeking in an ideal job candidate. In this chapter, we turn the tables and ask the question: What qualities define an ideal recruiter? In our experience, you're likely to succeed where others fail if you live by these ten principles.

Focus on Relationship-Building Rather Than on Resumes

In recruiting, who you know is as important as what you know — and the more people who know, like, trust, and respect you, the better the reputation you'll build for yourself and your company. That reputation will translate, down the road, into more great candidates and successful hires. So cultivate your candidates and your contacts, treat them fairly and courteously, and do good turns for them whenever you can. Base your relationships on sincere good will and long-term cooperation, rather than on short-term gains, and you'll establish relationships that will benefit you for years to come.

Establish a Network of Top-Notch Candidates

You won't find the people you need simply by depending on job boards and resume banks. Instead, build your own network of great candidates, and add to it weekly. Your network will provide you with three essentials: great employees to satisfy your demanding hiring managers, referrals to other stellar candidates, and valuable information when you have questions.

Use Technology in as Many Ways as You Can

Everyone needs to be a bit of a techie these days — and that includes recruiters. To recruit effectively on the Internet, conduct sophisticated database searches, stay in touch with candidates through e-mail and e-newsletters, and conduct online assessments and skill testing, you need to have a good grasp of computer technology and how it's changing. Hone your skills every chance you get, by taking classes, attending workshops, and taking advantage of the information on Internet recruiting forums.

Understand the Need for Speed at All Levels of the Recruiting Process

A successful recruiter posts open jobs quickly, begins networking with contacts immediately, schedules phone screens and interviews with top candidates right away, and extends offers to winning candidates without delay. Every day you shave off your hiring process doubles or triples your chances of success.

Recruit All the Time

There's no such thing as a 40-hour week in recruiting! Instead, be willing to spend extra time and effort to research where the talent is hiding, and then go there to start building relationships. This means talking to people everywhere — airplanes, professional events, conferences, you name it. It means hanging out at happy hours, attending charity events, maybe even going to karaoke bars. (Hey, we didn't say this job is easy.) It also means joining recruiting groups, and using recruiting forums where you can network with others willing to share advice and offer help.

Develop an In-Depth Understanding of Your Company and the Jobs You Need to Fill

When you know your stuff, your candidates will see you as smart and savvy — and they'll get a good impression of your company as well. Moreover, you'll have a better feel for the candidates who best suit your needs. So get to know your industry, and cultivate a working knowledge of the skills needed for your jobs. Develop an extensive knowledge of your company's (and your competitors') products and customers, as well as your (and their) strengths and weaknesses.

Get Everyone Involved in the Recruiting Process

A successful recruiter enlists hiring managers and other employees in the effort to get jobs filled. How? By encouraging every employee to spread the word about how great the company is, and by educating hiring managers on the current job marketplace, the market value of certain skill sets, and the need to move quickly to capture good employees.

Measure Your Efforts

To refine your recruiting efforts, you need to know what's working and what isn't. Which recruitment and advertising efforts were most successful in attracting talent? What's the company's retention rate, and is it changing? How many positions did you fill last month? What was the time to fill? How many interviews did you conduct? What was your interview-to-hire ratio? There are plenty of relevant statistics to measure, but don't just measure for the sake of measuring. Instead, use your results to fine-tune your recruiting process and make changes where they're needed.

Develop Strong Sales, Marketing, and Communication Skills

A huge part of recruiting involves marketing your company and your job openings to your candidates, and marketing your candidates to your hiring managers. In addition, to attract and win great candidates, you need to write dynamic job descriptions and outstanding offer letters. What's more, you need to impress candidates and persuade hiring managers with your verbal skills. And, last but not least, you need to know when to be quiet and listen wisely. If you think you can use some improvement in any of these areas, take a writing class, sign up for a communications course, attend a marketing workshop, or read books on effective writing, marketing, or speaking.

Use Multiple Recruiting Resources

A successful recruiter doesn't rely on a single source to find the best talent. By combining an in-house database, employee referral programs, outside recruiting agencies, advertising, campus recruiting efforts, and online recruiting, you'll maximize your recruiting power.

Chapter 32

Ten Biggest Interviewing Mistakes

*M*any a candidate arrives for an interview bright-eyed, eager, and full of cheer, and leaves an hour or two later saying, "I wouldn't work for those people for a million dollars." And many an interviewer makes the wrong moves and, as a result, overlooks a great candidate and hires a poor one instead.

To prevent these disasters, take pains to avoid interview goofs that can undo weeks of recruiting work. We talk about interviewing no-no's in Chapter 20, but here's a concise list to share with your hiring managers — or anyone else who needs a quick refresher on the biggest mistakes to avoid on interview day.

Being Unprepared

"Oops — where's the key to the conference room? Sorry I forgot to get you the parking directions. Fred will be here in a minute — he didn't get the note about the time change. But let's go ahead and get started without him. So, uh, what exactly did you do in your last position? I'm afraid I can't remember what your resume said..."

Beginning an interview on an unprepared footing can be fatal to your chances of making a hire, because you'll appear incompetent, disorganized, or even discourteous. To avoid making a bad impression, get your ducks in a row before the interview starts. Review the individual's resume or application before the interview. Prepare a list of questions to ask, and make sure your questions don't overlap with those of other interview team members. Know what position the candidate is interviewing for, and review your other openings in case your candidate is qualified for a different role in your company. And, on a practical note, verify that your candidate received the interview schedule and parking directions, have someone set up your meeting room, notify your receptionist to welcome the candidate, and confirm that your interview team is ready to go.

Being Late

Nothing creates a bad impression like leaving your candidate waiting for an hour in the lobby. If you're unavoidably delayed, ask a co-worker to greet and apologize to your candidate. But short of a flat tire or other life crisis, nothing should make you tardy.

Asking Illegal Questions

Don't even schedule an interview until you know that everyone on your team understands which questions are legally taboo (see Chapter 21). Asking an illegal question is the mother of all interviewing errors, because it can do more than just lose you a candidate: It can cost your firm a small fortune in legal fees and generate bad publicity that will hurt your hiring statistics for years to come.

Talking Too Much

If you spend the entire interview doing all the talking, how will you ever determine if this candidate is a good match for the job?

Asking Too Many Yes-No Questions

"Did you like your last job?"

"Yes."

"Do you have the skills we need?"

"Yes."

"Do you have any problems working in a team?"

"No."

This sort of boring and uninformative interview happens every day, and must waste a million hours of interviewers' and candidates' time each year. Granted, you may need to ask a few yes/no questions ("Do you have a driver's license?"), but keep them to a minimum. The idea is to draw your candidate out, so ask open-ended questions such as, "What do you think about Microsoft's new .NET technology?" or "Why did you choose to specialize in pediatric nursing?"

Not Taking Notes

You'll probably interview several candidates for each job opening, and if you don't take any notes during the interview (or at least write down some comments right after the interview), you'll have a hard time comparing candidates fairly and effectively. Don't rely on your memory — it's always better to get it in writing. Moreover, good documentation to support your hiring choices can protect you in the event of a lawsuit.

Being Swayed by Biases

Don't let irrelevant characteristics such as weight, height, attractiveness, accents, or clothing get in the way of hiring a good candidate. Focus on skills and experience, and judge candidates fairly.

Not Treating the Interview as an Equal Exchange

Treat your interview not as an interrogation, but rather as an equal exchange of information. Remember: While you're trying to decide whether your candidate would be good for your company, the candidate is trying to decide whether your company and position would be a good match for her. Give her plenty of time to ask questions, and go out of your way to provide her with information.

Failing to Sell Your Company and Your Job throughout the Interview

Too often a job interview consists of *grilling* the candidate, without any thought given to *selling* the candidate. While most managers and interviewers aren't salespeople, it's important to remember that today's candidates usually have several job offers from which to choose. Thus, selling your candidates on your company and the job is as crucial these days as selling your customers on your products or services.

Rushing Through an Interview

No matter how tired you are, or how many candidates you've interviewed, each candidate deserves equal time. When you hurry through an interview, you're likely to offend a prospect, fail to spot an outstanding candidate, or miss the warning signs that would steer you away from a bad hire.

Chapter 33

Ten Great Referral Program Ideas

In This Chapter

▶ You can never go wrong with cold, hard cash
▶ Appealing to your employee's inner child
▶ Selling your company with prizes

A high-powered employee referral program (see Chapter 9) brings in top-quality new hires and rewards current employees — and if you're really creative, it can also advertise your company as a great place to work. When you plan rewards for employee referrals, think fun, be creative, and focus on the image you hope to project. Among the best draws are the rewards we discuss in this chapter.

Cash

Okay, so it's not that creative — but it's universally loved. Offer enough money to generate excitement, and increase the amount for hard-to-fill positions. If you have well-connected employees, consider offering an extra incentive for bringing in multiple new employees for crucial spots; for example, offer a big cash bonus for bringing in three people, and an even larger bonus for five.

Stock Options

Although they've lost a little of their luster recently, stock options can still be a tempting incentive — especially if you're not in a position to offer large cash awards or big prizes. Moreover, stock options give your employees a feeling of ownership in the company.

Gift Certificates

These are another favorite if you can't offer large cash referral bonuses, and a nice extra even if you can. Popular gift certificates include those to restaurants, major department stores, and well-known online stores such as Amazon. Offer a selection, so you'll be sure to please everyone.

Contests

Give away cars, boats, expensive exercise equipment, or any other major prizes that you can afford. Offer one entry for each successful hire stemming from a referral, or for each referral of a qualified applicant, and hold a drawing every 3, 6, or 12 months. But use contests to supplement other rewards, not to replace them; otherwise, employees who don't win the big prizes may feel that their efforts are wasted.

Extra Paid Time Off

Like cash, this is a reward that everyone loves, and it's relatively inexpensive. But be generous, because an extra vacation day or two isn't much of an incentive. To really motivate your volunteer recruiting army, offer every Friday off for a month, or an extra week of paid vacation, in exchange for a referral that generates a new hire.

Airline Tickets

If your company can obtain good deals from airlines, round-trip tickets to Las Vegas, Hawaii, or other vacation "hot spots" will woo many employees. If possible, also offer employees a few hundred dollars worth of fun money to spend on their holidays.

High-Tech "Toys"

Electronic gadgets are especially popular with employees in high-tech companies or departments. But who wouldn't want a new TV? Other tantalizing prizes include computers, stereos, Palm Pilots, laptops, DVD players, global positioning systems, video-game systems, or cell phones. (Again, consider offering a choice of prizes to attract a wide range of employees.) Another alternative: Offer a high-speed Internet connection subscription.

Tickets to Local Sporting Events, Concerts, or Amusement Parks

A family trip to a major-league game, a big concert, or Disneyland can cost an employee a minor fortune, but it's a fairly inexpensive prize from a corporate point of view. Offer at least four tickets, if possible, so you won't cause more problems than you solve. ("What do you mean, you and Dad are going to Disney World, and I have to stay home?")

Company T-shirts, Hats, Sports Bags, and Other Apparel

Offer these as fun additions to your prize package. A T-shirt alone won't motivate an employee to refer anyone, but if you offer an employee and his or her entire family T-shirts, hats, or other apparel as one part of your reward, you'll gain lots of free publicity. It's an especially good (and often overlooked) idea to have some company shirts in baby sizes; as advertisers are fond of saying, babies sell, and people are likely to remember your name if they see a little tyke sporting your logo.

A "Loaner" Prize

If you can't afford to give away a big prize, "lend" one to the employee who brings in the most good referrals each month. Let your winner have the use of a company car or a boat for a month, or allow him or her to use the company condo for a week. Another related idea that appeals to working moms and doesn't require a big budget: Offer maid service for a month.

Index

• D •

● *X* ●

FOR DUMMIES
BOOK REGISTRATION

Register This Book and Win!

We want to hear from you!

Visit **dummies.com** to register this book and tell us how you liked it!

- ✔ Get entered in our monthly prize giveaway.

- ✔ Give us feedback about this book — tell us what you like best, what you like least, or maybe what you'd like to ask the author and us to change!

- ✔ Let us know any other *For Dummies* topics that interest you.

Your feedback helps us determine what books to publish, tells us what coverage to add as we revise our books, and lets us know whether we're meeting your needs as a *For Dummies* reader. You're our most valuable resource, and what you have to say is important to us!

Not on the Web yet? It's easy to get started with *Dummies 101: The Internet For Windows 98* or *The Internet For Dummies* at local retailers everywhere.

Or let us know what you think by sending us a letter at the following address:

For Dummies Book Registration
Dummies Press
10475 Crosspoint Blvd.
Indianapolis, IN 46256

™

**BESTSELLING
BOOK SERIES**